No Surrender

writings from an anti-imperialist political prisoner

David Gilbert

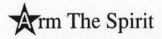

It's This Way

I stand in the advancing light,
my hands are hungry, the world beautiful.

My eyes can't get enough of the trees,
they're so hopeful, so green.

A sunny road runs through the mulberries,
I'm at the window of the prison infirmary.

I can't smell the medicines,
carnations must be blooming nearby.

It's this way:
being captured is beside the point,
the point is not to surrender.

Nazim Hikmet
Turkish political prisoner
1948

No Surrender
writings from an anti-imperialist political prisoner
by David Gilbert

ISBN 1-894925-26-2

copyright 2004 David Gilbert

1st edition, 1st printing
published in Montréal, Canada, May 2004
by Abraham Guillen Press and Arm The Spirit

Abraham Guillen Press
C.P. 48164
Montréal, Québec
H2V 4S8, Canada
email: abrahamguillenpress@yahoo.com

Arm The Spirit
Box 6326, Stn. A
Toronto, Ontario
M5W 1P7, Canada
email: ats@etext.org

Distributed in the United States by:

AK Press Distribution
674-A 23rd Street
Oakland, California
94612-1163
phone: (510) 208-1700
email: akpress@akpress.org
website: www.akpress.org

cover design by Lisa Roth
back cover photo by Roz Payne
visit Roz Payne's Archives: www.newsreel.us

Printed in Canada

In memory of Kuwasi Balagoon,
Albert Nuh Washington,
and Jah Teddy Heath.

The struggle continues.

Acknowledgements

From the beginning of my time upstate, two different individuals greatly encouraged me to write and worked hard to find outlets: Bob Feldman and Jeff Jones. I'm indebted to editors who were willing to publish me in periodicals like *Toward Freedom* and *Metroland*, and especially to James Rensenbrink and Allison Mass, who gave me a regular, completely uncensored book review column in *Downtown*. Jamie M. (of Abraham Guillen Press) was the one who proposed collecting some of those writings into a book, and he has done the lion's share of the formidable production work. When our very limited resources inevitably led to major production obstacles, many political supporters and friends rallied to help: Matt Capri, Jonathan Cohen (who sadly passed away from cancer), Linda Evans, Sam Green, Peter Clapp, Richard Clapp, Helen Hudson, Claude Marks, Matt Spurlock, Callie Williams, Donna Willmott, the Anti-Colonial Working Group (Concordia QPIRG-Montréal), Arm the Spirit, Jericho Amnesty Movement (Bay Area), Political Prisoner Calendar Committee (Montréal), Prairie Fire Organizing Committee (Chicago), !Presente! performance troupe (Richard Cambridge, Myriam Ortiz, Dana Woodruff, chill breeze, and Jamey Smythe), Resistance in Brooklyn, and Socialism & Democracy. A special thanks to Lisa Roth for designing the beautiful cover of this book, and to Teresa Agrillo and Betsy Mickel for their arduous copy editing. Throughout the years in prison, I've been sustained and enriched by a wonderful community of family and friends — much stronger and more vibrant than I could have imagined. I won't try to list all the names here. I hope that I regularly express, and that each person involved feels, my love and appreciation. Among that community an additional thanks for specific help with writing goes to Naomi Jaffe, Elana Levy, Herman Bell, Dan Berger, Terry Bisson, Anthony Cisco, Susie Day, Dave Dellinger, Tynan Jarrett, Judy Jensen, Lise Kuhn, Vicki Legion, Karl Levesque, Betty Liveright, Jackie Malone, Matt Meyer, J. Sakai, Barbara Smith, Meg Starr, Janet Stavnezer, Becky Thompson, Victor Wallis, and Ken Yale. A special lifetime thank-you to Chesa, Kathy, Bernardine, and Bill.

David Gilbert

Contents

Sundiata Acoli (Clark Squire)
39794-066
P.O. Box 3000
USP Allenwood
White Deer, Pennsylvania
17887, USA

Marilyn Buck
00482-285
5701 8th. St. Camp Parks, Unit B
Dublin, California
94568, USA

David Gilbert # 83A6158
Clinton Correctional Facility
P.O. Box 2001
Dannemora, New York
12929, USA

(address subject to change without notice)

Foreword—Sundiata Acoli

The reader will find *No Surrender* a remarkable excursion into the mind of David Gilbert on a diversity of topics of acute interest to all concerned about the pressing political issues of our times. David has judiciously selected and reviewed a series of books on each important question of our day for the edification of the reader and quick penetration to the heart of the matter, whereupon David forthrightly states his position on the issue—and moves on. In addition, he employs an enjoyable parade of personal interviews, autobiography, letters, telephone conversations, haiku, skits, children stories, and humor to diversify the means but accomplish the same end.

It's refreshing, even breathtaking, to witness David's masterful handling of the material. He touches all the bases: race, class, gender, women, nationalism, white supremacy, armed struggle, political prisoners, AIDS, imperialism, human rights, the environment, and many more. In the end, the reader comes away with a thorough political education in both global and local affairs, painlessly and pleasurably delivered. Even in those rare instances where I found myself in disagreement, they were but minor differences of opinion or questions in which the definitive jury is still out, one being the extent of unnecessary AIDS deaths among Blacks, and other people of color, due to their belief in AIDS conspiracy theories.

David provides a unique insider's view into the history of Students for a Democratic Society (SDS) and the Weather Underground Organization (WUO) and the latter's armed propaganda actions in solidarity with the then ongoing armed struggles of peoples of color and other revolutionary groups in the U.S. and abroad. He sums up by drawing lessons from the past that provide the reader with valuable insights to approaches that will help liberate the future.

No Surrender is a much needed and highly relevant work for which I'm honored to write this preface in tandem with, and for, two of my most beloved PP/POW comrades, Marilyn Buck and David Gilbert, respectively.

Foreword—Marilyn Buck

I met David Gilbert in 1967 at a Students for a Democratic Society (SDS) conference. He had been a student at Columbia, I a recent University of Texas dropout. He was one of the acknowledged ideologue-activists within the legions of SDS where many of us were led more by our outrage against the war in Vietnam and racism inside Amerikkka than by ideology and strategy. In a grueling debate over the inclusion of women's liberation as part of the SDS program, David stood out as one of the men supportive of women's liberation. That impressed me; I first had been moved to political activism because of my own experience as a young woman in this society.

That fall I worked at the SDS national office on *New Left Notes*, the SDS newspaper. There, I read an ideological piece on "Praxis," written by David

Gilbert, Bob Gottlieb, and Gerry Tenney. Though I know I didn't agree with the new working class analysis or how it has been interpreted since, the fact that I remember reading such an article 35 years later is significant to me. The need for analysis slapped me in the face; I was one of the ardent Texas anarcho-hippy anti-intellectuals in those heady days of liberatory possibility and dreams. Youthful enthusiasm and desire for "revolution now" were not enough.

More significant is that David Gilbert was a young radical who had already grasped the importance of the relationship between theory and practice as indispensable to any potential revolutionary victory. His heart for battling injustice and his mind for understanding the system and ideologies challenging that system were probably as attuned as was possible for a 22-year-old youth. The 1960s were a time when clarity of heart and mind were difficult; we, the young student radicals, were outraged at the failure of U.S. democracy as we struggled against its war in Vietnam, as well as against the domestic war against the internal colonies. Today, David continues to nurture that unity between his heart of love and solidarity with oppressed peoples and his mind of revolutionary ideology.

Many of our radical activist generation were inspired by Che Guevara and his often-cited words, "Let me say, at the risk of seeming ridiculous, that a true revolutionary is guided by great feelings of love." I would say that David so internalized this ethic that it is reflected in everything he writes and does. It is *the* starting point, whether he is critiquing his and our errors and serious breaches of our own visions in the past, or he is exposing the anti-human strategies and ideology of U.S. imperialism, its allies, and other unjust institutions. He understands, from long practice and history that when one is struggling against an enemy of humanity and opposing injustice, it is easy to lose perspective or to be seduced by indignation and hatred of those evils, and so to relinquish one's own humanity, compassion, and heart. He is not afraid to address these issues.

In *No Surrender* David writes about the lessons of history. There are not yet many books written by white U.S. radicals who speak clearly about white and male supremacy, about national liberation and anti-imperialism. David is not merely an observer or detached intellectual; he is engaged and speaks from our collective struggle. His court statements are vocal in challenging white and male supremacy and fighting the colonial imperial system that is this nation-state we live in. But David has not rested on this history; he continues to examine his and our practice and ideas. He is critical, but always out of a love for the struggle and a desire to contribute to our collective understanding of the past and the present—in order to stir the imagination and vision of new, liberated societies free from oppression and corruption. In his histories of SDS and the Weather Underground, he looks at the many strategic and analytical errors, as well as at the role that our white privilege played in thwarting our ability to further social change and equality between nations and peoples, and women and men. Then in selections from *Enemies of the State*, an interview with David, Laura Whitehorn, and myself, he discusses his thoughts for building a contemporary movement and reminds us that revolutionaries act out of love. David's writing is an act of love and resistance.

David begins with his own political development. He does so with insight and even humor. After all, how does one express one's politics in seventeen syllables, in a haiku poem! He realizes that he, a man capable of many words, must also be able to distill his words for clarity. Humor and humility are important threads in David's writings and reflect the breadth of who David is, locked away from society at large.

After 20 years of imprisonment for his political acts and stance in support of the Black national liberation struggle, David has not stopped growing intellectually or as a human being. His intelligence and unwavering commitment to social and economic justice echo beyond the walls of Attica prison, one of Amerikkka's notoriously cruel dungeons, his present location. His voice is strong. As a prisoner myself for nearly 20 years, I know how difficult it is to create and to engage with the world. It is a never-ending effort to get hold of reading materials and to keep them, or to do research, much less to read, study, and think. Thought is constantly disrupted; arbitrary rules and interruptions create a chaos in which sorrow, discontent, and rage are the generalized response to and currency of the harsh cruelty, brutality, and absences of imprisoned women's and men's lives. Noise, stress, fear, even mental breaks fill the time and space of the prison world. But in reading his words, that in and of theselves are a triumph of the human spirit, we experience resistance, commitment, and courage.

David is present. Like Mumia Abu-Jamal, a former Black Panther and notable journalist, even from Death Row where he has resided for over two decades, David comments on the most current of events. He offers a sharp political analysis of the attack on the World Trade Center and Pentagon on September 11, 2001. He mourns the loss of life and condemns the U.S. financial-military empire that created the very forces that have now turned against their sponsors. He reminds us that we must measure the value of all human life, in every nation of the world, not only the lives of particular populations here in the U.S.

David is not only a prison intellectual. He is an activist. Along with other brave prisoners, he played an important role in the early days of the AIDS/HIV crisis that inundated the whole country, especially the prison system. These early, inside-the-walls activists challenged ignorance, prejudice, and the cruel mistreatment of prisoners who were HIV positive. They went up against the New York State prison system and fought for AIDS education, adequate medical treatment, and peer counseling. That work was important not only in New York prisons, but also in prisons nationwide. Because that work threatened the status quo, David and his comrades were separated, ultimately transferred to more hostile prison situations, and hindered in doing AIDS education. But David did not stop. He didn't take the easy path and rest on that which had been accomplished; he continued to challenge misinformation and to expose the right-wing origins of the more popular views about the origins of AIDS, in *AIDS Conspiracy Theories: Tracking the Real Genocide.*

One of David's principal vehicles for analysis and commentary are the numerous book reviews he has written over these many years. He is a voracious reader. His reviews not only do justice to the content of the books he reviews; he also brings insight, compassion, and interest to whatever he reads. You meet the writers, as well as David, face-to-face. His love for justice and liberation is seen through these reviews; that is, in what he chooses to read and review: books that analyze and challenge white supremacy, women's oppression, and the relations between race and class. He argues that the interests of oppressed nations are not separate from the interests of oppressed women, and that the struggle for the earth's environment is not separate from internationalism and the struggle against neoliberalism and global imperialism.

David offers us, the readers, more than historical analysis or book critiques; he offers us possibility, the power of the creative, of engagement in the world, to change it, no matter what one's situation might be. We should never minimize creativity—artistic, intellectual, or physical. Creation is possibility. A viewer, a reader, another activist may pounce upon an idea, or a historical encounter or practice, and not only make it her or his own but also use it as a springboard for a collective vision of how to move forward. We can never know what may awaken any one of us to participate actively in the world, to embrace other peoples in solidarity, and to struggle for the life of the planet. David's history, my history, our history, offers lessons and possibilities, especially for the generations that follow in our footsteps to seek justice and liberation worldwide.

These articles, statements, essays, book reviews, and poetry present the reader with a principled, clear view of the radical and revolutionary political activism from the 1960s to the present. You may find that you have a different starting point, you may bring a different ideological foundation and orientation, and you may not agree with all his analysis or conclusions, but you will be moved to reflect. You will gain insights, and perhaps become curious about the politics and world that motivated David and so many others of us.

No Surrender nears its close with several selections of David's humor. He is very funny at times: sometimes corny, sometimes subtle. By the time you reach this section, you will have seen that his seriousness is leavened with humor. I recognize in his development and use of humor my own. Humor is essential to survival in this prison world that we inhabit along with other political prisoners and a monumental number of men and women from oppressed nationalities and the working class. Humor is subversive, and enables us to hold on to humility, humanity, and imagination. There are many days in prison when imagination flees to the corners to hide from the grim sorrows of our days. Humor bolsters imagination, sets it free to fly beyond the walls to join with women and men worldwide who struggle against the grimness of oppression, starvation, death, and humiliation. Our imaginations flow through the veins of sorrow to erupt into the possibility of new days.

This ability to hold on to humor enhances David's humanity, his ordinariness, and his uniqueness of spirit as a thinker and an actor on this human stage of struggle. David's voice is a joyful voice of liberation and resistance. Listen.

Introduction—David Gilbert

My warm welcome and greetings. My appreciation goes out to you, the reader. To even find and pick up this book, you most likely are someone who finds conditions in this world intolerable and who believes in struggle for qualitative change. My hope for this book is that it can contribute in some small way to the dialogue needed to build more effective revolutionary movements.

The title *No Surrender* comes from the Nazim Hikmet poem (see page 3) and was chosen to stress that even after capture, prisoners of war and political prisoners (POW/PPs) try to find ways to continue to contribute to the struggle. POW/PPs in the U.S. have managed to do so in a variety of creative and courageous ways: from artwork to AIDS education, from sponsoring outside community self-reliance projects to insightful strategy initiatives. Political writing has been a major vehicle. Jalil Muntaqim and Ray Luc Levasseur, to name just a few, have produced valuable bodies of work. A POW/PP who particularly inspired me in the decade before my October 1981 arrest is Sundiata Acoli. I appreciated both his political clarity and his regular use of book reviews as a format. It struck me that, despite the prison obstacles to the intense collective discussions political people crave, analyzing specific books was a way both to keep learning and to offer some critical insights.

I had a book review column from 1992–1997, writing close to 100 in that period for *Downtown* and its sister publication *Agrarian Weekly.* These small counterculture papers were read predominantly by white youth, who were the people I most wanted to engage around racism. I can't say if my writing had much—or any—impact. I also placed a number of pieces in *Metroland* and *Toward Freedom.* In addition to book reviews, I've produced many pamphlets, interviews, articles, and solidarity statements over the years.

The difficult process of paring down the selections to make a volume of reasonable size has been guided by a main criterion: what would be of most use to activists in today's emerging movements? For the same reason, I divided the book into topic sections. Such divisions are, of course, artificial in that all forms of oppression and resistance interrelate to form one whole cloth of social reality. But I realize that not everyone will want to go through this book page by page. The topic headings are meant to help readers zero in on what they find most interesting and useful. In addition, I've included sections on my political starting points, humor, and children's stories to offer a fuller sense of myself as an activist, writer, and human being and because both a sense of humor and the nurturing of children are integral to a sustainable and loving movement.

In putting these selections spanning 20 years into one volume, I have done some minimal editing to avoid excessive repetition and for accuracy and clarity. Where updates and explanations are needed, there are brief introductory comments in italics. I've not changed the political content in the entries themselves, even when they could benefit considerably from hindsight. Once again, a warm welcome and an appreciative salute to you, the reader.

Chapter 1

Starting Points: Becoming Politically Conscious

About David Gilbert—Political Autobiography

The starting point for me is identifying with other people. That solidarity, that tenderness, mandates standing with the oppressed—the vast majority—against the power structure. The 50 percent of children in sub-Saharan Africa suffering from severe malnutrition, the women and girls sold into sexual bondage in Thailand, the homeless kids scavenging in the streets of Saõ Paulo, the prisoners with AIDS locked in isolation cells in Alabama . . . they are all precious human beings whose lives matter.

Reality burst into my consciousness when I was 15, with the Greensboro sit-ins of February 1960. I guess I had been unusually naive in that I fervently believed in America's rhetoric about democracy and equality. This promise was totally belied by the patent racism, as well as by the U.S. practice of imposing brutal dictators on Third World nations around the globe. The Civil Rights Movement also showed me more of a sense of humanity and nobility of purpose than I found in the white suburbs where I had grown up.

In 1962 I joined the Congress of Racial Equality, and in 1965 I started the Committee Against the War in Vietnam at Columbia University. I was one of the founding members of the SDS (Students for a Democratic Society) chapter there, and in 1967 I wrote the first national SDS pamphlet that named the system as "*U.S. imperialism.*" I participated in the Columbia strike against the Vietnam War of 1968.

The rise of the Women's Liberation Movement and determined efforts by women comrades showed me the importance of struggling against sexism and of striving to live our humanist values in our personal relationships.

In response to the murderous government assault on the Black Liberation Movement and the unending, massive bombing of Vietnam, the Weather Underground formed in the early 1970s. I spent 10 years in underground resistance. On October 20, 1981, I was captured when a unit of the Black Liberation Army and allied white revolutionaries attempted to take funds from a Brinks truck with the unfortunate result of a shoot-out in which a guard and two policemen were killed. Mtayari Shabaka Sundiata was subsequently killed by police, while numerous other comrades were captured and given long sentences. I was sentenced under New York State's felony murder law (even with no allegations of doing any shooting, a participant in the robbery can be given full legal responsibility for all deaths) to 75 years to life, which makes my earliest parole eligibility in 2056.

Kathy Boudin and I have a thoughtful, magnificent, loving son. I also am very fortunate to have many fine family and friends who have stood by me. In prison, I have tried to continue to contribute through political writings. In addition, after my codefendant Kuwasi Balagoon died of AIDS on December 13, 1986, I became intensely active as an advocate and educator around AIDS in prison.

[from *Can't Jail the Spirit*, 4th edition, March 1998]

Coming of Age Politically at Columbia:
Political Development in Relationship
to the Black Movement, 1962-1968

My first voluntary act after arriving at Columbia University was to join the Congress of Racial Equality (CORE) chapter there. That was in the fall of 1962. CORE was the most militant northern-based civil rights group of that time (the contemporary CORE is quite a different story and of questionable integrity). They were sponsoring the electrifying "freedom rides" of the day. Integrated groups were riding the bus lines into the South. They were brutally attacked by Ku Klux Klanners (it has recently been exposed that FBI agents organized some of those attacks). I didn't have the courage/commitment to volunteer to go on a freedom ride, but I wanted to lend my support to these efforts.

The guy sitting at the table on Low Plaza introduced himself as the chairman of the chapter. I remember thinking, but not saying, *What's wrong with these activists? Why can't they pick a good old American title like "President"? "Chairman" sounds like it's from the Soviet Union.* That's how strong anti-communism was coming out of the 1950s. And it was used as a bludgeon against any social stirrings against the system. Of course, anti-communism is still very powerful, but it has been breached considerably since then; today, the authorities are wielding the same type of bludgeon with the label "terrorist."

I grew up in Brookline, a white, middle class suburb of Boston. I was one of those people who really believed what they taught us in school—that this system provided justice and equality for all. I assumed that, like me, everyone had access to good housing, nutrition, medical care, and education as a matter of course. At the same time, I felt restless with the cultural sterility and lack of community in suburbia.

These assumptions and feelings were dramatically exploded by the emergence of the Civil Rights Movement, which burst into national focus in 1955: on December 4, Mrs. Rosa Parks refused to give her seat up to a white man on a Montgomery, Alabama, bus and was arrested. This act initiated a massive Black bus boycott led by Rev. Martin Luther King Jr. The beginning of sustained direct action came with the February 1, 1960, lunch counter sit-in in Greensboro, North Carolina; this action became the impetus for forming the Student Nonviolent Coordinating Committee (SNCC pronounced "Snick"). So, by 1960, I began to see that many people in the U.S. didn't even have the necessities of life, let alone equality and justice.

I was also inspired by the nobility of purpose of the Civil Rights Movement, which stood in stark contrast to the individualism and careerism that predominated in my community. I remember seeing Dr. King on television, and a ripple went through my chest as I felt, *This is what it's like to be human, to be moral, to care about other people.* So, in many ways, I came to Columbia looking to get involved in civil rights.

Before school started, there was a week of orientation for freshmen. I only remember two things about it. First, that all the student activities skits were obsessed with sex—sex in the sense of "scoring" rather than as an expression of caring and intensity between people. Really, the impression they gave you was that you should go up to the first Barnard woman you saw and tear her blouse open (I assume that there have been significant changes on this since 1962). The second thing was that the dean got up and said, very dramatically, "Don't go into Harlem, especially with a Columbia sweatshirt on."

So, of course, on the very next night, a friend and I cut the regular program and went into Harlem (*sans* Columbia sweatshirts, however). For us, coming straight from the surburbs, it was like stepping into another country. Certain blocks were alive with activity, teeming with people out socializing at night. Some people were clearly reeling from being high, others were in little groups singing doo-wop, others playing cards, whatever. People were speaking a language that I couldn't understand.

The next morning, my same friend and I went down to Wall Street. There, we saw chauffeurs sitting in long, sleek limousines. We rapped with the chauffeurs. The price of one limousine alone was much more than the cost of four years at Columbia, an education the youths we had seen in Harlem could never afford.

A year or two later, I had the opportunity to spend a good deal of time in Harlem. This experience proved central to my development into a revolutionary.

In those days, there were a number of liberal, do-good projects emanating out of Columbia. Most of the programs brought ghetto kids to the university for tutoring. We used to joke—with incipient consciousness that something was seriously wrong—that the programs were designed to mold Harlem Blacks to think like Brooklyn Jews. However, one of the projects had the position that learning best took place in the child's own environment. That's the one I chose. So, in 1964, I was going into Harlem once or twice a week to tutor.

Despite my civil rights consciousness, I was still shocked by the level of oppression that I saw. A friend's uncle died because of lack of access to basic medical care; some buildings didn't have heat during the winter; police intimidated and abused the people. In my naiveté, I was running to the Human Rights Commission, but I soon learned that that route did not accomplish much.

If the experience had only been of the starkness of oppression, I think that I would have remained a militant liberal. But I saw the other side, too, the strength of Black people and the vibrancy of the culture they developed in the face of that oppression. There was a much greater sense of community, of the extended family, of helping each other out, of openness and expression of human feelings, than anything I had experienced in Brookline or at Columbia. I don't mean to romanticize Black culture; the strains from oppression were there, too: internal violence, drugs, absent fathers. But there was a strength from the resistance to oppression and a basic humanism that really struck me.

This experience helped me understand that Black people could run their own communities far better than any outside force—including well-meaning liberals like myself—could run it for them. I was in transition from a liberal, who wanted to "uplift" the oppressed (to make them more like me), to a revolutionary, who

19

realized that oppressed people like themselves must become the arbiters of their own destiny. The other side of becoming a revolutionary was realizing that things were far from ideal in the society I came from. I did not want to hand on to my children a society wracked by racism and unjust wars, a society where the almighty dollar was valued far above human beings. Joining with the Black struggle for human rights was a key to achieving a more humane society for white people also.

The understanding of U.S. society was much more advanced in Harlem than at the Political Science Department at Columbia. I was still tutoring when the U.S. started bombing North Vietnam. Actually the first bombing was in August 1964, with the famed Tonkin Gulf Resolution. This was an initial flurry to prepare public opinion and establish a "legal" justification for an undeclared war. The sustained bombing did not begin until February 24, 1965, shortly after Johnson's election as the "peace" candidate. I had, by fortuitous circumstances, been part of the small percentage of people in the U.S. who had been aware of Vietnam since 1961. I knew that the U.S. had imposed an unpopular dictator on South Vietnam, although I couldn't understand why "our democratic government" would do this. So, on a February day in 1965, reading the news of the new bombings as I rode a train into Harlem, I was extremely upset.

The families who would have me tutor their kids were far from the most militant. When I got to the door, the child's mother could see from my face that I was terribly upset. "Dave, what's the matter?" "I can't believe it. Our government is bombing people on the other side of the globe for no good reason." At that point, she had never heard of Vietnam nor did she know the background, but her response was immediate: "Bombing people for no good reason, huh? Must be colored people who live there." She made the connection in a very direct way that I had had trouble seeing even though I had been working on both fronts (civil rights and peace) for some four years. I was still blinded by defining our system as a "democracy" (with some faults), while she understood it as, in its essence, a racist and exploitative system.

The basic connection between Black liberation here and national liberation struggles throughout the Third World was developed and expressed in its most crystalline and powerful form by Malcolm X. At a time when "well-meaning liberals" were cautioning Blacks that they were a 10 percent minority who might provoke a white backlash, Malcolm demonstrated that Black people were part of the vast majority in the world-oppressed peoples. At a time when most Americans didn't yet know the war in Vietnam was going on, Malcolm already saw that the U.S. would be defeated there. Some analysts feel that as soon as Malcolm X traveled to Africa and directly connected the Black struggle here to Third World struggles abroad, the CIA signed his death warrant. Within a year of those travels, he was assassinated.

Malcolm's thinking is an essential reference for revolutionary politics within the U.S. There is no way that I could adequately summarize it here. People who haven't read *Malcolm X Speaks* (Grove Press) really should.

On February 18, 1965, Malcolm spoke to a capacity audience in the Barnard gymnasium. Of course I was there, although with some mixed feelings. Mainly, I felt favorably toward him because I supported Black militancy. But the nationalism made me a little uneasy—would I be rejected just because I was white? What role did we have in the struggle?

It is very rare that a mere speech has lasting impact on one's consciousness. But seeing Malcolm speak was one of the formative experiences of my life. I had never seen such a clear exposition of social reality. He explained that the division in the world wasn't between Black and white but rather between the oppressed (who were mainly people of color) and the oppressors (who were mainly white). He also put forward a positive role for whites—but not within the Black struggle—who really fought the system and organized within their own communities. Three days later, he was dead.

On that day at Barnard, the most persistent questions from the audience were all about "Black anti-Semitism." The insistence on this charge both surprised and upset me. I certainly hadn't experienced such an issue during my work in Harlem. I felt that the tension expressed was being used to evade fundamental issues of white supremacy in America. It was like blinders used to shut out the sunlight of Malcolm's lucid exposition of social reality.

The history and development of this highly charged controversy is worth an essay in itself. Here, I just want to indicate that this charge of "Black anti-Semitism" did not arise as a spontaneous response to some general position in the Black movement. The tension had been developed and promoted in a very conscious fashion. As early as 1963, Norman Podhoretz wrote an article (for *Commentary*, I believe) arguing that Black anti-Semitism was a major problem. At the time, he had a certain amount of "left" cover for his charge. Since then, Podhoretz has come out as a stalwart among a grouping of "neoconservatives" who prepared the intellectual groundwork for much of Reagan's program. I have no way of knowing whether Podhoretz was working directly with a government agency at the time. But it is clear to me that his position was part of a counterinsurgency strategy to destroy Jewish support—which was considerable at the time—for the Civil Rights Movement.

The year 1967 brought the issue of Zionism into the open here. With the Six-Day War, the state of Israel stood in much clearer relief as an enemy of Third World people. SNCC and some other Black organizations came out, quite justly, in opposition to Israel at that time. Actually, so did SDS, but the furor and backlash was overwhelmingly against the Black movement. I experienced the reality of Zionism as a form of racism in a very painful and personal way: A few very close friends from the movement vehemently turned against both the Palestinians and the Black struggle, seemingly overnight. With other activists whom I knew, Zionism worked as a right-wing influence more subtlely over time. For myself and many other Jews in the movement, the bedrock lesson from the Holocaust was to passionately oppose all forms of racism; we could never join in the oppressing of another people.

A major theme in the 1960s was the Black struggle for a decent education for their children. Actually, it wasn't just in the 1960s—it is a struggle that goes back to the laws against slaves learning how to read. After the Civil War, the two main demands among Black people were for land and free education (see W. E. B. Du Bois, *Black Reconstruction*).

The approach in the early '60s was to fight for school integration. The white schools had the best-trained teachers, the best resources, far more money. Rev. Milton Galamison led a popular movement to integrate the New York City schools that included conducting a massive school boycott. There was one particular high point, a march of thousands to the Board of Education. I remember the exhilaration of crossing the Brooklyn Bridge among such a large and spirited group of people. Eighteen years later, I found out that also marching across the Bridge on that sunny day was a junior high school girl named Judy Clark, later my comrade and codefendant. The city was adamant against school integration, and the movement was defeated for the time being.

After "Black Power" became a popular slogan, people tried a new strategy, community control. The idea was for the Black community to supervise its schools to ensure that their children received a relevant, respectful, and quality education in their own neighborhoods. Despite strong community support, this program was smashed through a combination of a frontal attack led by the teachers' union (UFT) and a sophisticated cooptation effort led by the Ford Foundation. In 1968, during the height of the struggle, the UFT called a teachers' strike in direct opposition to community control; some white "left" groups actually supported this racist strike as a "working class struggle." During the strike, a number of teachers, including some led by Columbia SDS graduate Ted Gold, broke into the locked schools to help teach freedom classes (Ted died on March 6, 1970, with two other comrades, in the tragic townhouse explosion that resulted from an early and marred effort to initiate armed struggle).

The city, having blocked school integration, also smashed community control to upgrade education within the Black community. The system, as it had for 350 years, again proved adamantly opposed to Black people getting a decent education. Of course these demands, if won, would have also helped to create a higher quality of education for many white children—both through the struggle to improve the educational system in general and through providing us with more of a true history of this country and a broader understanding of the world.

When the slogan "Black Power" erupted in the summer of 1966, it sent shock waves throughout the country. First shouted by a SNCC field-worker, Willie Ricks, it became publicized and developed by Stokely Carmichael. Actually, the concept is much older. Richard Wright, for example, wrote a book in the 1950s entitled *Black Power*, inspired by the struggles for independence in Africa. But the slogan became a breakthrough in 1966 because it expressed the necessity of moving to a higher level of clarity and struggle.

I supported the slogan, but, like many white activists, I was also afraid of it. Whites had a lot of power within the Civil Rights Movement. Whether consciously or not, white educational background and prestige in society were manipulated to gain disproportional control, while the development of Black leadership was being stifled. Whites had something to protect. It was comfortable to be at the peak of a morally prestigious movement for change while Black people were taking the main casualties for the struggle. On the other hand, the challenge presented to us to organize within our own communities was a very difficult one to take on. Also, behind the "Black Power" slogan was a struggle around nonviolence. Most whites in the movement tended to be ideologically committed to nonviolence. The young Black fieldworkers of SNCC had seen too many Blacks murdered; many began to advocate armed self-defense. The name was soon changed so that the "N" of SNCC stood for "National" rather than "Nonviolent."

Despite my initial defensiveness, "Black Power" made fundamental sense on many levels. First, it expressed the basic reality that Black people had to develop their own leadership and set the terms of their own liberation. Second, it challenged us to organize a revolutionary consciousness within the white community, thus focusing us on our primary responsibility. "Black Power" also taught a very important political lesson: the need was not, as we had thought, to "shake the moral conscience of America." Those in power knew very well what they were doing. The point, rather, was to shift or overturn who had power—from the handful of oppressors to the vast numbers of oppressed people. So the slogan "Black Power" also became a fountainhead for the development of a revolutionary tendency within the white student movement.

Meanwhile, the war in Vietnam was growing as a major issue on campus. I'm really not documenting this aspect of the struggle in any detail in this article. But it is important to remember that the Civil Rights Movement had done a lot to open up consciousness and create a more fertile soil for the growth of the anti-war movement. Where civil rights and the war were synthesized, we would tend to have the strongest politics and action. For example, at Columbia University in May of 1965, a coalition of CORE and the International Vietnam Committee blocked the Naval ROTC ceremony. I believe this was the first such campus action in the country (of many more to come) directed specifically against the war.

When "Black Power" came out, it helped to set a more militant context and direction for the anti-war movement, too, expressed in such things as draft resistance and disruption of the war machine. Unfortunately, a large segment of the anti-war movement lost that sense of connection to the struggle for Black liberation. It seems a lot easier for people to support self-determination overseas than it is to support it right here at home. This failure to develop solidarity with the Black and other liberation struggles within the U.S. (Native American, Chicano/Mexican, Puerto Rican) is one of several factors that caused our movement to fall apart in the mid-70s.

The revolutionary sector of the student movement continued to develop in response to the Black Liberation Movement. After 1966, several Black organizations tried to put the teachings of Malcolm X and the electricity of "Black Power" into programmatic form—SNCC, the Black Panther Party (BPP), the Republic of New Afrika (RNA), the Revolutionary Action Movement (RAM), and others. The Panthers were the most widely known and in the sharpest

23

confrontation with the police. All these groups were revolutionary nationalists. The "nationalism" meant, most basically, that Black people must direct their own struggle and that the goal was to achieve control of their own communities and/or land, as well as the other means of livelihood. The "revolutionary" meant that this could not be achieved without a struggle, including violent struggle, and that independence had to serve the interests of the most oppressed sectors of the nation, not those of a new Black bourgeoisie. These groups also tended to identify with and support national liberation struggles in the Third World.

As with previous periods of history, Black Nationalism inspired a high tide of militancy, especially within the ghettoes. This piece is not the place to chronicle the upsurges of that period. The reader is probably aware of the many urban uprisings that rocked the U.S. in 1964, 1965, 1966, 1967, and 1968. Hundreds of Black people were shot down by the National Guard and police, who valued protecting private property way above Black human lives. The U.S. government found itself facing the prospect of fighting a two-front war—in Vietnam and at home.

There were many different trends in the white student movement. Some activists argued that we could only organize people around their "immediate needs"—such as student power. Others argued that we should go to the working class and organize them around their "immediate needs"—such as a shorter work week and higher wages. But reality showed that people were most motivated to move around the issues most reflecting the general crises in society—the war, the Black struggle. Some of the politically most advanced and militant struggles were those that synthesized these two issues. When that connection could be related to the concrete realities of the institutions or communities where we lived, there were good conditions for sustained, militant struggle. These were some of the conditions that produced the famous Columbia strike of 1968.

I won't try to tell the history of the strike here (there is a factually accurate account in the book *Up Against the Ivy Wall* by the 1968 staff of the Columbia *Spectator*). I just want make a couple of basic political points about the strike. The strike cannot be understood solely in terms of events and developments on campus; we were very much catapulted forward by world events. The Tet offensive—the turning point in the war because it showed that the U.S. could not win in Vietnam—started in February of 1968. Martin Luther King Jr. was assassinated on April 4, which was followed by Black uprisings in cities across the country. These events provided both the urgency and the inspiration for a higher level of struggle. The Columbia strike began in late April.

The burning issues in society also had very specific expression at Columbia. While the administration initially lied outright, we subsequently proved that the university was doing war research (as part of the Institute for Defense Analyses). Also, Columbia, which we already knew to be one of the main slumlords of the city (the old Columbia fight song, "Who Owns New York," is meant quite literally), moved to take over scarce parkland in Harlem to build a school gym. Students, in addition to taking a stand on the great issues of the day, were saying something about what kind of institution we wanted to be part of. We could not be free, grow, acquire the knowledge we needed in a structure based on oppressing other people. We demanded that Columbia stand on the side of humanity.

The Columbia strike was an event of tremendous importance for our movement. Spurred on by the actions of the Black students, large numbers of white people participated in shutting down a major institution, in solidarity with Third World peoples (Vietnam and Harlem). This development was significant enough for ruling-class elements to do their best to defeat and deflect it. Strike leaders and many participants were kicked out of school, the press grossly distorted the goals and methods of the strike, and the Ford Foundation moved in as a "friend" of the students (this is the same Ford Foundation that later that year moved to co-opt the Black community control of schools movement). They funded a group called "Students for a Restructured University" (SRU). This group argued that the real issue of the strike was student participation in the decisions of the university. The Ford Foundation was willing to let us have all sorts of "democracy" within this elite, white institution as long as it could sever us from solidarity with national liberation struggles. SRU then became a base to try to create a liberal vs. radical split among the strikers over the questions of militancy and on the centrality of the demands around war research and the gym.

This contradiction around a white, upper-class form of "democracy" (which, after all, had been the basis of the American Revolution) produced an amusing personal anecdote from the strike. As an alumnus who knew many professors, I was sent as a strike representative to a faculty assembly meeting. I had been up the whole preceding night. Most of the faculty were hostile to the strike, which threatened their bread and butter. Some of the slicker professors set a trap for us based on our commitment to, but confusion around, democracy. They had surveys showing that, while about two-thirds of the students supported us on the issues, a comparable majority would vote against the strike as a tactic.

In the large and diverse University community, many students were not aware of our long series of pre-strike efforts to get Columbia to stop the gym and the war research. I was questioned: "Would the strikers abide by a democratic vote of the entire university as to whether to end the strike?" Torn between their definition of "democracy" and the fundamental principles of the strike, I stammered out an answer: "We believe in democracy, we will abide by the results of a vote...uh, as long as the people of Vietnam and Harlem can vote, too, since it is their lives that are most affected by these decisions." My statement was later cited by the Columbia alumni magazine as a prime example of the "irrationality" of the strikers.

The Columbia strike, a wave of similar campus actions across the country, and the confrontation with the Chicago police at the Democratic Convention all served to bring our movement to a certain plateau. It was beyond protest; we were in confrontation with an entrenched and ruthless power—a lesson that the

Black movement had articulated a couple of years earlier.

Black Nationalism was the spearhead for revolutionary development within the U.S. The government recognized this and intensified its attacks with the then secret but now infamous COINTELPRO (Counterintelligence Program). All the revolutionary nationalist groups I mentioned earlier, especially the Panthers, came under withering attack. Scores of Black cadres were murdered and literally thousands put in jail, usually set up on standard "criminal" charges. At the same time, police infiltrators waged a campaign, taking advantage of real weaknesses and contradictions within the movements, to create antagonistic splits as well as to break off white solidarity.

Meanwhile, the Nixon administration was responding to the prospect of defeat in Vietnam by widening the war to Laos and Cambodia and by intensifying the genocidal policy of bombings and chemical warfare. Six million people were killed, wounded, or made homeless in Indochina during the Nixon years. And still, the Indochinese people fought on to victory.

With the war raging at that level, with Black Panthers being attacked in their offices and murdered in their homes, any white movement worthy of the name "revolutionary" had to take on the task of building an underground that could carry on armed struggle against this criminal government. At the same time, we needed to develop a militant mass movement that would fight against imperialist war, support Black liberation, oppose male supremacy, and organize increasing involvement of working class sectors of our population. These pressing tasks would set the terms for the successes and failures of the 1970s. Beyond the '70s, the same underlying themes of oppression and struggle are very much alive in the world and on the campuses today.

[This memoir of the 1960s was never published; it was written for and sent to anti-apartheid activists at Columbia University, April 1985]

First Court Statement

This statement came at our first opportunity to speak in court at the beginning of pre-trial hearings. It is here that Kuwasi Balagoon, Judy Clark, and I refused to recognize the legitimacy of the court and refused to participate in any "criminal" proceedings. Throughout the trial, we only spoke when there were opportunities to raise the fundamental political issues; on several occasions we were physically ejected for doing so.

The government that dropped napalm in Vietnam, that provides the cluster bombs used against civilians in Lebanon, and that trains the torturers in El Salvador calls us "terrorists." The rulers who have grown rich on generations of slave labor and slave wages violently imposed on Black people label us "criminals." The police forces of Amerika who have murdered 2,000 Third World people in the last five years and who flood the communities with drugs say that we "have no respect for human life."

We are neither terrorists nor criminals. It is precisely because of our love of life, because we revel in the human spirit, that we became freedom fighters against this racist and deadly imperialist system.

The lesson of history is that oppression calls forth rebellion; social structures that live off plunder, exploitation, and degradation mandate revolution. The 400 years of the rip-off of the labor and ingenuity of African people in the New World created their absolute right of self-determination and national liberation; the 400 years of brutal repression created the necessity of armed struggle to achieve those rights. White people with any sense of justice and with any hope for living in a humane and cooperative society must fully ally with Black liberation.

There should be no illusions that these proceedings will be fair and impartial. The courts, along with the army and the police, are very much a part of the repressive apparatus that maintains this criminal and thoroughly illegitimate social system—imperialism—in power. This court has no right to try us. I will not participate in these hearings. The mass media, controlled by big money, serve these same ends. The FBI/police/media have waged a massive campaign of slander against us, a campaign highly political and reactionary in character. Can we now expect that the courts and media will provide us a comparable forum to answer their lies and racism?

Let no one be fooled by their cries of "law and order" and "stop crime." If those were the real concerns, war criminals like Nixon and McNamara would be in prison, killer cops would no longer be walking the streets, the Ku Klux Klan would have been wiped out, the corporations that grow fat from apartheid in South Africa and from racism would have been seized long ago.

The only way we will get justice is to build a revolutionary movement that fights for it.

[September 13, 1982]

Opening Trial Statement

This opening was written for the first day of trial. I never got to say it in court. Kuwasi Balagoon made the first opening to affirm the history and right of the struggle for New Afrikan independence (this brilliant statement has been reprinted in "A Soldier's Story: Writings by a Revolutionary New Afrikan Anarchist" published by Solidarity in Montréal, 2001). Kuwasi was stopped and ejected halfway through his statement; Judy and I walked out with him.

David Gilbert's mugshot 1981

27

My name is David Gilbert. I am a revolutionary and a freedom fighter. I fully support and ally with the struggle of Black people for human rights, for self-determination, for land and independence. The courts in the U.S. function to maintain the current social order at all costs. They certainly aren't about "justice" because they actually serve and protect the worst criminals, the biggest criminals of all: the war criminals and mass murderers like Nixon and General Westmoreland, the big corporations who rob billions of dollars from the sweat and blood of the people, the FBI and police forces who plotted the assassinations of numerous Black leaders.

While they proclaim the U.S. a "democracy," in reality the U.S. is the richest and most extreme empire in world history—the conquests and plunder by Genghis Khan, Julius Ceasar, Alexander the Great, and Xerxes are peanuts in comparison. The U.S. was first built on chattel slavery and on the massive theft of Native and Mexican lands. It went on to directly conquer Puerto Rico and the Philippines. Today the U.S. has a military presence in something like 60 countries around the world; it rakes in economic plunder—at great human costs—across the continents of Latin America, Africa, and Asia. And within the colonizing nation, within white Amerika, this same government and corporations control and exploit the working class.

This system is most accurately defined as imperialism. The U.S. is not alone but it is the leader of the imperialist countries, which include Western Europe and Japan. Imperialism can be most simply described as the relentless quest for profits, operating on a world scale—profits primarily for the large corporations and banks, that is—conquered and protected by the government and military apparatus. This relentless and expanding quest for profits displays no sentimentality about the human lives that may be trampled on the way.

What are the human costs of this system in the Third World? 40 million people—half of them children—die of malnutrition and starvation every year. That is seven times the number of people who died in all the Nazi concentration camps, a holocaust each and every year because of the economy of imperialism. Five hundred seventy million people are suffering from malnutrition; 1.5 billion people have little or no access to medical care; 800 million adults are illiterate; 250 million children do not attend school. And the imperialists want to accuse us of crimes!

Human beings don't just accept such intolerable conditions. They are imposed upon them by force and violence. That is why the U.S. government builds up military elites and brutal dictatorships in these countries. It is not so much that the U.S. tends "to back the wrong side in the Third World"—rather the U.S. *is* the wrong side.

There is not a single example of people in the Third World being able to achieve qualitative economic and social change by peaceful means. Not in Chile, not in India, not in the Congo, not in South Africa, not in Palestine. Nowhere. Imperialism has too much of a stake in the current economic order and is willing to use force and violence wherever needed. So revolution has become the only path for survival, for life, for self-respect in these nations. And in the process of participating in the development of people's war, the wretched of the earth also transform themselves, take history in their own hands, create collective social forms, develop the participation and leadership of women, lay the basis for a new society.

The control of the labor and resources of whole nations—in essence, colonization—is not something that happens only in faraway places. When they massacred the Native Americans, drove them off their land, and confined them to reservations—that's colonization. When they kidnapped millions of African people, assigned them specific economic roles and social status, continue to exploit and abuse them as a people for 400 years—that's colonization. When they sent an army in to conquer and steal the northern half of Mexico and then took over the land and the lives of the people—that's colonization. When they invaded Puerto Rico with 15,000 troops, then went to massacre and imprison the opposition, covering 13 percent of the land with U.S. military bases, and extracting incredible wealth—that's colonization.

Nor is all of this ancient history by any means. My comrade Kuwasi Balagoon has just eloquently described the history and conditions of New Afrikans in Amerika. If you're Black in Amerika, it is twice as likely (compared to whites) that your baby will die in infancy, three times as likely that your family will live below the poverty level, 10 times as likely that you will go to jail, 22 times as likely that you will be shot dead by the police.

The ongoing colonization against New Afrikan people, the continual violent repression, and the courageous resistance that Black people have upheld throughout history all constitute a state of war. This war is not nearly as developed as Vietnam or El Salvador, but the same broad terms apply.

The continuity of intolerable oppression and violent repression against New Afrikan people reveals why there is an absolute necessity for a Black Liberation Army. A BLA that not only carries on the tradition of resistance but that also becomes a spearhead for the mobilization and participation of the masses of New Afrikan people in their own liberation.

The events of October 20, 1981, can only be understood in this context. The attempted expropriation was part of a response to generations of robbery and murder on the grandest scale possible. It was an effort to reclaim an infinitesimal portion of the wealth stolen from the labor of Black people and to use it for the needs of the Black community and to advance the struggle for land and independence. Most importantly, the action is in the context of an absolutely just struggle for national liberation—a right that is recognized by international law and by progressive people around the world.

It is imperialism itself that has made armed struggle a necessity. But revolutionary violence can in no way be equated with the violence of the system; they are quite the opposite. Since imperialism lives by the suppression of the vast majority of humankind, the violence it uses must be massive and designed to intimidate. It is terrorist violence! For example the dropping of napalm in Vietnam, the dropping of cluster bombs on civilians in East Beirut, the "disappearing" of left-wing activists in Latin America, the gunning down of 2,000

Third World people over five years by police forces in the U.S.

Revolutionaries, on the other hand, focus violence on finding the most effective means of destroying the power structure. The revolution could and would never match the system's colossal weaponry and ruthlessness. Revolution only wins through the support and participation of oppressed people themselves. So revolutionary action must be geared toward winning and mobilizing the oppressed; this is the opposite of the state's terroristic violence.

We have tremendous respect for human life. That is what compelled us to become freedom fighters against this deadly imperialism in the first place.

The responsibility and risks of fighting are great; the cost of not fighting—the human toll from the ongoing rule of imperialism—is infinitely greater.

Everything changes. Today we live in the age of the victory of national liberation and the advance of socialism. This cracks open qualitatively new potential for revolution. Conditions have been changing radically in Amerika since the U.S. defeat in Vietnam. Today we live in a country where the Ku Klux Klan is on the rise; a country where white supremacist mobilizations are also being led from the highest echelons of society in the form of "law and order" campaigns and "anti-immigration" crusades. We live in a period of economic dislocation and—despite minor swings up and down—economic crisis will deepen over the decade. We are witnessing a sinister mobilization for war, and new imperialist wars are inevitable as long as this system survives.

White working class people will be increasingly called upon to be the shock troops against Third World people here and called upon to be the cannon fodder for the new imperialist wars.

These realities set the context for the type of movement we must build within the oppressor nation. The emergence of white anti-imperialist freedom fighters—those in the field as well as those captured—is important because it represents some of the qualities our movement must develop on a much wider scale: full commitment to and alliance with national liberation, the development of armed struggle and mass militancy, the building toward the ability to wage class war against imperialism. We need to win increasing numbers of working people to fight white supremacy, oppose imperialist war, struggle for the equality of women, and, most fundamentally, fight for the liberation of all oppressed nations and for socialism.

[August 8, 1983]

Our Politics in 17 Syllables

love for the people
means nonstop struggle against
imperialism

[October 1997]

Chapter 2

Fighting White Supremacy

Savage Inequality

OTA BENGA: *The Pygmy in the Zoo*
by Phillips Verner Bradford and Harvey Blume
New York: St. Martin's Press (1992)

> *There were 40,000 visitors to the Bronx Zoo on Sunday. Nearly
> every man, woman and child of this crowd made for the monkey
> house to see the star attraction in the park— the wild man from
> Africa. They chased him about the grounds all day, howling,
> jeering, and yelling. Some of them poked him in the ribs, others
> tripped him up, all laughed at him. Then, when the keepers had
> caught him once again, they asked him how he liked America.*

—*New York Times,*
September 18, 1906

The man in the zoo was Ota Benga, a pygmy from the Congo who stood about
4 feet 10 inches tall and weighed around 100 pounds. The pygmies were known
in Africa for their superb hunting skill, lovely dance, gift for mimicry, and lively
sense of humor. Ota did not arrive at the zoo as an exhibit, but was lured into
the monkey cage by the zoo's director, William T. Hornaday. A determined
protest by a group of Black ministers ended that degradation after 19 days.

Ota came to the United States with his friend, Samuel Phillips Verner (each
had saved the other's life in Africa). Verner, the scion of an old slave-owning
family in South Carolina, first went to Africa as a missionary in 1895. His direct
experience with Black missionaries there blew away his white supremacist
preconceptions. He never advocated Jim Crow again, and when Africans later
saved his life, Verner vowed to work to benefit their race: "May God forget me
and mine when I forget them and theirs."

Whether he forgot or not, any good intentions became secondary to Verner's
pursuit of career and fortune. He maintained an inexcusable silence on the
atrocities of colonialism in the Congo (such as the widespread practice of
chopping off the hands of natives who failed to bring in their quota of rubber)
and was later rewarded with a large land grant there. Neither did Verner object
when his friend was exhibited in the monkey cage.

Co-author Phillips Verner Bradford is Samuel Phillips Verner's grandson and
had access to a treasure trove of sources. The nuanced and complex portrait of
Verner does not skew the terms, but rather underscores that racism is much
more than a question of personal beliefs; it pervades the culture and is totally
embedded in the social and economic structures. The one weakness of the book
is the apparently limited source material available on Ota Benga, whose
perspective is central to humanizing the story. We tend to trust Bradford and co-
author Harvey Blume's instincts, because they do such a careful and sensitive
job overall, but they should have provided a fuller explanation on what part of

33

their presentation of Ota is documented and what part is their own thoughtful projection.

The glory of the writing is in the rich historical detail. *Ota Benga* provides fascinating background in a range of areas: new technologies from Edison and Bell, the rise of financiers such as Bernard Baruch, the real historical basis of Stanley's legendary African explorations, Sir Arthur Conan Doyle's role in the Congo Reform Movement, how a fusion of African and Western music created New Orleans jazz, the birth of the Ferris wheel and Coney Island, the crucial debate on Negro advancement between Booker T. Washington and W. E. B. Du Bois. These events and names are not dropped like undigested lumps. Rather, each is a thread that is woven with splendid craft into a colorfully patterned and extremely durable whole cloth.

The authors never rail abstractly against the evils of racism. Instead, a starkly powerful indictment emerges out of their perceptive attention to detail. A stellar example is their description of the St. Louis World's Fair of 1904. The Anthropology Wing displayed a panoply of "inferior races": the Congo pygmies, the Ainus of Japan, Eskimos [Inuit], the Igorots of the Phillipines. The Inuit were forced to wear their furs during the hot St. Louis summer; the pygmies were not allowed to don clothes in the chilly fall.

The main attraction in the American Indian exhibit was the 75-year-old Geronimo, dubbed "Hayer Tyger," who sat in a booth making arrows to sell to the tourists.

Despite the humiliations, a quiet dignity also emerges from these people's poignant efforts to maintain their humanity. Over the course of the description, we can't help but see that the real "savagery" here is among those who display, prod, and jab other human beings. As Ota's compatriot in the African exhibit, Latuna, pointedly remarked about hospitality:

> When a white man comes to our country, we give them presents...and divide our elephant meat with them. The Americans treat us as they do our pet monkey. They laugh at us and poke their umbrellas into our faces. They do the same to our monkey.

After Ota was freed from the zoo in 1906, he lived in Black institutions that managed to carve out some degree of independence and self-respect in segregationist America. By 1916, however, abandoned by Verner and penniless, Ota despaired of ever being able to return to his native land. Singing a traditional song, he shot himself through the heart. He is buried in an unmarked grave in Lynchburg, Virginia.

[published in *Metroland*, January 7, 1993]

Malcolm X's Message

MALCOLM X SPEAKS:
Selected Speeches and Statements
Edited by George Breitman.
New York: Grove Weidenfeld (1990)

> *There is a tendency to drain the radical message of a dynamic, living activist into an abstract icon, to replace radical content with pure image.*
>
> — Manning Marable

The hit movie and the best-selling autobiography have revived widespread interest in Malcolm X. He towers as a powerful symbol of Black pride and dignity. Treatments of Malcolm's life have tended to focus on two aspects: his heroic rise from the depths of ghetto vice to become an inspiring voice for African American rights and his evolving attitude toward white people. Unfortunately, very little attention is being given to the actual content of his penetrating political positions—positions that the establishment found very threatening indeed. We are now in danger of being left with a Malcolm as a benign symbol, gutted of his insightful analysis and revolutionary approach that are still so urgently relevant today. The best source for the content of Malcolm's politics is his speeches, and the fullest collection of speeches from the last year of his life is *Malcolm X Speaks*.

What made Malcolm the most brilliant thinker of the era was his bold ability to cut through the conventional wisdom that was so dominant that few dared to even imagine different terms. He understood how the media systematically inverts reality: "The press is so powerful in its image-making role, it can make a criminal look like he's a victim and make the victim look like he's a criminal... [they] will have you hating the people who are being oppressed and loving the people doing the oppressing." Malcolm tore off the blinders. At a time when even protesters wrapped themselves in the American flag, he made a clean break: "No, I'm not an American. I'm one of the 22 million black people who are victims of Americanism. I don't see any American dream; I see an American nightmare."

His core philosophy was Black Nationalism, which he defined in essence as Black people controlling the politics and economy of the Black community and at the same time getting together to remove the afflictions destroying the moral fiber of the community. He moved the debate beyond integration vs. separation by identifying the central feature of segregation as outside control and oppression. "When you're under someone else's control, you're segregated." And he trenchantly defined the situation of Blacks as basically a colony within the U.S., with the police functioning as an occupying army.

As a Black Nationalist, Malcolm saw the major struggle as one for independence; throughout history independence was based on land, and it almost always took a revolution to achieve land and independence.

He recognized that differences existed within the Black nation. His ripping riff on the house slaves (who got a few privileges and therefore tended to identify with the master) and the field slaves (the vast majority, who did the backbreaking work and hated the master with a passion) is a classic. Malcolm's vitriolic attacks on reformist Black leadership burned to the bone. At the same time, he called for unity in the face of an enemy who thrived on creating divisions. This contradiction between the need to attack reformism and corruption and yet to avoid promoting splits in public was not one he was able to transcend in his tragically truncated lifetime.

In one central area, these speeches do sound dated. There is no discussion of women, their oppression, and their role in the struggle. Malcolm often used the term "the Black man" to stand for Black people as a whole. He was advanced for his day in recognizing and extolling such grassroots leaders as Gloria Richardson and Fannie Lou Hamer, but this book presents no explicit struggle against sexism.

Malcolm used the term "the white man" to sum up the oppressor. "Now in speaking like this, it doesn't mean that we're anti-white, but it does mean we're anti-exploitation, we're anti-degradation, we're anti-oppression." While Malcolm increasingly came to recognize that there were some anti-racist white people, he was clear that they could not help by joining or trying to lead Black organizations, which had to develop internal unity and their own leadership. Concerned whites needed to attack racism at its source: "Whites who are sincere should organize among themselves and figure out some strategy to break down prejudice that exists in white communities." "They have to take a stand, but not a compromising stand, not a tongue-in-cheek stand, not a nonviolent stand." The hypocrisy of the oppressors preaching nonviolence to the oppressed evoked Malcolm's most caustic scorn. The same government that drafted black men and ordered them to unleash terrible violence in Vietnam insisted that black people were duty bound to respond nonviolently when beaten and murdered for simply trying to vote in Mississippi. "Why, that's the most hypocritical government since the world began!" Malcolm demanded that the proponents of nonviolence preach it first to the Klu Klux Klan and to the racist police. "I'm nonviolent with those who are nonviolent with me."

Malcolm's masterstroke was moving the issue of civil rights to the qualitatively higher level of human rights. "Whenever you are in a civil-rights struggle, whether you know it or not, you are confining yourself to the jurisdiction of Uncle Sam...the criminal who's responsible [in the first place]." "Expand the civil-rights struggle to the level of human rights, take it to the United Nations, where our African brothers...our Asian brothers...our Latin American brothers can throw their weight on our side." His initial success in interesting some African governments in such an approach prompted deep consternation in high levels of the U.S. government during what turned out to be the last year of Malcolm's life.

The human rights perspective was not just a clever maneuver but rather was rooted in Malcolm's heartfelt internationalism. He deeply identified with oppressed people throughout the Third World. Some of his most stunning speeches involve cogent explanations of what was happening in the Congo, and how the press was manipulating people to side with colonialism and totally depreciate the value of African lives. At a time when almost no one questioned U.S. foreign policy, Malcolm condemned the war in Vietnam. He understood the U.S. as the center of an imperialist system, with global reach, that is economically dependent on cheap raw materials, starvation wages, and captive markets in the Third World: "Washington...exercises the same forms of brutal oppression against dark-skinned people in...Vietnam, or in the Congo, or in Cuba or in another place on earth where they are trying to exploit."

Malcolm's internationalism broke through the constant intimidation of African Americans as a small, isolated minority within the U.S. by placing them squarely as a part of a large world majority: "the oppressed people of this earth make up a majority...we [can] approach our problem as a majority that can demand, not as a minority that has to beg." And he grasped that in the modern world, "real power is international."

In these 1990s days of "new world order," it may be hard to feel the explosiveness of his 1960s message: The combination of the national liberation struggles raging around the world and the rising of people of color within the U.S. could revolutionize society. But Malcolm illuminated a real and volcanic potential, one that made rulers tremble. His passionate internationalism is sorely needed today, as oppressed groups are so bitterly played off against one another. The very power of imperialism—the vast number and range of people it exploits—still constitutes the heart of its ultimate vulnerability. For Malcolm's birthday, on May 19, give yourself a precious gift—read *Malcolm X Speaks*.

[published in *Downtown*, May 12, 1993]

Petrified Pioneers

REMEMBERING BABYLON
by David Malouf
New York: Pantheon Books (1993)

> *A black! That was the boy's first thought. We're being raided by the blacks! After so many false alarms it had come.*
> *...But it wasn't a raid, there was just one of them; and the thing, as far as he could make out...was not even maybe human. The stick-like legs, all knobbed at the joints, suggested a wounded waterbird, a brolga, or a human that in the manner of the tales they told to one another, all spells and curses, had been changed into a bird, but only halfway, and now, neither one nor the other, was hopping and flapping toward them out of a world over there, beyond the no-man's land of the swamp, that was the abode of*

> *everything savage and fearsome, and since it lay so far beyond*
> *experience...of nightmare rumors, superstitions and all that*
> *belonged to the Absolute Dark.*
> *...It was a scarecrow...stumbling about over the blazing earth,*
> *its leathery face scorched black, but with hair, they saw, as it*
> *bore down upon them, as sun-bleached and pale-straw coloured*
> *as their own.*
> *...The creature, almost upon them now and with their dog at its*
> *heels, came to a halt, gave a kind of squawk, and leaping up*
> *onto the top rail of the fence, hung there, its arms outflung as if*
> *preparing for flight. Then the ragged mouth gapped.*
> *"Do not shoot," it shouted. "I am a B-b-british object!"*

Thus does Gemmy Fairly come tumbling into the small community of white settlers in the bush on the East Coast of mid-19th-century Australia. As a barely 14-year-old cabin boy and deathly ill, he had been set adrift from a British ship. Washing ashore, he was saved by the tribe of native Australians who found him. Now, 16 years later, curious about the whites who have recently arrived, he stumbles into their settlement. His hazy and faulty memory of English—using "object" for "subject"—is unintentionally prescient about the British attitude toward the aborigines.

While Gemmy is totally pivotal, this novel isn't mainly about him. As the Australian author David Malouf said in an interview in the *New York Times*, "No white person here understands the aboriginal world enough to write about it." Nor does the author ever clarify to what degree Gemmy's docile and fragile nature represents tribal culture or instead resulted from the traumas and abuse he suffered as a street urchin in England. But the presence of Gemmy—this "white black man"—is a glittering foil for flashing light on the white community he lives in for two years. Malouf, the author of numerous previous novels and books of poetry, sets his crafted and subtle writer's art to this intentional examination.

Gemmy's presence brought the whites to the edge of a world where "all their education, their knowledge, their know-how, yes, and the shotguns they carried—might not be enough against—against what? Some vulnerability to the world that could only be measured, was measured still, by the dread it evoked in them?" They lived in a strange and unruly land, that had never been plowed, where nature ran amok with a "lushness and quick bloom followed by a dank putrescence." And their unacknowledged recognition of the wrong they did to the natives weighed on their conscience in the form of nightmares about hostility and retaliation.

"Good reason, that for stripping [the land] as soon as you could manage of every vestige of the native." No wonder Gemmy gradually loses strength from the choice between paranoid distrust or condescending pity the whites offer him and flees back to his tribe. But this novel isn't limited to a broad-strokes sketch of collective social consciousness. Malouf's forte is detailed attention to individual characters, in their variety and complexity. For example, the description of the changes in the father of the most humane of the pioneer families:

> *And Jock, in his disappointment, his shame too, perhaps, at having promised [his wife] so much and provided so little, began to refine in himself the stringy, hard-bitten qualities of dourness and harsh self-discipline that the land itself appeared to demand, and which, for all the fierceness of its own sunlight, dashed out the last of sunniness from him.*

Malouf draws the settlers with considerable sympathy, taking us back, for example, to the suffocating life of the Scottish coal mines, or revealing the intense sense of worthlessness frantically denied through vehement disdain for the Blacks, or taking us on the field trips of the minister with a genuine love for botany. And there is an almost magical moment of soulfulness when the pubescent Janet finds the calmness to stand statue-still while covered by a swarm of bees, able to see the moment through Gemmy's eyes.

Malouf, with a skill reminiscent of Nadine Gordimer but without her intensely political context, is deft at drawing out the internal thoughts—the self-consciousness, insecurities, unreal hopes—at counterpoint to the verbalized conversation in social situations. For example,

> *George sensed the little catch of interest in her and felt his confidence lift. If he was let down by anything it was the state of his shirt cuffs, which were very grubby. He pulled the sleeves of his jacket down to hide them, and noticed, as he did, the dirt that was ingrained in the knuckles of his big hands; even Hector's, he saw, were cleaner. How careless he had allowed himself to become!*

The author has the annoying habit of occasionally using a pronoun that doesn't refer to the antecedent noun and of offering portents of dramatic events that never really come in the book, but these are small faults in a textured writing that otherwise does a seamless job at drawing us into the feelings of the characters and the feel of the place.

This novel is not a strident polemic against white settler colonialism in Australia, although such would be justified and even necessary for understanding that country. But it is an insightful and nuanced look into the psyche of the pioneers who fled hardship and oppression in Europe to struggle to establish a new life, but who are haunted by their fears of the people and the land they subdue in the process. They can't appreciate the potential Eden they have found because they are all too anxious to reshape it as the Babylon they remember.

[published in *Downtown*, June 8, 1994]

The Paper Trail to Genocide

THE FBI FILES
Leonard Peltier Defense Committee
Lawrence, Kansas: self-published (1996)

On March 20, 1996—the very day that activists engaged in nonviolent civil disobedience in Washington, D.C. to demand Leonard Peltier's freedom—the U.S. Parole Commission denied parole to this preeminent Native American political prisoner. After serving 20 years for murders he didn't commit, he was told his next reconsideration hearing would be in December 2008.

Those demonstrators aren't the only people outraged about this epitome of government prosecution. During his incarceration, 27 million people worldwide have signed letters and petitions, and Amnesty International has expressed grave concerns about the improprieties and injustices of his conviction, as have the European Parliament, Nelson Mandela, numerous congresspersons, and many Native American groups.

The case's basis lies in the continuation of genocidal wars against American Indians. Responding in February 1973 to a long pattern of insufferable abuses, traditionalist Indians, accompanied by the American Indian Movement (AIM), occupied the Wounded Knee trading post on the Pine Ridge Reservation in South Dakota. A 72-day siege ensued, during which the FBI and U.S. Marshals used armored personnel carriers, helicopters, and assault weapons. This was followed by a far-less-publicized reign of terror.

Within three years, 60 AIM members or supporters were killed and hundreds were wounded. The FBI never solved—in fact, never bothered to investigate—any of these murders. But on June 26, 1975, they did send two armed guards—with lots of backup—to the home of AIM supporters on the pretext of finding a pair of stolen cowboy boots. The agents didn't even have the warrant the FBI claims they were trying to serve.

Given the atmosphere of violence, this armed FBI incursion led to a shoot-out. AIM member Joe Stuntz Killsright and FBI agents Jack Coler and Roland Williams were killed. On the same day, puppet "tribal president" Dick Wilson was in Washington, D.C., illegally signing away an eighth of the reservation (the uranium-rich Sheep Mountain area) to the U.S. Park Service. The shoot-out served as a launchpad for the intensified waves of repression that finally decimated AIM.

Whenever police or FBI agents are killed, the government imperative is to obtain rapid convictions and harsh punishments to set an example—even if they can't find the actual perpetrators. In this case, AIM activists Dino Butler and Rob Robideau were charged, but later acquitted on the basis of self-defense. After that, the government's full fire was concentrated on Leonard Peltier, who was extradited from Canada based solely on affidavits later admitted to be fraudulent.

At the trial, evidence of the prevailing climate of fear that had proven decisive in the Butler/Robideau trial wasn't allowed. For the prosecutors, the "convincing evidence" was the claim that ballistics analysis showed that a bullet casing at the scene came from a rifle they linked to Peltier. But documents illegally withheld from the defense—and only uncovered years after the trial—state that the FBI's tests actually showed that the casings didn't come from Peltier's rifle or any other weapon linked to him. Other exculpatory evidence may be hidden in the thousands of pages of FBI documents yet to be released. Nevertheless, this leader of the movement for Native American self-determination is still serving a double life sentence.

Peltier's defense committee recently published a fascinating booklet called *The FBI Files*, which contains 50 of the 13,799 pages of documents released thus far, along with relevant excerpts from affidavits and court proceedings. A short introduction sets the context; tags indicate each document's significance. Unfortunately, too much emphasis is placed on the point that there were other likely suspects and not enough on the political context that justified self-defense for whoever did shoot back.

In such a crucial case, a collection of documents isn't an adequate substitute for thorough description and analysis; fortunately, this was provided by Peter Matthiessen's *In the Spirit of Crazy Horse*. Ward Churchill and Jim Vander Wall presented a shorter but very cogent summary in *Agents of Repression*. Yet for those already familiar with the background, the committee's booklet is an invaluable supplement. Here are some of the salient points revealed by the documents:

- The government claimed that it considered Peltier a "nobody" and therefore had no motive to frame him. But an FBI memo, written 10 months before the shoot-out, lists his occupation as "Manager—American Indian Movement."

- Two months prior to the incident, the FBI developed a position paper on acting "in lieu of the use of troops...to deploy FBI Special Agents in a paramilitary law enforcement situation." The defense position—that the incursion was a planned provocation—is bolstered by a memo indicating that another eight armed agents were in the area, as well as 30 lawmen able to quickly respond.

- A memo from the Rapid City FBI office to the director of the FBI describes the prosecution's knowledge that they were legally required to make FBI lab reports and expert's notes available to the defense—and their intention to withhold apparently exculpatory material.

- Several pages deal with the suppressed FBI lab reports concerning the casings.

What even more glaring evidence of a frame-up might be unearthed in the

6,589 pages the Bureau still refuses to divulge? One can only wonder. Yet enough has already been exposed to make the overturning of Peltier's conviction imperative.

To learn more about the Peltier campaign, write:

Leonard Peltier Defense Committee (LPDC)
  P.O. Box 583
  Lawrence , Kansas
  66044, USA
  email: lpdc@freepeltier.org
  website: www.freepeltier.org

[published in *Toward Freedom*, June 1996]

Mumia Must Live

LIVE FROM DEATH ROW
by Mumia Abu-Jamal
New York: Addison-Wesley (1995)

> *Perhaps we can shrug off and shred some of the dangerous myths laid on our minds like a second skin—such as...the "right" to a fair trial even. They're not rights—they're privileges of the powerful and rich. Don't expect the media networks to tell you, for they can't. Because of their incestuousness...with government and big business.*
> *I can.*
> *Even if I must do so from the valley of the shadow of death, I will.*
> *From death row, this is Mumia Abu-Jamal.*

This preface sets the tone for the immediacy and hard-hitting reality of *Live from Death Row*. The author had been a member of the Black Panther Party as a youth and later became a supporter of the radical MOVE organization. By 1981, Mumia Abu-Jamal was an award-winning journalist and an outspoken critic of police brutality in Philadelphia, when he was given the death penalty for the murder of police officer Daniel Faulkner. Despite a plethora of apparent injustices and legal irregularities in his case, Mumia is now stalked more closely than ever by an execution date of August 17, at 10 pm [since reversed].

As of October 1994, there were 2,948 people locked in death rows in the U.S. Some 40 percent are African Americans, who constitute only 11 percent of the U.S. population. And the disparity based on the race of the victims—whose lives are or are not deemed valuable—is even starker. Meanwhile the death penalty is exceedingly rare for anyone with money and resources no matter how heinous the crime.

Last year National Public Radio (NPR) contracted Mumia to do a series of recorded commentaries about life on death row—and then, after intense political pressure, canceled them for "editorial reasons." Now, thanks to the publishing house Addison-Wesley, you can read for yourself what NPR censored. *Live from Death Row* comprises those commentaries along with several of Mumia's previously published essays. In addition, the book includes an insightful introduction by acclaimed novelist John Edgar Wideman and an informative afterward by Mumia's [then] attorney, Leonard Weinglass.

The invaluable heart is the raw power of Mumia's description and analysis. In my scores of book reviews over the years, I've never used the following phrase, so I don't use it lightly: this book is a *must-read*. The government carefully shields its citizens from glimpsing any human qualities in the condemned and from learning of the glaring inequities as the justice system grinds forward with the most premeditated of serial murders. Mumia Abu-Jamal's eloquent writing lifts the shroud hiding some 2,948 souls inhabiting the netherworld of our death rows and thus exposes a darkness and leads to understanding our society as a whole.

What is death row like?

> *Mix solitary confinement, around-the-clock lock-in, no-contact visits, no prison jobs, no educational programs by which to grow, psychiatric "treatment" facilities designed only to drug you into a coma; ladle in hostile, overtly racist prison guards and staff; add the weight of the falling away of family ties and you have all the fixings for a stressful psychic stew designed to deteriorate, to erode one's humanity.*

Pennsylvania's new death row maintains virtually around-the-clock solitary confinement, with a mere five hours a week for recreation in outside cages. For many, there is no psychological life. Mumia, always with a sharp eye for irony, notes that the prison permits the inmates TVs, which numbs the mind, but not typewriters, which could be tools for legal liberation.

Even family visits are turned into exercises in humiliation. In many states, non-contact visits are the rule, preventing the family and the condemned convicts from touching. The denial of physical contact, along with all the other difficulties of making a visit, can atrophy emotional ties over time.

The author recounts, with great poignancy, the visit of his young daughter:

> *She bursts into the tiny visiting room, her brown eyes aglitter with happiness; stopped, stunned, staring at the glass barrier between us; and burst into tears at this arrogant attempt at state separation. In milliseconds, sadness and shock shifted into fury as her petite fingers curled into tight fists, which banged and*

pummeled the plexiglas barrier, which shuddered and shimmied but didn't shatter. Why can't I hug him? Why can't we kiss? Why can't I sit in his lap? Why can't we touch? Why not?

Mumia, the father, summons up extraordinary creativity to soon have his daughter laughing gleefully.

In addition to vivid, human detail on the conditions, Mumia challenges the broader politics of capital punishment. He shreds the pretense of "deterrence" by showing that the states that have led in executions have the highest murder rates. He provides a sobering example—the systematic perjury of a medical examiner who provided key testimony in thousands of criminal cases—of just how easy it is to condemn an innocent defendant to death. He dissects the McClesky v. Kemp (1987) decision, where the U.S. Supreme Court accepted the data showing extreme racial disparity in the application of Georgia's death penalty but let it stand nonetheless. He sounds an alarm about the rapid march to eviscerate habeas corpus (the traditional right by which prisoners can bring constitutionally based challenges to their convictions before the federal courts).

Unlike other prisoners, "death row inmates are not 'doing time.' Freedom does not shine at the end of the tunnel. Rather, the end of the tunnel brings extinction. Thus, for many here, there is no hope."

But there are also many continuities. Indeed, while Wilbert Rideau and Ron Wikberg's *Life Sentences* (see the review in *Downtown*, February 3, 1993) was so loudly promoted as providing the "real story inside prison," *Live from Death Row* does a much better job. Mumia provides graphic examples of vicious beatings of inmates by guards, of psychological deterioration and suicides, and of medical neglect tantamount to attempted murder. Yet the perpetrators in the well-documented cases presented have not been indicted. As the author explains, "words like 'justice,' 'law,' 'civil rights,' and, yes, 'crime' have different elastic meanings depending on...whether one works for the system or against it."

While these violent incidents are the most dramatic, Mumia maintains perspective in explaining that violence is not the pressing daily issue for most prisoners:

> *The most profound horror of prison lives in the day-to-day banal occurrences. Prison is a second-by-second assault on the soul, a day-to-day degradation of the self, an oppressive steel and brick umbrella that transforms seconds into hours and hours into days.*

The strength of Mumia's writing is best seen in his vivid descriptions of prison life and his ability to always educe the human element, even in brief sketches. The broader political essays in this collection are also short and crisp, usually to spotlight one key point or to expose a glaring hypocrisy rather than to present a comprehensive analysis. Thus "Musings on Malcolm" doesn't attempt a complete exegesis of his entire politics but does confront the latter-day efforts to water down his message. Mumia forcefully reclaims the real Malcolm, the uncompromising scourge of American racism who died for the human rights of self-defense and self-determination.

The book includes numerous other short essays on politics and criminal justice that are well worth reading: the persuasive national pattern underlying the infamous beating of Rodney King in Los Angeles; the danger, nonetheless, of double jeopardy entailed in the federal retrial of the four police perpetrators who had been shamefully acquitted in a state trial; the sham behind the "get tough on crime" mania, which is a proven failure at reducing crime but a great success as a social program of public employment for a predominantly white sector of workers; the dark, repressive trend toward "Super Max" prisons in the U.S. with conditions of almost total lockdown and solitary confinement.

Mumia perspicaciously cautions against writing off today's youth as "a lost generation," as he limns the social and cultural conditions to which they are responding and indicates the potential seeds for positive rebellion. "If they are lost, find them."

His two pieces on Huey Newton and the Black Panther Party show a rare ability to appreciate both the brilliance and the shortcomings of the man. Mumia also brings back into focus the crucial role that the murders of 38 Panthers played in destroying the party and makes an impassioned appeal to revive the Panther Party 10-point program: "The very conditions that gave rise to the party in the 1960s—brutal cops, racist courts, ineffective education, joblessness and the like—still plague our people to this day."

The release of *Live from Death Row* ignited a public controversy. The same forces that generated the pressure to cancel the NPR series—the Fraternal Order of Police and Officer Faulkner's widow (who understandably is antagonistic to the man she believes killed her husband)—tried to stop publication of this book. They protest that the murderers should not be allowed to profit from the notoriety of their crimes. The only counterpoints acknowledged in the mainstream media are the right to free speech and the interest in writings about death row.

As happens so often, the terms of debate turn reality on its head. It was not the notoriety of the case that created, spanking-new, a broadcast or publishing opening for Mumia. He was an award-winning journalist and had already appeared on NPR before the 1981 incident occurred. It was precisely his articulate voice for the African American community and his sharp critique of police brutality that made Mumia a target of police harassment and attack. The result was December 9, 1981, when Mumia was gravely wounded and beaten and then charged with the murder despite several witnesses who say they saw the actual shooter flee.

The armies that occupy the ghettos and barrios can't abide an effective tribune for human rights and Black self-determination. They tried to silence him in 1981; they are trying to silence him today. This vibrant human being, with his robust voice for freedom, must live.

Demand that the execution of Mumia Abu-Jamal be stopped.

To contact Mumia's Defense Committee:

International Concerned Family
and Friends of Mumia Abu-Jamal
4601 Market Street
Philadelphia, Pennsylvania
19143, USA
phone: (215) 476-8812
email: icffmaj@aol.com
website: www.mumia.org

[published in *Downtown*, July 19, 1995]

3 Haiku for Mumia Abu-Jamal

Young Panther, then
bold journalist. His crime?—speaking
the truth to power.

With huge heart, wry wit,
and ardent analysis—
a torch for freedom.

Sunny, slightly sly
smile slips through barren bars to
sprinkle us with life.

[published in The Black Panther, Winter 1995]

Chapter 3

Lessons from History: Race and Class in America

Looking at the White Working Class Historically

One of the supreme issues for our movement is summed up in the contradictions of the term "white working class." On one hand, there is the class designation that should imply, along with all other workers of the world, a fundamental role in the overthrow of capitalism. On the other hand, there is the identification of being part of a ("white") oppressor nation.

Historically, we must admit that the identity with the oppressor nation has been primary. There have been times of fierce struggle around economic issues, but precious little in the way of a revolutionary challenge to the system itself. There have been moments of uniting with Black and other Third World workers in union struggles, but more often than not an opposition to full equality and a disrespect for the self-determination of other oppressed peoples. These negative trends have been particularly pronounced within the current era of history (since World War II). White labor has been either a legal opposition within or an active component of the U.S. imperial system.

There have been two basic responses to this reality by the white Left: (1) The main position by far has been opportunism. This has entailed an unwillingness to recognize the leading role within the U.S. of national liberation struggles, a failure to make the fight against white supremacy a conscious and prime element of all organizing, and, related to the above, a general lack of revolutionary combativeness against the imperial state. More specifically, opportunism either justifies the generally racist history of the white working class and the Left or romanticizes that history by presenting it as much more anti-racist than reality merits. (2) Our own tendency, at its best moments, has recognized the leading role of national liberation and the essential position of solidarity to building any revolutionary consciousness among whites. We have often, however, fallen into an elitist or perhaps defeatist view that dismisses the possibility of organizing significant numbers of white people, particularly working class whites.

There is very little analysis, and even less practice, that is both real about the nature and consciousness of the white working class and yet holds out the prospect of organizing a large number on a revolutionary basis. This fissure will not be joined by some magical fusion of abstract thought—either by evoking classical theories of class or by lapsing into cultural or biological determinism. We must use our tools of analysis (materialism) to understand concretely how this contradiction developed (historically). But a historical view can not be static. In seeing how certain forces developed, we must also look (dialectically) at under what conditions and through what means the contradiction can be transformed.

In this review, I want to look at three historical studies that contribute to the needed discussion: (A) Ted Allen's two essays in *White Supremacy* (a collection printed by the Sojourner Truth Organization); (B) W. E. B. Du Bois, *Black Reconstruction* (New York:1933); and (C) J. Sakai, *Settlers: The Mythology of the White Proletariat* (Chicago:1983).

Ted Allen's *White Supremacy in the U.S.: Slavery and the Origins of Racism*

Allen's two essays provide us with a very cogent and useful account of the development of the structure of white supremacy in the U.S. He shows both how this system was consciously constructed by the colonial ("Plantation Bourgeoisie") ruling class and what the initial impact was on the development of white laborers. Contrary to the cynical view that racism is basic to human nature and that there has always been (and therefore will always be) a fundamental racial antagonism, Allen shows that systematic white supremacy developed in a particular historical period, for specific material reasons.

> Up to the 1680s little distinction was made in the status of Blacks and English and other Europeans held in involuntary servitude. Contrary to common belief the status of Blacks in the first seventy years of the Virginia colony was not that of racial, lifelong, hereditary slavery, and the majority of the whites who came were not free. Black and white servants intermarried, escaped together, and rebelled together. (p. 3)

A rapidly developing plantation system required an expanding labor supply. The solution was both to have more servants and to employ them for longer terms. A move from fixed-term servitude (e.g., seven years) to perpetual slavery would be valuable to the ruling class of the new plantation economy. The question for analysis is not so much why there was a transition to chattel slavery but why it was not imposed on the white servants as well as on the Blacks. To analyze this development, we need to understand that any method of exploiting labor requires a system of social control.

There was a series of servile rebellions that threatened the plantation system in the period preceding the transition to racially designated chattel slavery and white supremacy. Allen cites numerous examples. In 1661 Black and Irish servants joined in an insurrectionary plot in Bermuda. In 1663, in Virginia, there was an insurrection for the common freedom of Black, white, and Indian servants. In the next 20 years, there were no fewer than 10 popular and servile revolts and plots in Virginia. Also many Black and white servants successfully escaped (to Indian territories) and established free societies.

Allen places particular emphasis on Bacon's Rebellion, which began in April 1676. This was a struggle within the ruling class over "Indian policy," but Bacon resorted to arming white and Black servants, promising them freedom. Allen says "the transcendent importance" of this revolt is that "the armed working class, Black and white, fought side by side for the abolition of slavery." He mentions, but doesn't deal with the reality, that Bacon's cause was to exterminate the Indians. Allen's focus is on the formation of chattel slavery, but it is a problem that he doesn't analyze the other major foundation of white supremacy: the theft of Native lands through genocide.

The 20-year period of servile rebellions made the issue of social control urgent for the plantation bourgeoisie, at the same time that they economically needed to move to a system of perpetual slavery. The purpose of creating a basic white/Black division was in order to have one section of labor police and control the other. As Allen says, "the non-slavery of white labor was the indispensable condition for the slavery of black labor." [1]

A series of laws was passed and practices were imposed that forged a qualitative distinction between white and Black labor. In 1661 a Virginia law imposed twice the penalty time for escaped English bondservants who ran away in the company of an African lifetime bondservant. Heavy penalties were imposed on white women servants who bore children fathered by Africans. One of the very first white slave privileges was the exemption of white servant women from work in the fields and the requirements through taxes to force Black children to go to work at 12, while white servant children were excused until they were 14. In 1680, Blacks were forbidden to carry arms, defensive or offensive. At the same time, it was made legal to kill a Black fugitive bondservant who resisted recapture.

What followed 1680 was a 25-year period of laws that systematically drew the color line as the limit on various economic, social, and political rights. By 1705, "the distinctions between white servants and Black slavery were fixed: Black slaves were to be held in life long hereditary slavery and whites for five years, with many rights and protections afforded to them by law." (p. 6)

We can infer from these series of laws that white laborers were not "innately racist" before the material and social distinctions were drawn. This is evidenced by the rulers' need to impose very harsh penalties against white servants who escaped with Blacks or who bore them children. As historian Philip Bruce observed of this period, many white servants "had only recently arrived from England, and were therefore comparatively free from... race prejudice."

The white bondservants now could achieve freedom after five years service; the white women and children, at least, were freed from the most arduous labor. The white bondservant, once freed, had the prospect of the right to vote and to own land (at the Indians' expense).

These privileges did not come from the kindness of the planters' hearts nor from some form of racial solidarity (Scottish coal miners were held in slavery in the same period of time). Quite simply, the poor whites were needed and used as a force to suppress the main labor force: the African chattel slaves. The poor white men constituted the rank and file of the militias and later (beginning in 1727), the slave patrols. They were given added benefits, such as tax exemptions, to do so. By 1705, after Blacks had been stripped of the legal right to self-defense, the white bondservant was given a musket upon completion of servitude. There was such a clear and conscious strategy that by 1698 there were even "deficiency laws" that required the plantation owners to maintain a certain ratio of white to African servants. The English Parliament, in 1717, passed a law making transportation to bond servitude in the plantation colonies a legal punishment for crime. Another example of this conscious design is revealed in the Council of Trade and Plantation report to the king in 1721 saying that in South Carolina, "Black slaves have lately attempted and were very nearly succeeding in a new revolution—and therefore, it may be necessary to propose some new law for encouraging the entertainment of more white servants in the future."

It would be important to have a concomitant analysis of the role of the theft of Indian land and of the impact of the slave trade itself. Allen's analysis[2] of early plantation labor, however, provides an invaluable service. When Black and white labor were in the same conditions of servitude, there was a good deal of solidarity. A system of white supremacy was consciously constructed in order to (1) extend and intensify exploitation (through chattel slavery) and (2) have shock troops (poor, but now privileged, whites) to suppress slave rebellions. Thus the 1680–1705 period[3] is a critical benchmark essential to understanding all subsequent North American history. As Allen tells us, "It was the bourgeoisie's deliberately contrived policy of differentiation between white and Black labor through the system of white skin privileges for white labor that allowed the bourgeoisie to use the poor whites as an instrument of social control over the Black workers." (p. 5)

Allen refers to, but doesn't fully develop, the impact of white supremacy on the white laborers. His general analysis is that by strengthening capitalist rule it reinforced exploitation of whites too: "white supremacy [was] the keystone of capitalist rule which left white labor poor, exploited and increasingly powerless with respect to their rulers and exploiters." But since "the mass of poor whites was alienated from the black proletariat and enlisted as enforcers of bourgeois power" (p. 40), it would be useful to have more analysis of the interplay of these two contradictory roles: exploited/enforcers. In any case, the overall effect was to break the white workers from their proletarian class struggle alongside Blacks and to bind them more tightly to their own ruling class.

W. E. B. Du Bois's *Black Reconstruction 1860–1880*

Du Bois's work is a classic study, and absolutely essential to understanding U.S. history. The book deals not only with the Reconstruction period that followed the Civil War but also with the war itself and the period of slavery preceding it. This review will only focus on the insights about the relationship of white labor to Black people and their struggles. There are, however, two essential theses that Du Bois puts forward that should be pointed out here.

1. The slaves were not freed by Lincoln's or by the Union's benevolence. The slaves essentially freed themselves. First they fled the plantations in great numbers, depleting the South of labor for its wartime economy. Second, they volunteered to fight with the Union to defeat the slavocracies. The Emancipation Proclamation of 1863 came only when Lincoln realized that he needed to use Black troops in order to win the war (it applied only to states at war with the Union). Two hundred thousand Black troops made the decisive difference in the war.

2. Reconstruction was not the period of unbridled corruption and of heartless oppression of the noble (white) South that has since been depicted by the propaganda of history. Not only did Reconstruction see the active role of Black people in the government, but also, based on that, it was an era of democratic reform that brought such things as free public education, public works, and advances in women's rights to the South. At the same time, Du Bois shows how Reconstruction was defeated by a systematic campaign of terror, with the complicity of the capitalist North.

Du Bois's analysis of the pre-war South starts with the basic structures (whose origins Allen described) in place and well developed. The system of slavery demanded a special police force, and such a force was made possible and unusually effective by the presence of poor whites. By this time, there were "more white people to police the slaves than there were slaves." (p. 12)

Still, there were very important class differentiations within the white population. Seven percent of the total white Southern population owned three-fourths of the slaves. Seventy percent owned no slaves at all. To Du Bois, a basic issue is why the poor whites would agree to police the slaves. Since slavery competed with and thereby undercut the wages of white labor, wouldn't it seem natural for poor whites in general to oppose slavery?

Du Bois presents two main reasons: (1) poor whites were provided with non-laboring jobs as overseers, slave-drivers, and members of slave patrols (Du Bois doesn't indicate what percentage of whites held jobs like these). (2) There was the "vanity" of feeling associated with the master and the dislike of "Negro" toil. The poor white never considered himself a laborer; rather, he aspired to himself own slaves. These aspirations were not without some basis (about one-fourth of the Southern white population were petty bourgeois, small slave-owners).

The result was that the system was held stable and intact by the poor white. Gradually the whole white South became an armed and commissioned camp to keep Negroes in slavery and to kill the black rebel. (p. 12)

There was another factor that had heavy impact on both poor whites in the South and the Northern working class. In early America, land was free (based on genocide of the Indians), and thus acquiring property was a possibility for nearly every thrifty worker. This access to property not only created a new petty bourgeoisie emerging out of the white working class, it also created an ideology of individual advancement rather than collective class struggle as the answer to exploitation.

The Northern working class tended to oppose the spread of slavery but not oppose slavery itself. If slavery came to the North, it would compete with and undercut free labor. If the plantation system spread to the West, it would monopolize the land that white workers aspired to settle as small farmers. But there was very little pro-abolition sentiment in the white labor movement.

Northern white labor saw the threat of competition for jobs from the fugitive slaves and the potentially millions behind them if abolition prevailed in the South. There was considerable racism toward freed Blacks in the North.

The most downtrodden sector of white workers—the immigrants—might seem to have had the least stake in white supremacy. But the racism had its strongest expression among these sections because at the bottom layer of white labor, they felt most intensely the competition from Blacks for jobs[4] and blamed Blacks for their low wages. During the Civil War, the Irish and other immigrant workers were the base for the "anti-draft" riots in the Northern cities. These were really straight-out murderous race riots against the local Black population.

For Du Bois, the position of the Northern working class appears somewhat irrational. Freed slaves did represent, it's true, potential competition for jobs. However, Du Bois argues, "what they [white workers] failed to comprehend was that the black man enslaved was an even more formidable and fatal competition than the black man free." (p. 20)

This analysis seems inadequate. As materialists we have to wonder why such a formidable consensus[5] of a class and its organizations would hold a position over a long period of time that was opposed to their interests. In addition to the issue of competition, we must ask if the superexploitation of Black labor was used to provide some additional benefits for white labor—in a way, did the formation of the U.S. empire anticipate some of the basic oppressor/oppressed worker relations described by Lenin with the development of imperialism? Certainly the issue in relationship to the Native Americans is clear: genocide provided the land that allowed many white workers to "rise" out of their class (which also strengthened the bargaining power of remaining laborers). This reality firmly implanted one of the main pillars of white supremacy. There were undoubtedly also some direct benefits from the superexploitation of slave labor for the white working class that Du Bois does not analyze. Data presented in *Settlers: The Mythology of the White Proletariat* indicates that white American workers earned much higher wages than their British counterparts.

Du Bois sees the material basis of white labor antagonism to Blacks as based in competition for jobs and its impact on wage levels. On the other hand, he sees the existence of a slave strata as even worse competition. But how did this second aspect play itself out? Perhaps as direct competition only for the white working class in the South. But here there was the counterforce of slavery being the direct basis for a large section of whites to become petty bourgeois, while others got jobs overseeing and controlling Black labor. It isn't clear how slavery in the South would directly compete with Northern labor; on the contrary some benefits might be passed on as a result of the superexploitation of Black labor. Certainly first the wealth generated by King Cotton and then the availability of the cheap raw materials were cornerstones of the Northern industrialization that provided and expanded jobs.

Further, this issue cannot be treated in isolation from the other main pillar of white supremacy—the availability of land based on genocide of the Native Americans. It is doubtful that the capitalist class would have opened up the West for settlement without the guarantee of still having an adequate supply of cheap labor for industrialization. Earlier in England, to prepare the way for manufacturing, there had been the brutal enclosure movements that forced peasants off their land in order to create a large supply of cheap labor. In North America, the movement was in the opposite direction: people were actually "settling" the land, becoming peasants, while manufacture was developing. It is unlikely that this would have been allowed without (1) slavery to guarantee cheap labor for the main cash crops and raw materials and (2) an influx of immigrant labor into the Northern cities. In any case, the predominant position among Northern labor opposed the spread of slavery but did not favor abolition; these positions were punctuated by occasional race riots with a white working class base. In addition to the aspiration to rise to the petty bourgeoisie, a labor aristocracy began to develop in the prewar period, usually based in longer-established white settlers as opposed to immigrant workers. After 1850, unions of skilled labor began to separate from common labor. These skilled labor unions established closed shops that excluded Blacks and farmers.

After the Civil War the defeat of the slavocracy, the presence of the Union Army, and the reality of thousands of armed Black troops, all should have created radically new conditions and possibilities for Black/poor white alliance in the South. Du Bois, in his very positive view of Reconstruction, goes so far as to describe it as "a dictatorship of labor" (p. 187) in the South. Reconstruction with the important Black role in Southern politics did mean a lot of democratic reforms while it lasted. There are some significant indications of poor whites allying. For example, early on in Reconstruction, Mississippi and South Carolina had popular conventions with significant poor white involvement. The Jim Crow laws, later passed in Mississippi, found it necessary to place severe strictures against whites associating with Blacks. But there isn't much evidence of a solid alliance from any large sector of poor whites.

The basis for an alliance seems clear. The basic problem of Reconstruction was economic; the kernel of the economy was land. Both freed slaves and poor whites had an interest in acquiring land. It would seem logical to have an alliance to expropriate the plantations. Du Bois gives several reasons why this alliance didn't come to fruition: (1) Poor whites were determined to keep Blacks from access to the better land from which slavery had driven the white peasants (i.e., if people took over ownership of land they had worked, the ex-slaves would get the choice plantation land). (2) Poor whites were afraid that the planters would control the Black vote and thus be able to politically defeat the poor whites' class aspirations. (3) Petty bourgeois whites still wanted to have cheap Black labor to exploit. (4) White labor was determined to keep Blacks from work that competed with them; poor whites were desperately afraid of losing their jobs. (5) White labor, while given low wages, was compensated with social status, such as access to public parks, schools, etc.; the police were drawn from its ranks; the courts treated whites leniently. In short, white labor saw a threat to its racial prerogatives in every advance of the Blacks.

These reasons were all very real. However, it is not clear on the face of it why they should have overriden the potential for joint expropriation of the plantations. We must also look at a factor that Du Bois mentions but does not develop sufficiently: the power backing Reconstruction was the Union Army. Despite the importance of Black troops, there is no indication that the Union Army as a structured institution was ever anything other than an instrument of Northern capital. Northern capital wanted to break the national political power of the old plantation owners (hence the Black vote), but it certainly didn't want to support the liquidation of private property, even in the South. In fact, by 1868 the Union Army had forcibly retaken almost all the plantation land seized and worked by communities of freed slaves (see Vincent Harding, *There Is a River*). Thus died the promise of "40 acres and a mule."

Therefore, Du Bois's characterization of Reconstruction as a "dictatorship of labor" backed by the Union Army seems overdrawn. He is much more on the mark when he says, "It was inconceivable, therefore, that the masters of Northern industry, through their growing control of American government, were going to allow the laborers of the South any more real control of wealth and industry than was necessary to curb the political power of the planters." (p. 45)

It seems to me that with the presence and dominance of Union troops, the joint expropriation of the old plantations did not appear as a very tangible possibility. It is in that context that the poor whites' overwhelming choice was to try to reconsolidate their old white privileges. This would also be the natural spontaneous choice given the history and culture. The power context also reflects on the question of alignments on a national scale.

Looking nationwide, Du Bois reasons, "there **should** have been [emphasis added]... a union between champions of universal suffrage and the rights of freedmen, together with the leaders of labor, the small landholders of the West, and logically the poor whites of the South" against the Northern industrial oligarchy and the former Southern oligarchy. This union never took place. Du Bois cites two main reasons: (1) The old anti-Black labor rivalry and (2) poor whites' old dream of becoming small farmers in the West, hoping to benefit from land speculation and the small-scale exploitation of Black labor.

Here again Du Bois's explanation, while helpful, does not seem to be sufficiently materialist; the implication seems to be white workers going against their more basic material interest. We need to also specify some of the concrete benefits that accrued to white labor at the expense of Black (and Indian) subjugation. Also, to reiterate, these choices took place in the context of a vigorous and rising U.S. capitalism. The prospect of white supremacist rewards that capitalists could offer must have seemed very real and immediate, while the prospect of overthrowing private property (which would necessitate alliance with Blacks) must have seemed difficult and distant.

By the 1870s, the labor movement in the North saw the growth of craft and race unions. "Skilled labor proceeded to share in the exploitation of the reservoir of low-paid common labor." The position of common labor was greatly weakened since their strikes and violence could not succeed with skilled labor and engineers to keep the machinery going.

In the South, the poor whites became the shock troops for the mass terror that destroyed the gains of Black Reconstruction. Du Bois explains that the overthrow of Reconstruction was a property—not a race—war. Still, the poor whites involved were not simply tools of property. They perceived their own interests in attacking the Black advances. In fact, some of the early examples of Klan-style violence that Du Bois provides show such bands attacking the old planters as well as the freed slaves.

Du Bois documents, state by state, the war of terror that defeated Reconstruction. Here, I will indicate it with one example: In Texas, during the height of the war, there was an average of 60 homicides per month. Black Reconstruction was also defeated with the complicity of Northern capital, which agreed to the withdrawal of Union troops in 1877. The defeat of Reconstruction meant that the color line had been used to establish a new dictatorship of property in the South. For Black labor, this meant a move back toward slavery in the form of sharecropping, Jim Crow laws, and violent repression. For white labor, their active support of the "color caste" (white supremacy) immeasurably strengthened the power of capital, which ruled over them.

J. Sakai's *Settlers: The Mythology of the White Proletariat*

While Allen and Du Bois focus on specific periods, Sakai sketches the whole time from the first European settlement to the current time. Also, Sakai examines the relationship of the white proletariat to Native Americans, Mexicanos, and Asians, as well as to the Black nation.

This, of course, is quite a scope to cover in one book. Sakai starts from an explicit political perspective: what is called the United States "is really a Euro-american settler empire, built on colonially oppressed nations and peoples." In this light, a lot is revealed about U.S. history that not only is quite different from what we learned in school but also debunks interpretations generally put out by the white Left.

Even for those of us who think we understand the white supremacist core of U.S. history, reading *Settlers* is still quite an education. To take one stark example, when the Europeans first arrived, there were an estimated 10 million Natives in North America. By 1900, there were only 300,000. Sakai also critiques the white supremacist nature of movements mythologized by the Left such as Bacon's Rebellion, Jacksonian Democracy, and the struggle for the eight-hour workday. Sakai shows that integral to most advances of "democratic" reform for white workers was an active consolidation of privileges at the expense of colonized Third World peoples.

Because it covers such a range, there are some points of interpretation that could be questioned. Overall, it is a very revealing and useful look at U.S. history. For this review, I just want to look at one period, the 1930s. Then we also will examine the overall political conclusions that Sakai draws.

The Great Depression of the 1930s was a time of intensified class struggle, the building of the CIO[6], the famed sit-down strikes such as in Flint, Michigan, the height of the Communist Party U.S.A. The CIO of this period has often been praised by leftists as exemplary in including Black workers in its organizing drive.

Sakai sees the essence of the period as the integration of the various European immigrant minorities into the privileges of the settler nation (white Amerika). In return, as U.S. imperialism launched its drive for world hegemony, it could depend on the armies of solidly united settlers (including the whole white working class) serving imperialism at home and on the battlefield. The New Deal ended industrial serfdom and gave the European "ethnic" national minorities integration as Amerikans by sharply raising their privileges—but only in the settler way: in government-regulated unions loyal to U.S. imperialism.

Where the CIO organized Black workers, it was utilitarian rather than principled. By the 1930s, Black labor had come to play a strategic role in five industries (usually performing the dirtiest and most hazardous jobs at lower pay): automotive, steel, meat-packing, coal, and railroads. Thus, in a number of industrial centers, the CIO unions could not be secure without controlling Afrikan (Black) labor. "The CIO's policy, then, came to promote integration under settler leadership where Afrikan labor was numerous and strong (such as the foundries, the meat-packing plants, etc). and to maintain segregation and Jim Crow in situations where Afrikan labor was numerically lesser and weak. Integration and segregation were but two aspects of the same settler hegemony." (p. 86)

At the same time, it was CIO practice to reserve the skilled crafts and more desirable production jobs for white (male) workers. For example, the first UAW/GM contract that resulted from the great Flint sit-down strike contained a "noninterchangeability" clause that in essence made it illegal for Black workers to move up from being janitors or foundry workers. Such a policy came on the heels of Depression trends that had forced Blacks out of the better jobs. Between 1930 and 1936, some 50 percent of all Afrikan skilled workers were pushed out of their jobs.

Roosevelt's support of the CIO came from a strategy to control and channel the class struggle. A significant factor in the success of the 1930s union organizing drives was the government's refusal to use armed repression. No U.S. armed forces were used against Euro-Amerikan workers from 1933–1941.[7]

This policy was in marked contrast to, for example, the attack on the Nationalist party in Puerto Rico. In 1937, one month after President Roosevelt refused to use force against the Flint sit-down strike, U.S. police opened fire on a peaceful Nationalist parade in Ponce, Puerto Rico. Nineteen Puerto Rican citizens were killed and more than 100 wounded. While leftists committed to organizing in the '30s might want to bring in different examples and argue Sakai's interpretations, I think that overall the subsequent history of the CIO has been clear: it has both reinforced white monopolies on preferred jobs and has been a loyal component of U.S. imperial policy abroad.[8]

What conclusions about the white working class can we draw from this history? Sakai takes a definite and challenging position. *Settlers* is addressed, internally, for discussion among Third World revolutionaries. Still, it is important for us to grapple with its politics and to apply those lessons to our own situation and responsibilities.

Sakai's general view of history is that the masses of whites have advanced themselves primarily by oppressing Third World people—not by any means of class struggle. Also that for most[9] of U.S. history, the proletariat has been a colonial proletariat, made up only of oppressed Afrikan, Indian, Latino, and Asian workers. On top of this basic history, U.S. imperial hegemony after World War II raised privileges to another level. "Those expansionist years of 1945–1965... saw the final promotion of the white proletariat. This was an en masse promotion so profound that it eliminated not only consciousness, but the class itself." (p. 47)

Thus, for Sakai, there is an oppressor nation but it doesn't have a worker class, at least not in any politically meaningful sense of the term. To buttress this position, Sakai (1) discusses the supra-class cultural and ideological unification in the white community; (2) points to the much higher standard of living for white Americans; and (3) presents census statistics to indicate that whites are predominantly (over 60 percent) bourgeois, middle class and labor aristocracy. Here, Sakai enumerates class based solely on white male jobs in order to correct for situations where the woman's lower-status job is a second income for the family involved. This method, however, fails to take account of the growing number of families where the woman's wages are the primary income. The methodological question also relates to the potential for women's oppression to be a source for a progressive current within the white working class.

In a way, Sakai puts forward a direct negation of the opportunist "Marxist" position that makes class designation everything and liquidates the distinction between oppressed and oppressor nation.

Sakai's survey of U.S. history understates the examples of fierce class struggle within the oppressor nation that imply at least some basis for dissatisfaction and disloyalty by working whites. Still, these examples—defined primarily around economic demands and usually resolved by consolidation of privileges relative to Third World workers—cannot be parlayed into a history of "revolutionary class struggle."

Class consciousness cannot be defined solely by economic demands. At its heart, it is a movement toward the revolutionary overthrow of capitalism. "Proletariat internationalism"—solidarity with all other peoples oppressed and exploited by imperialism—is a necessary and essential feature of revolutionary class consciousness. In our condition, this requires up-front support for and alliance with the oppressed nations, particularly those within the U.S. (Black, Mexicano, Native). Thus white supremacy and class consciousness cannot peacefully coexist with each other. One chokes off the other. An honest view of the 350-year history clearly shows that the alignment with white supremacy has predominated over the revolutionary class consciousness.

Furthermore, the culture of a more or less unified, supra-class, white supremacist outlook is also a very important factor. That culture is a reflection of a common history as part of an oppressor nation; it also becomes a material force in perpetuating that outlook and those choices. Common culture is a format to organize even those whites with the least material stake in white supremacy.

All the above considerations, however, do not provide a complete class analysis. There are other aspects of people's relationship to the mode of production that are important. A central distinction is between those who own or control the means of production (e.g., corporations, banks, real estate) and families who live by wages or salaries, i.e., by working for someone else. Those who live by the sale of labor power have little control over or access to the basic power that determines the purpose of production and the direction of society as a whole. In the best of times, most white workers may feel comfortable; in periods of crisis, the stress might be felt and resolved on qualitatively different lines within the oppressor nation (e.g., which class bears the costs of an imperialist war or feels the brunt of economic decline). Even among whites, those who aren't in control have a basic interest in a transformation of society. It may not be expressed in "standard of living" (goods that can be purchased) as much as in the quality of life (e.g., war, environment, health, and the impact of racism, sexism, decadence). Crises can bring these contradictions more to the surface, expressing the necessity to reorganize society.

In my view there definitely is a white working class. It is closely tied to imperialism; the labor aristocracy is the dominant sector, and the class as a whole has been corrupted by white supremacy; but the class within the oppressor nation that lives by the sale of its labor power has not disappeared. This is not just an academic distinction; under certain historical conditions it can have important meaning.

A dialectical analysis goes beyond description to look at both the process of development and the potential for transformation. This is the great value of the Ted Allen essays. They show how white supremacy was a conscious construction by the ruling class under specific historical conditions. This implies that, under different historical conditions, there also can be a conscious deconstruction by oppressed nations, women, and the working class. Our analysis has to look for potential historical changes and movement activity that could promote revolutionary consciousness within the white working class.

In approaching such an analysis, we must guard against the mechanical notion that economic decline will in itself lessen racism. The lessons from Du Bois's description of the "anti-draft" riots of the 1860s (as well as our experience over the last 20 years) show the opposite to be true. Under economic pressure, the spontaneous tendency is to fight harder for white supremacy. While the absolute value of privilege might decrease, the relative value is usually increasing as Third World people abroad and within the U.S. bear the worst hardships of the crisis. The white workers closest to the level of Third World workers can be the most virulent and violent in fighting for white supremacy.

Rarely have major sectors of the white working class been won over to revolutionary consciousness based on a reform interest. Imperialism in ascendancy has been able to offer them more bread and butter than the abstraction of international solidarity. But a more fundamental interest could emerge in a situation where imperialism in crisis can't deliver and where the possibility of replacing imperialism with a more humane system becomes tangible.

Some Lessons from the '60s

In the '60s and '70s, it appeared as though the rapid advance of national liberation was remaking the world in the direction of socialism. In the past 12 years, the painful setbacks have shown just how difficult it is to create a viable alternative to underdevelopment in the Third World. Today we are at a historical juncture of crisis in social practice and theory. Nonetheless, given prevailing conditions, the contradictions and social struggles are likely to continue to be most intense in the Third World. Now, however, we have no clear guidelines as to when, how, or even if these struggles can lead to socialism in the world.

While it is discouraging to no longer have a defined outline for the triumph of world revolution, the human stake in the outcome of the social crises and struggles does not allow us the luxury of demoralization. We have to make our most intelligent and concerted effort to maximize the potential for humanitarian and liberatory change.

Solidarity with the Third World struggles has to become our top priority for both humanitarian and strategic reasons—the more we can do to get imperialism off their backs, the better the chances for their potential for leadership toward world transformation to bloom. But solidarity cannot be ethereal; it cannot be developed and sustained with any scope without some sort of social base within the oppressor nation. Class may very well not be a primary form for such a social base, but we still need to establish more realistic and useful terms for the role class can play in the next period of social upheaval and motion. The historical lessons we examined make it clear that it would be unreal to talk about the white working class "as a whole" or even the majority of it, as a revolutionary force.

But, on the other hand, the predominance of white supremacy is not genetically determined nor is it carved in stone historically. We need to look for what conditions and movement activity can promote anti-imperialist organizing within the white working class—both to build solidarity forces and to point the direction toward a genuine long-term emancipation of working people from a system based on exploitation, dehumanization, and war.

The movement of the 1960s showed the potential for positive response from whites to the rise of national liberation struggles, along with a desire for a more humane and cooperative society. It is true that this response came first from elite students, the children of the petty bourgeoisie and professionals. These sectors felt more secure in their privilege and felt less immediately threatened by advances for Black people than did the poorer sectors of whites. Also, students and intellectuals are frequently the group that early on, albeit subjectively, responds to emerging contradictions in a given society. The movement was a real reflection of the objective advance of national liberation and the need to transform U.S. society. As the war in Vietnam dragged on, increasing numbers of working-class youth became involved in the movement.

This fledgling success and glimmer of potential of the '60s also provided some historical lessons that we have not done nearly enough to analyze and codify. The movement involved more than the traditional unrest of students. Broader cultural identification played a major role in generating a larger youth movement. First and foremost, it was the impact of Black culture, with its more humane values of social consciousness, emotional expressiveness, and sense of community—primarily through the genesis of rock 'n' roll. The cultural rebellion also importantly involved an opening of sexual expression that challenged the prevailing straitjacket of repression. Paradoxically, and counter to the grim realities we've come to understand, at that time drugs (particularly marijuana and LSD) were seen as liberation from repressive control and promoting anti-authoritarianism.

Civil rights and anti-war activity among whites started mainly on the campuses, and the student movement was a spearhead for political consciousness throughout the '60s. Most white working-class youth were initially indifferent if not downright hostile to these first stirrings. But over the years there were increasing cultural links that laid the basis for a broader movement. For example, white working-class youth who dropped out of the daily work grind and were often into drugs gravitated to communities near campuses. Anti-draft counseling offices brought many into more direct political contact with the movement. The burgeoning of community colleges meant that more working-class youths were themselves students.

By the late 1960s the growing disenchantment with and anger about the war in Vietnam provided a unifying focus and sense of identity for all the disaffected. When soldiers in Vietnam started to turn against the war, that added a new dimension to the movement, as well as significantly deepening its class composition.

The main base for the anti-imperialist movement of the '60s was a social movement of youth, heavily impacted and in many ways generated by Black culture. As the movement developed, it involved increasing numbers of working-class youth, who played a major role in the movement's growth and heightened militancy. This extension showed (1) the ability of culture to be a bridge to deepening the class base of a social movement; (2) the increasing ways the draft, in the context of a bloody and losing war, made the interests of some working-class people intersect with those of national liberation; and (3) the contagious effect of victorious revolutions and liberatory vision.

The New Left did have an intelligent strategy for extending the movement and deepening its class base, but abandoned it at the very moment it was achieving stunning success. The Revolutionary Youth Movement (RYM) strategy called for the extension of what had started as a primarily elite student base to a broader, particularly working-class youth base by doing more work around the draft, with GIs in community colleges, and among youth in working-class neighborhoods. The movement, still heavily male supremacist, had little sense of the role of women and often lapsed into very negative sexist posturing. However, even here, the freedom, energy, and rhetoric of the movement provided a new opening for women's liberation. Women active in the Civil Rights Movement and in SDS (Students for a Democratic Society) provided a major impetus for the new wave of feminism that emerged in 1967. Unfortunately the reaction of men within the movement was so sexist that it led to what has become an ongoing and destructive stasis that pits anti-imperialism and women's liberation against each other. But RYM did offer a vision extending the movement to involve broader working-class sectors without losing the political focus on anti-war, anti-racism, and militancy.

Large numbers of working-class youth did get involved in the movement. At the high point, millions took to the streets in the wake of the 1971 invasion of Cambodia and the killing of students at Kent State. This movement was, of course, not magically free of racism, as painfully illustrated by the failure to make issues of the killings at Jackson State and of Chicano anti-war activists in Los Angeles. But it was a movement that could, with political leadership, have strong anti-imperialist potential.

SDS, which correctly formulated the RYM strategy in December 1968, was already splintered by May 1971. The dissolution of SDS shortly before the triumph of its strategy was not simply a question of stupidity or even just a matter of the pervasive power of opportunism. The student movement had reached a crisis in 1969 because its very successes had moved it from simply "shocking the moral consciousness of America" to realizing that it was in fundamental opposition to the most powerful and ruthless ruling class ever. The murderous attacks on the Black movements we supported (dozens of Black activists were killed and a couple of thousand were incarcerated from 1968 through 1971) drove the point home graphically at the same time that the dictates of solidarity urgently pressed us to qualitatively raise our level of struggle. The movement went into a crisis in 1968 because it came face-to-face with the terrifying reality of imperialism's power.

RYM was a creative and realistic strategy to extend the base and power of the movement, although it needed to be joined by an equally strong politics on women's liberation. But for all of its value as a transitional strategy, RYM was in itself nowhere near an adequate basis for overthrowing bourgeois power. So, looking for immediate answers in the crisis, the Left floundered on the perennial dilemma in white supremacist society. The majority looked for a magic solution to the problem of power by mythologizing the white working class as "revolutionary"—in reality this position meant a retreat into white supremacy and away from confronting imperialism. The minority tried to maintain purity around racism and the war by seeing ourselves as exceptional whites, separated from any social base—in reality this position meant abandoning responsibility for building a movement that could sustain militant struggle against imperialism.

While a youth movement in itself can't be sufficient, the promising success of RYM within its realm does suggest some lessons:

1. the role culture can play in building cross-class movements;

2. the value of looking for potential points of intersection of interests of whites with the advance of national liberation—e.g., (a) costs of imperialist wars, GIs, draft, taxes, social priorities, (b) situations of common oppression where there is Third World leadership (welfare, prisons, some labor struggles), and (c) situations where a vision of a revolutionary alternative can be most readily perceived (youth, women);

3. the likelihood that social movements can play more of a role in involving white working people in a progressive struggle than traditional, direct forms of class organizing. The social movements though—youth, lesbian-gay-AIDS, anti-war and anti-nuclear, ecology, and potentially around housing, health, and education—have typically had a middle-class leadership and a primarily middle-class base ("middle class" meaning people from college-educated backgrounds—mainly professionals and petty bourgeois).

While the Women's Liberation Movement is usually labeled as a social movement because it is not one of the traditional struggles for state power, it should be more appropriately be grouped with national liberation and class as responding to one of the three most fundamental structures of oppression. No movement can be revolutionary and successful without paying full attention to national liberation, class struggle, and the liberation of women.

After the collapse of the anti-war and youth movements in the 1970s the Women's Movement provided the most sustained and extensive impetus for social change within white America. Like the social movements, the leadership and main active base was middle class. With the ebbing of the radical women's liberation tendency that identified with national liberation, the apparent leadership of contemporary feminism has a more pronounced middle-class character—at the same time that many more working-class women, while eschewing the name "feminism," have actively adopted and adapted the goals and struggles of the movement.

I would argue that the Women's Movement and the social movements, to be revolutionary, must relate to racism, national liberation, and Third World leadership. But I should add that, as with the youth movement, each should be looking for ways to extend its base into the working class on an anti-racist and pro-women's liberation basis.

The lesbian-gay-AIDS movement has been of particular urgency, militancy, and importance in this period. The struggle around AIDS has pushed the radical sector toward the need to ally with Third World and poor white communities impacted by intravenous drugs and poor health care. The AIDS movement has also provided leadership in breaking through the sterile conservative (cut back services to the poor) versus liberal (defend state bureaucracy) definition of political debate. ACT-UP and others have provided an excellent example of mobilization and empowerment from below for self-help while at the same time demanding a redistribution of social resources to meet these social needs.

Peace, ecology, the homeless, health care, and education all speak to important pieces that express the inhumanity and ineffectiveness of the whole system. Of course these movements have been, almost by definition, reformist. But that doesn't mean that they have to be reformist under all circumstances: e.g., (1) a deeper crisis in imperialism where it has less cushion from which to offer reforms; (2) a situation where revolutionary alternatives are strong enough to be tangible; (3) a political leadership that pushes these movements to ally with national liberation, promote women's liberation, and deepen their class base, while at the same time drawing out the connections among the different social movements into a more coherent and overall critique of the whole system. Under such circumstances and leadership, the social movements could not only involve far more white working-class people in anti-systemic struggles, but could also serve to redefine and revitalize class issues and class struggle itself.

Lessons from the '60s certainly don't offer a blueprint for the '90s, which are a very different decade. Clearly we are not now in a period of progressive social upheaval. Economic dislocation, at least initially, provides fertile ground for white supremacist organizing. National liberation struggles are not at this point achieving a clear path to socialism.

What is certain is that there will be changes and, at points, crises. We can't afford to repeat the old errors of once again floundering on the dilemma of either "joining" the working class's white supremacy or of abandoning our responsibility to organize a broader movement. While there is no blueprint, the basis for a real starting point is an analysis of actual historical experience.

In sum, revolutionaries must be realistic about the history of white supremacy, the impact of material wealth and dominance, and the mushrooming of job and status differentials among workers, both nationally and internationally. There is nothing approximating the Marxist revolutionary proletariat within white America. At the same time, the distinction between those who control the means of production and those who live by the sale of labor power has not been completely obliterated.

A system of white supremacy that was historically constructed can be historically deconstructed. A key factor for whites is the tangibility of a revolutionary alternative as opposed to the more immediate relative privileges that imperialism has had to offer. In this regard we have no map of what the future will bring. The experience of the '60s does offer some possible lessons for when the system is under stress: (1) Anti-imperialist politics are more important than initial class composition. (2) Culture, especially with ties to Third World people, can be an important force for building progressive cross-class movements. (3) In seeking to extend such movements, revolutionaries should look for intersection points of white working-class interests with the advance of national liberation, such as the draft. (4) Women's liberation must play a central role in all movements we build. (5) The various social movements, if we can fight for an alliance with the national liberation and the presence of women's politics and leadership, can be important arenas for extending our base to include working-class people, mutually redefine class and social issues, and make the connections to an overall anti-systemic perspective.

Notes

1   There were several reasons why Blacks were the planters' choice for perpetual slavery: (1) after the English revolution of 1640-1666, the demand for labor expanded in England and limited the supply of English labor available to the colonies; (2) the alliance against feudalism that the English bourgeoisie had by necessity forged with the lower classes limited their ability to impose wholesale slavery; (3) in the colonies, it would be harder for escaped Black slaves to blend in with the dominant white settler population.

2   He notes that Black historian Lerone Bennett Jr., also developed the same basic analysis.

3   Many Black Nationalists cite this period as when an oppressed Black (or New Afrikan) Nation was within North America. This set of laws and color restrictions clearly went beyond the class exploitation of laborers to the systematic oppression of Afrikans as a people.

4   The most frequently cited examples of "competition" are Black workers lowering wages or, in later years, being used as strike breakers. But in reality the role of the white immigrants wasn't that passive. Before 1850, Black workers predominated in many trades in both Northern and Southern cities. A huge influx of white foreigners, particularly after the Irish famine in 1846, caused a radical change. The unskilled Irish, in particular, pushed Blacks out of these occupations (Philip Foner, *Organized Labor and The Black Worker*, New York: 1982, p. 6).

5   Even prominent European Marxists who came here soon dropped the demand for abolition.

6   Initially "Committee for Industrial Organization," then "Congress of Industrial Organizations."

7   This point could be misleading. There were several bloody clashes between workers and local and/or state police forces—e.g., at Flint and during the general strike in San Francisco. Here, though, Sakai is emphasizing the role of the federal government and the broader ruling-class strategy led by Roosevelt.

8   For a version of the same history that emphasizes the CIO's commitment to organizing Black workers, see Philip Foner, op. cit., chapter 16. Foner emphasizes that after five years of the CIO's organizing (1935–1940), the number of Black trade union members rose from 100,000 to 500,000, with many trade union benefits for those workers. He admits, however, that "such militant activities made no real dent in Negro joblessness" and that "the CIO also did little to break down the discriminatory lines in industries where blacks were employed." (p. 233)

9   For certain periods, immigrant Europeans were genuine workers until they, too, were integrated into the settler privileged.

[September 18, 1984]

Chapter 4

Truth and Roses: Voices of/for Women of Color

Subtle and Lovely
Her Writing Invisibly
Caresses Our Hearts

SEVENTEEN SYLLABLES
AND OTHER STORIES
by Hisaye Yamamoto
Latham, NY: Kitchen Table—Women of Color Press (1988)

Haiku is a form of Japanese writing where the entire poem is exactly 17 syllables long. When well done, it can express an amazing density of meaning and feeling within that diminutive space. The impact is accomplished as much by elliptical suggestion as by the intensity of the imagery.

Seventeen Syllables is not a volume of poetry, but Hisaye Yamamoto does write with a verbal economy and an elegance of connotations that is reminiscent of haiku. This book brings together 15 of her short stories, written over a period of 40 years, including two that served as the basis for PBS's 1991 film *Hot Summer Wind*. Yamamoto draws deeply from her own life experience as a second-generation Japanese American woman: the relationship between immigrant parents and their American-born children, the constraints on the lives of women, internment in the concentration camps, and other encounters with racism. But there are no social treatises or soap-box speeches here, just keen observation with a nuanced appreciation of interior emotional life.

The title story is about a Japanese immigrant, a housewife and hard-working farmer, who finds her outlet for beauty and self-expression in writing haiku. This flowering lasts for only three months. Her husband becomes increasingly resentful and surly about the time she devotes to her art. The climax comes during peak harvest day as they are rushing to pack up the tomatoes before the heat ruins them. The editor of the Japanese paper in San Francisco arrives to award the housewife first place in the haiku contest, and she, elated, invites him in for tea as she unwraps her prize—a beautiful drawing. Her husband, sorting tomatoes in the heat, rushes into the house and furiously smashes the picture frame with an axe and burns the artwork.

While the theme is moving, the power of the story comes from being narrated by the daughter. Rosie, a sophomore in high school, is experiencing the sexual awakening of her first kiss with Jesus Carrascos. We have the ignition of the romantic hopes of the daughter juxtaposed to the event that defines what a total trap marriage has become for the mother. But even more, the understatement entailed in the indirect narration actually works to puissantly underscore the poignancy of the mother's situation. The concluding paragraph is brilliant.

Suddenly, her mother knelt on the floor and took her by the wrists. "Rosie," she said urgently. "Promise me you will never

> marry!" Shocked... Rosie stared at her mother's face. Jesus, Jesus, she called silently, not certain whether she was invoking the help of the son of the Carrascos or of God, until there returned sweetly the memory of Jesus' hand, how it had touched her and where. "Promise," her mother whispered fiercely, "promise." "Yes, yes, I promise," Rosie said... her mother, hearing the familiar glib agreement, released her. Rosie, covering her face, began at last to cry, and the embrace and consoling hand came much later than she expected.

In one compact encounter, we see the mother's desperation about her life; the totally different perspective of a girl newly touched by sexual stirrings; the connection yet great gulf between the two generations, papered over by glib agreement, "Yes, I promise." The last sentence is virtuoso subtlety. The mother, except for her urgent importuning of Rosie, has been incredibly stoic throughout the story. But the uncharacteristic delay in consoling her crying daughter reveals what a body blow had been delivered to her own inner soul.

Yamamoto's most effective narrative voice is of a girl or a young woman. "Yoneko's Earthquake" is another beautiful example of how the obliqueness of the daughter's perspective, oblivious to most adult concerns, does a brilliant job of slowly leading us to see, through indirect hints, just how great the emotional turmoil in the adult's life must be. The opening story of the collection, "The High Heeled Shoes, A Memoir," is a masterpiece on sexual harassment written in 1948, decades before the modern feminist movement publicly defined the issue. Typical of Yamamoto, there is no raging drama or bloody physical violence. A lewd phone call from a man calling himself Tony sets the woman narrator off on a reverie about a slew of incidents of sexual harassment.

> There was a man in the theater with groping hands. There was a man on a streetcar with insistent thighs. There was a man who grinned triumphantly and walked quickly away after he trailed one down a drizzly street at dusk and finally succeeded in his aim of thrusting an unexpected hand under one's raincoat.

What emerges is the tremendous constraint these persistent, threatening accostals place on the lives of females, what the author calls "the ubiquitous womanly fear." The true drama here is in the impact on the woman's psyche. "The telephone rings. Startled, I go warily, wondering whether or not is might be Tony again. I hold my breath after I say 'Hello?'" It turns out to be Aunt Mine with plans to come over for dinner. "It is possible she wonders at my enthusiastic appreciation, which is all right, but all out of proportion."

The other memoir in this collection, "Life Among the Oil Fields," turns out to be a quietly stunning piece of work. It starts off as a pleasant and meandering Depression Era reminiscence of a young girl growing up on a family farm amid the oilfields south of Los Angeles. Then, seemingly by random free association, the narrator mentions her accident-prone younger brother, Jema. As they are running along the side of the road one day, he gets knocked over by a cavalierly speeding car, which doesn't deign to stop. Stunned, with a concussion and confusion, he fortunately doesn't have any more serious injuries.

The parents pay a visit to the white couple who hit and ran to ask for some kind of settlement, but the couple refuses to accept any responsibility. "Mama and Papa were indignant. Were we Japanese in a category with animals then, to be run over and left beside the road to die?" The concluding paragraph softly screams out the internal damage caused by such racism. "When I look back on that episode, the helpless anger of my father and mother is my inheritance." But Yamamoto, always aware of the complexity of and the contradictions in human feelings, also recognizes her own born-in-the-U.S.A attraction to the images of American glitter and glamour.

> *But my anger is more intricate than theirs, warped by all that has transpired in between. For instance, I sometimes see the arrogant couple...as young and beautiful, their speeding open roadster as definitely and stunningly red. They roar by, their tinkling laughter, like a long silken scarf, is borne back by the wind.*

During World War II, more than 110,000 Japanese Americans, most of them U.S. citizens, were forced to abandon homes, farms, and businesses and were placed in concentration camps (Bank of America became the giant corporation it is today partly by gobbling up those properties at low prices).

The camps are neither directly denounced nor vividly described in *Seventeen Syllables*. But they do provide the background in two stories about personal disintegrations. "The Legend of Miss Sasagawara," another intriguing use of oblique narration, deals with one family's deterioration into mental illness. "Las Vegas Charley," the longest story in the book, spans the life of one man and at the same time personifies the history of that generation of immigrants. Kazuyuki Matsumoto ("Las Vegas Charley") found the Arizona concentration camp "not too unbearable" and grew content with the free food and card games with friends. But, removed from his family farm after losing a son on the Italian front of the war, he slides back into the obsessive gambling that he had earlier put aside for the sake of his family. Matsumoto typifies a decent-hearted but very flawed and limited human being. In old age, he becomes a burden to his remaining son, whose conflicting emotions about his father conclude the story:

> *Hate for rejecting him as a child; disgust and exasperation over that weak moral fiber; embarrassment when people asked what his father did for a living; and finally, something akin to compassion, when he came to understand that his father was not an evil man, but only an inadequate one with the most shining intentions, only one man among so many who lived day*

> *to day as best they could, limited, restricted, by the meager gifts*
> *Fate or God had doled out to them.*

"The Brown House" is a lively, variegated, and wryly humorous account of how the Hattori family is debilitated by the husband's gambling addiction. The gambling house is a rare island of racial integration. Yet Mr. Hattori ultimately beats his wife for her sheltering of his fellow gambler, a Black man, during a police raid on the illegal casino. The story ends with what would be a much-too-facile resignation to—even embracing of—her lot by Mrs. Hattori, if not for the closing observation from the vantage point of the proprietress of the gambling den: "Mrs. Wu... decided she had never before encountered a woman with such bleak eyes."

Yamamoto paints with a multihued palette of pastels. As in any collection, there is some unevenness, but it is surprising how many of these stories are superb. Yet, this book is the exact opposite of a page-turner. You will want to read slowly to catch the graceful hints and exquisite human timbres. As in tasting a series of quality wines, it helps to clear the palate in between stories, so as to be fully sensitive to the very specific bouquet of each one.

A note must be added about the excellent quality of this edition. The introduction by Professor King-Kok Cheung is a refreshing break from the usual platitudinous praise. Instead we are treated to a substantive essay that provides valuable biographical and historical background and helpful literary interpretation. Additionally, the striking cover of this paperback won first prize in its category in the New York Book Show. This award is quite a coup for a small independent publisher.

Kitchen Table Press is worth special mention in its own right. It is the only publisher in the U.S. run by and committed to writings by women of color. As with most ventures of the oppressed, they are always scrambling for economic survival. They have published many outstanding works, including the excellent anthologies *The Bridge Called My Back* and *Home Girls*.

Kitchen Table—Women of Color Press folded, due to lack of funds, in 1997

[published in *Downtown*, April 13, 1994]

Descent into Hell

A MODERN FORM OF SLAVERY:
Trafficking of Burmese Women and Girls into Brothels in Thailand
by Asia Watch and Women's Rights Project
New York: Human Rights Watch (1993)

> *"Lin Lin" was 13 years old when she was recruited by an agent*
> *for work in Thailand. Her father took $480 from the agent with*

the understanding that his daughter would pay the loan back out of her earnings...three days later she was taken to the Ran Dee Prom brothel. Lin Lin did not know what was going on until a man came into her room and started touching her breasts and body and then forced her to have sex. For the next two years, Lin Lin worked in various parts of Thailand in four different brothels. The owners told her she would have to keep prostituting herself until she paid off her father's debt (by the age of 15, she had contracted HIV).

"Lin Lin" is just one of 20,000 Burmese women and girls pressed into sexual bondage in Thailand. With a rapid turnover, an estimated 10,000 new recruits come in every year. The Burmese are only a fraction of the between 800,000 and two million prostitutes—women, girls, and boys—working in Thailand. As immigrants—often illegal, not speaking the language, and with no local resources—they are subject to some of the worst conditions within an inherently abusive trade.

The Women's Rights Project and Asia Watch, both divisions of Human Rights Watch (HRW), have performed an invaluable service by bringing this contemporary descent into hell to our attention. Their research was based on interviews with 30 of the Burmese females in Thailand, as well as on written sources and on the work of nongovernmental organizations.

Forget all the Broadway plays and Hollywood movies about the happy hooker with the heart of gold. There is absolutely nothing sexy about forced (physically or economically coerced) prostitution. *What A Modern Form of Slavery*'s (AMFOS) detailed report makes painfully clear is just how exploitative and brutal the trade is at each stage—from fraudulent recruitment to rape to harsh and punitive lock-ups to repression when returning to Burma to, in the majority of cases, a death sentence from AIDS.

The pull for this giant economic machine that devours human flesh is the lucrative sex trade in Thailand. This industry got a big boost in the late '60s when Thailand became a rest and recreation area for U.S. armed forces stationed in Vietnam. Now $3 billion a year from "sex tourism," including men from Japan, Europe, and the U.S., is Thailand's leading source of foreign exchange. The domestic use of prostitutes by Thai men is even bigger.

The push on the young Burmese females is the tremendous poverty of and repression against peasant families and ethnic minorities in eastern Burma, under harsh military dictatorship (which has renamed the country "Myanmar"). "Lin Lin" didn't know she was being recruited into prostitution; only four of the 30 interviewees did. Most thought they were going to Thailand for jobs as maids or waitresses that would enable them to send money home to their families.

When they get to Thailand, sometimes having been raped en route, they find themselves in brothels where they have to work off the debt for the money given to their families. Usually there is a 100 percent interest charge, and any costs above their meager daily allowance, such as rare medical attention, are added to their debts. Since the brothel owners keep all the accounts, as with most forms of debt bondage, these women and girls are in fact held as long as the owners want them. If they try to escape, they are beaten up by pimps. If they do get away, they are likely to be returned by police, who work closely with the brothels, or to be turned over for deportation to Burma, with rumors that HIV-positive prostitutes are executed there and more certain prospects of prison time or being impressed as porters for the army operations against ethnic minorities. "Going home is the greatest hope of most of the Burmese women and girls we interviewed, but deportation as illegal immigrants is one of their greatest fears."

HRW goes to great pains to show how all aspects of the Thai and Myanmar governments' policies violate provisions of national and international law. Suffice it to say here that there is official collusion at every step of the way. The Thai police are frequent users and protectors of the brothels. The young, immigrant females, among the most vulnerable members of society, are also subjected to inhuman prison conditions and sexual abuse when arrested or in deportation centers.

The enslaved females are young. Those interviewed ranged from 12 to 22 years old, with the average age 17. Client fears about AIDS (even while it is those forced into prostitution who are the most likely victims of AIDS) drive the brothel owners to find even younger girls to create an image of virginity. Working conditions are inhuman. The women and girls work about 12 hours a day, 25 days a month. They see something like 10 clients a day and can also be hired out for an entire night or day. Each lives and works in a small cubicle; they are rarely allowed out and have little access to health care. While condoms are usually available, it is completely the client's choice whether to use them.

This book is written in a very dry and repetitive fashion that almost numbs the reader to the unimaginable suffering. This style is typical of HRW, with its focus on enumerating all the legal categories of human rights abuse. The 30 interviews must contain raw material for a searing oral history that could burn the human reality into our consciousness. Here, we just get little glimpses. Even women who have been in brothels for years are still haunted by the trauma of their first days.

> "Swe Swe" did not even realize it was a brothel until she was brought to a room, still with her sarong on. She said she screamed and kept hitting her head against the wall as her first client forced himself on her. Afterwards, her head was bleeding badly, she said she remembered little else. A 10-year-old girl from Shan State...whose kidnapper received 35,000 baht, said she was given to a farang (Westerner) who paid 5,000 baht ($200) for her virginity. It hurt so much she passed out, and the brothel owner later beat her with a stick.

AMFOS does not give details beyond the first experiences of the regular sadism to which prostitutes in such vulnerable positions are commonly subjected. But we can that infer this reality applies to these Burmese in debt bondage from the reports that they have no right to refuse any client and are beaten for trying to do so.

As if such horrors weren't enough, these women and girls are also stalked by the specter of AIDS. While HRW hasn't done a scientific survey, they estimate that 50 to 70 percent of the Burmese trafficked into Thai prostitution are HIV-positive. Of the 30 interviewees, 19 had been tested, of whom 14 were infected. The tests are done without informed consent; the results go to the brothel owners and to immigration authorities but not to the persons tested. More fundamentally, as long as there are such unequal power relations and inability to negotiate terms of sex, there will be no way to stop the wildfire spread of AIDS among these young Burmese females.

AMFOS ends with a series of recommendations, basically changes in law and policy for Thailand, Burma, and the international community. While these are decent reforms, they will never turn the problem around without a concerted political mobilization against the underlying forces of social inequality and economic exploitation.

It is hard to believe that people can treat other human beings so viciously. But these degradations are only the logical outgrowth of a world economic system where profits are sacred and people expendable. If we keep our heads in the sand, we deny our own humanity.

[published in *Downtown*, June 8, 1994]

Women's Plights and Fights Around the World

HUMAN RIGHTS WATCH GLOBAL REPORT ON WOMEN'S RIGHTS
by Human Rights Watch Women's Rights Project
New York: Human Rights Watch (1995)

Half of humankind, females fully share with their male counterparts the legion of human rights assaults rooted in racism, poverty, and political repression. But women and girls are also subject to another entire dimension of violations based on gender. Until fairly recently, "human rights" issues have been presented in predominantly masculine terms, while a universe of intolerable mistreatment—from rape to domestic violence to super-exploitation of labor—was either trivialized as "merely personal" or condoned as "only natural."

The shroud of silence that traditionally covered up the oppressions of women has slowly begun to be lifted. The revolutions that emerged in the Third World after 1944 made major, if partial, gains for women's liberation in countries such as China, Cuba, and Mozambique. Then the 1970s saw a strong re-emergence of feminism in the West. Today there are at least some movements and organizations that can be heard to insist, emphatically, that the widespread outrages against women and girls are imperative human rights issues.

The Women's Rights Project of Human Rights Watch (HRW) released its *Global Report on Women's Human Rights* in 1995. This volume does not attempt to be comprehensive—that would require an encyclopedia. But the report does present crucial examples that illuminate global problems.

Rape is a most vicious violation of a person's physical and emotional integrity. That rape is not a matter of "out-of-control sexuality" but rather a ferocious crime of power is made distressingly obvious by the ways it is used as a weapon in political conflicts such as civil wars, forced migrations, and police interrogations.

Whether in the now-publicized atrocities in Bosnia-Herzegovina or in the more "remote" (from media attention) assault by the brutal Burmese army on the ethnic Rohingya Muslims, mass rapes are used politically to degrade the victims, to demoralize their communities, to terrorize minorities into fleeing an area, and even to force women to carry babies fathered by the attacking group. To maximize the humiliation to all involved, women and girls of all ages are at times raped in front of their families, who are held helplessly at gunpoint.

When such a campaign of terror produces a mass exodus, the extreme vulnerability of the uprooted often results in widespread abuses at the refugee camps that receive them. For example, United Nations camps sheltering 200,000 Somali refugees in Kenya had 192 documented cases of rape—most by marauding bandits but many by Kenyan police—during just six months in 1993. Because victims are often unwilling to report such assaults, the actual incidence of rape may have been up to 10 times higher. For any woman previously subjected to genital mutilation, there is additional excruciating pain. In some cases, the assailants slit open the victim's vagina with a knife before raping her.

The government of Peru ushered in in 1997 portrayed itself as the beacon of civilization and decency as it faced off with a guerrilla group (Tupac Amaru Revolutionary Movement-MRTA) holding hostages to demand the release of its imprisoned members. Part of the unseemly underside of the government's claim to be the victim is that Peru is a prime example of how security forces use rape as a direct tool of torture during interrogations of political prisoners.

Rape during interrogation is committed in order to get information or to frighten the detainee into complying with the wishes of her captors. Frequently it is combined with other forms of torture: beatings, the "submarine" (near drowning), electric shocks, and the "little bird" (hanging the detainee from ceiling hooks by her elbows with her arms bound behind her back).

While rape is an attack on a person's physical integrity, it is typically treated instead as a crime against honor—the honor of the woman or girl and the honor of the man (husband or father) deemed to own her. Thus the victim is seen as immoral, or at least now "impure"—and is made to feel that way herself. The resulting emotional and social damage, on top of the initial assault, makes the way that rape is dealt with in patriarchal society an especially harrowing form of adding insult to injury.

The flip side of the concept of honor is the social repression to control women's sexuality and their reproductive lives. For example, in Turkey women are regularly subjected to coerced virginity examinations (presumptively decided by whether their hymen is intact). Such a medical examination may be requested by a girl or woman's family, and these forced invasions of bodily privacy are routine for women arrested on political charges. Those suspected of illegal prostitution or simply seen as acting "immodestly"—for example women dining in public without male escorts—may be arrested and subjected to such exams. As a Turkish women's rights activist explains, there is a basic reason for these gross intrusions: "This is a way for men to control women. Why do men want women to be untouched? It is a matter of power."

Sexual and physical assault is not limited to the arenas of public conflict. In Brazil, for example, surveys indicate that over 70 percent of all reported crimes of violence against women occurred in the home (and the percentage of unreported crimes would undoubtedly be even higher). At the same time, there is a nearly total failure to prosecute domestic battery or rape. The incidence of murder of women by their husbands or lovers is shockingly high—400 such murders there from 1987 to 1989. Yet the perpetrators regularly go free based on the "honor defense," the claim that the man was enraged by the woman's infidelity.

The United States diverges from almost all other countries, and from the standards of international law, by allowing male staff to be in positions of unsupervised contact with female prisoners. The extreme isolation and powerlessness makes these women particularly vulnerable. HRW investigated six prison systems in the U.S. and found verbal degradation, unwarranted visual surveillance while naked, inappropriate sexual contact, physical assault, and rape of female inmates by male staff to be widespread.

Even when sexual interaction does not appear to be forced, the gross power inequalities mean that it can never be truly consensual. Women prisoners who have nothing often feel compelled to trade sex for favors to meet pressing needs—from food to stamps to drugs. And any woman who wants to end such a sexual liaison can easily be subjected to harsh retaliation, from trumped-up disciplinary charges to physical beatings. What makes this all even worse is that many women prisoners—probably the majority—were previous victims of domestic violence and/or sexual molestation. The festering emotional wounds make the sexual exploitation of women prisoners the "dirty little secret of (U.S). corrections."

Women's labor is, of course, widely exploited, often more severely and injuriously than men's. Take the plight of domestic workers imported into Kuwait. These women are pushed to migrate by the poverty and unemployment in Sri Lanka, Bangladesh, the Philippines, and India. They work full time as live-in maids for about $100 a month in order to send money home to their families. As "aliens," they have virtually no political or legal protection.

These domestics often aren't allowed out of the house, where they may be subjected to forms of debt-peonage as well as beatings and rapes. Some of these maids became so desperate that they jumped out of second- or third-story windows to try to escape hellish conditions. The importation of such laborers as well as the incidence of violence and molestation against them have seen a marked increase since the U.S. "liberated" Kuwait in 1991.

As much of this survey reveals, it can't begin to cover the range and depth of human rights violations against women. For one thing, HRW barely touches on the general social and economic conditions that create so many life-and-death problems for women in the Third World. Those harsh realities also intensify the more gender-specific horrors such as sexual trafficking in women and girls. HRW even proffers the anomaly of progressive "international financial institutions" (the World Bank and the International Monetary Fund) without at all engaging the decisive role of such powers in creating the oppressive foundation of the problems.

Global Report is not simply a collection of horror stories. We can glimpse some reflected rays of light in how efforts by women's and human rights organizations have exposed and fought many of these violations. For example, revelations about rampant rape in the U.N. refugee camps in Kenya led to some improvements in physical security, the beginning of counseling and medical services, and the right of women in danger to request transfer to another camp.

The Brazilian women's movement's mass protests against domestic violence led to the creation of special police stations, wholly staffed by female officers, where such assaults can be reported. Women prisoners and advocates in the U.S. have initiated civil rights suits that have forced two of the corrections systems surveyed to begin remedial measures. But so far, the results in all of these areas have been mainly cosmetic: new regulations that sound better but that aren't implemented in practice. Achieving real change will take a much deeper transformation of attitudes and of power relations.

A tobacco company, evidently extolling women's right to equal rates of lung cancer, used to blare the trifling slogan, "You've come a long way, baby!" The human reality of women and girls throughout the world engenders an opposite, both weighty and urgent, call: the struggle has just begun.

[published in *Agrarian Weekly*, February 5, 1997]

Truth and Roses

THE TRUTH THAT NEVER HURTS:
Writings on Race, Gender, and Freedom
by Barbara Smith
New Brunswick: Rutgers University Press (1998)

The truth that never hurts is this: "Black lesbians and specifically Black lesbian writers are here to stay. In spite of every effort to erase us, we are committed to living visibly with integrity and courage and to telling our Black women's stories for centuries to come." This bold affirmation is fully embedded in a fierce and loving struggle against all the major ways human beings are demeaned and limited—race, class, gender, sexuality, disabilities—and provides a crucial cornerstone for building effective coalitions for justice.

Barbara Smith lives these principles: a pioneer of Black feminist literary criticism, a coauthor of the first statement of identity politics in 1977, an editor of the groundbreaking *Home Girls: A Black Feminist Anthology*, she's been a consistent activist from the streets of Chicago in 1968 to the movement against the war in Afghanistan today. And Smith writes with clarity and sparkle. This spare selection from her many essays over the last 30 years makes a rare and beautiful bouquet that becomes only more relevant and useful with time.

I'm not an "objective" reviewer. Barbara is a good personal friend. But I greatly admired her politics and writing for a decade before I had the opportunity to meet her. Even so, *The Truth That Never Hurts* overflowed my expectations by providing a fuller, richer whole to her politics and a delightful reminder of how much I can still learn.

The book opens with the 1977 "Toward a Black Feminist Criticism," a piece that itself played an important role in opening that field. It starts us on a four-essay, fascinating tour of literature: the crucial bonds between Black women that were so necessary to survival as seen in Toni Morrison's *Sula*; the powerful evocation of Black women's lives in Zora Neale Hurston's 1937 *Their Eyes Were Watching God*, with, for example, a grandmother's determination not to let men make a "spit cup" out of her Janie; and the complex, authentic, and passionate portrayal of Black lesbians in Audre Lorde's autobiographical *Zami*. These and other insightful discussions generate strong magnetic pulls back to these works themselves. The four essays give a strong sense of the pathbreaking work of such foremothers of Black women's literature as Audre Lorde, Pat Parker, and Alice Walker.

The catalytic role of her own essays notwithstanding, Smith understands that the fundamental basis for Black feminist literature is the development of a strong political movement to provide support and power for and interest in these emerging voices. It's no surprise, then, that most of the rest of the book is about political issues and building movements. Smith fights fully on four major fronts: race, class, gender, and sexuality.

From the daily hostilities, such as a waitress' nastiness, to a frightening attempt on Smith's life, the insults and dangers of white supremacy are always present: "To this day, racism is systematically institutionalized in every aspect of the United States' political, economic and social life." She sees both the resulting damage to relationships among Black people and the love and community they've forged. She's explicit about white supremacy's centrality to capitalism and the long-term need for revolution.

For Smith, feminism must be "the political theory and practice that struggles to free *all* women... Anything less than this vision of total freedom is not feminism but merely female self-aggrandizement." While fully affirming her identity, she cautions against equating lesbianism with separatism. She feels a strong bond with Black men in fighting racism and a core commitment to coalitions that work to free all the oppressed: women, poor and working-class people, and people of color [i.e., Blacks, Latino/as, Native Americans, Asians] in this country and in the colonized Third World."

At the same time, Smith directly confronts the heterosexual left's practice of trivializing homophobia with the unvarnished reality of: "the life-destroying impact of lost jobs, children, friendships, and family; the demoralizing toll of living in constant fear of being discovered by the wrong person; and the actual physical violence and deaths that gay men and lesbians suffer at the hands of homophobes." The counterpoint is the contribution that lesbian/gay/bisexual/transgender (l/g/b/t) liberation can make in challenging key buttresses of the capitalist system: "the imposition of rigid gender roles, the repression of sexuality, the negation of women's autonomy, the subordination of women and children within the nuclear family."

Smith has an amazing ability to battle on all fronts without sounding frantic or overwhelmed. She consistently and constantly confronts racism in the women's and l/g/b/t movements and sexism and homophobia in the Black community with anger but without rancor and without giving up on people. This strength must stem from her identification with all oppressed people and her bone-deep commitment to building coalitions. She's also conscious not to dismiss those whose identities are defined by privilege. The callousness and destructiveness of this system damages everyone's humanity. No one can be blamed for where she or he was born, nor can one emerge magically free of the prevailing racism and sexism. The real issue is one of choices: whether or not to be an active ally against oppression and for a more humane society.

Truth is striking in how clear, direct, and brief the writing is. For this review, I'd often flip back through an essay expecting, based on all it said, it to be 12 pages, only to find it was 5. This rare and refreshing ability comes from her firm grounding in activism. Smith deliberately avoids the abstract and convoluted formulations common in academia, instead making the conscious effort to be accessible and useful to grassroots organizers.

The one somewhat long and complicated entry is about the relationships between Blacks and Jews in the women's movement. This essay makes a rare contribution to dialogue by addressing the tangle of sensitive issues in an open and forthright way. Smith takes anti-Semitism very seriously as pervasive and pernicious. At the same time she's unequivocal that Jewish women of European descent must not exempt themselves from being part of white privilege and racism. Jews and other whites oppressed in various ways still have a core responsibility to struggle against the white supremacy at the heart of America.

Two selections are especially lyrical and moving. "We Must Always Bury Our Dead Twice" beautifully evokes the funeral of the superb writer James Baldwin. Smith transports us by capturing the rich emotional experience of this deeply spiritual Black funeral. This rapture is followed directly by starkness: "not a syllable was breathed that this wonderful brother, this writer, this warrior was also gay, that his being gay was indeed integral to his magnificence." The impact is a stunning, simultaneous sense of what was fully splendid and what was sorely lacking in this event.

The concluding essay, "A Rose," honors the author's dear friend Lucretia "Lu" Medina Diggs, who died in January 1997. The tribute is framed by an account of the horrifying brutalization of Haitian immigrant Abner Louima a few months later. New York City police beat and then tortured Louima in the stationhouse by ramming the wooden handle of a plunger up his rectum, causing life-threatening internal injuries. They then took the soiled handle and forced it into his mouth, breaking 2 teeth.

At first, it doesn't seem possible to combine in one essay such grotesque violence with a loving tribute to friendship. But her closeness with Lu, 20 years Smith's senior, was born in the trenches of the nearly impossible task of keeping the first women of color press in the U.S.—Kitchen Table—alive. Desperate financial straits meant that at times they worked, quite literally, out in the cold. Reeling from the gruesome police assault on Louima, Smith more deeply misses the discussions, emotional support, and practical help Lu always offered. "A Rose" concludes: "I am better able to face what life puts before me, both the brambles and the roses, because of knowing her."

Smith's analysis can help us cut through a contemporary debate: an "identity politics" seen as a very narrow, small-group mentality that creates divisions vs. a "universalism" that tacitly leaves the dominant values and culture in place. In a movement context, this tension is often expressed as a conflict between those who insist on explicit struggle and independent organization around race, class, gender, and sexuality and those who feel that such efforts detract from the common effort around globalization or war or the environment.

Identity politics did not arise as a way for every conceivable group to have its self-validating little niche, while disdaining other struggles. Instead it was a battle cry by those who had been crushed and silenced for far too long. Smith sees the concept as most useful with people whose "identities make them direct targets of oppression; and when they use their experience as a spur to active political work." In this regard, her starting point is the 1966 breakthrough of "Black Power" as an activist spearhead against white supremacy; and she is working toward a four-dimensional model of complexity and variations by also factoring in class, gender, and sexuality. (While Smith affirms the impact of Black Power, *Truth* only mentions subsequent Black nationalism twice, in the context of examples of sexism. This leaves a major gap in assessing the positive role, especially of revolutionary nationalism, as a formative force in building power for liberation.)

Speaking for the most oppressed is not at all about splintering into antagonistic fragments. All the "isms" are connected and reinforce each other. This unity was clearly articulated even in the very first salvo for identity politics, the Combahee River Collective statement, coauthored by Smith in 1977:

> *The most general statement of our politics at the present time*
> *would be that we are actively committed to struggling against*
> *racial, sexual, heterosexual and class oppression and see as our*
> *particular task the development of integrated analysis and*
> *practice based upon the fact that the major systems of*
> *oppression are interlocking.*

The way I see it, the only ultimate goal is the freedom and well-being of all humankind. But the crippling divisions are deeply rooted in oppression and inequality. That reality mandates independent power for and political leadership by the oppressed. That might seem like it entails an unbearably long and arduous journey through an uncharted thicket. Nonetheless, it's the shortest— indeed the only—way to get to a truly universal and liberated humanity. Barbara Smith's writings hand us a well-honed machete to start blazing the trail.

[written for this book collection, February 15, 2002]

Chapter 5

Thinking About Women: Challenging Male Supremacy

Thinking About Women

On the street I had women on my mind all the time, but that was nothing compared to being in prison. On many nights I lie in my cell just thinking about women—missing loved ones, remembering times together, dreaming about the future. A big, big part of the punishment of prison is separation from women.

Prison is not a natural environment. For some guys, who came in as youngsters, the main impression of women comes from "short-ice" [porn] magazines. But in real life, real women don't usually sit in provocative poses, ready to do our every bidding, with blank expressions on their faces and nothing in their minds. While they can certainly appreciate sexual love, real women (like us) also have minds, feelings, and goals of their own.

Sexual desire is only natural; the conditions of prison make the longings particularly intense. But sexually is only one of the important ways we miss women in our lives. We also miss their intellect, their companionship, their spirit, and their laughter. If we reduce women to "sex objects," we reduce ourselves to "sex maniacs." Some guys try to be lovers with every woman in the world—which they can't possibly do—and miss the many opportunities for solid friendships that can enrich our lives.

The isolation of prison is hard. Often we wish that our loved ones would visit and send packages a lot more than they do. But it works both ways; we frequently show little appreciation of the difficulties for our people on the outside. Raising children can be the most demanding job on Earth, and economic survival out there can be rough. We need to have enough heart to appreciate what our women are going through out there.

Our deepest responsibility is to look out for the children. There are serious problems that threaten their well-being and their future: racism, poverty, drugs, wars, and destruction of the environment. We will never overcome these grave problems if we disregard the intelligence, talent, and compassion of half of the human race.

We reveal a lot about ourselves in how we treat other people. A person who can only feel strong or important through disrespect for others based on their race or sex is a person with a weak sense of self-worth. As men, as human beings, we want to be treated with respect. Women, as human beings, want no less. If we show respect and appreciation for the women in our lives, it will also make us better men.

[July 30, 1990]

On Becoming Men

IRON JOHN—A BOOK ABOUT MEN
by Robert Bly
New York: Addison Wesley Publishing Company (1990)

Robert Bly's *Iron John* is a lot more than a book. It is both a rallying cry and a guide for a new "men's movement." Bly has appeared on TV and has led numerous "men's gatherings" across the country. *Iron John* was on the New York Times hardback best-seller list for all of 1991, and the paperback has been a best-seller so far in 1992. Several feminist reviewers have sharply criticized the book. In short, we are also dealing with a social phenomenon. The kernel of Bly's thesis can be found in a saying taken from New Guinean tribal life: "A boy cannot change into a man without the active intervention of older men." But in modern industrial society, fathers are remote, other older men don't act as mentors, and there is no ritual process of initiation. The result is men who haven't properly completed the transformation and are damaged in various ways.

The device of the book is an exegesis of the fairy tale "Iron John" as a paradigm showing the basic stages, and their importance, of the initiation of a boy into manhood. Bly brings in a plethora of other references from mythology, poetry, psychology, and personal anecdotes to illustrate and amplify his thesis. It isn't necessarily sexist to focus on men's needs, feelings, and changes. Bly is careful to say on a few occasions that his work on the development of men is not directed against women or the gains of the women's movement. But in these denials, the gentleman doth protest too much. His text is studded with references to an unhealthy male passivity in response to feminist anger: he complains that separatist feminists are trying to breed the wholesome fierceness out of men and bemoans that a major male response to feminism is to accept a role as recipient of anger. He goes so far as to say that we don't live under a patriarchy and also that "most contemporary men" are involved in some way at looking at their feminine side, trying to become "soft males" to please women.

I don't know where Bly lives, but on planet Earth there has been no such radical inversion of aggressiveness and power, and the majority of men have certainly not responded to feminism with a new softness and passivity (while passivity itself can be a hostile response by denying women the active engagement everyone needs for growth). It would have been healthier if Bly criticized feminism explicitly, for an open debate. His numerous side comments portray women and feminists as immediate obstacles for the "new man."

Yet, *Iron John* cannot simply be dismissed as a chauvinist tract. Some insights hit on real problems men have, and some themes resonate with the human soul. The book evokes something we feel deeply about how we've lost touch with "the wild man"—spontaneity, positive sexual energy, and most of all an appreciative and mutual relationship with nature. There is certainly a need for fathers to be more engaged in raising children, and for older men to act more as mentors.

There could be a great value in rituals that help each child pass into manhood or womanhood. Bly also occasionally has psychological insights that ring true.

But the valid bits and pieces come in the wrong context and lead in the wrong direction. Bly's position is flawed in a fundamental way: he is reactionary in the classic sense of reacting to the alienation of modern society by looking backward and yearning for some idealized version of earlier epochs. While Bly skips across time and place, often accepting at face value myths that had served to justify the ruling order of their day, he fails to do any relevant social analysis. His ranging references and images form an unreal conflation of the relationship to nature of the earliest human bands (in societies that were often matrilineal and nonhierarchic) with the values of the sacred king and the interior warrior (idealizations from societies that were thoroughly patriarchal and had rigid hierarchies).

For better or worse, we don't live in the world presented in myths and fairy tales. The real world is characterized by real structures of power and oppression. The situations of men and women are not simply balanced halves—yin and yang—that can be understood in parallel. It is not women, by and large, who rape men, who earn one-third more, and who predominate in every arena of power and decision-making. In this context, Bly's failure in his 271-page book about men to deal with homosexuality and the prevalence of homophobia—the terror men feel at the prospect of being placed in the "female" role—makes sense if you won't admit that society is vehemently male dominated.

If Bly's work was the first effort to draw men together to look at themselves, we may be able to view it as a mixed phenomenon—as naive and crude in not understanding the relation to the oppression of women but with some useful insights that could be strands toward a more positive development. But in fact the new men's movement arose as an alternative to a smaller movement that emerged in the '70s, men against sexism. In this approach, also, men get together to discuss their experiences, feelings, hurts, and desires to become whole—but in the definite context of examining and working against the oppression of women. In addition to talking about feelings on both these levels, men against sexism entails definite action such as taking on child care responsibilities or working against violence against women—which can be far more relevant and fulfilling than "wild man" dreams.

We cannot become whole men by perpetuating myths in the service of domination over women. To pretend that this problem doesn't exist or that models of masculinity can be analyzed without it is simply to accede to a culture formed by 7,000 years of male supremacy. This reality doesn't mean that all men are "the enemy" or that we have to reduce ourselves to quivering Jell-O bowls of guilt. The reality does mean, however, that there is no route to becoming whole men that does not involve examining actual power relations and working to change them. An active commitment to women's liberation can not only help overturn a terrible injustice but can also enrich all of society and in the process help us become better men.

[published in *Downtown*, June 10, 1992]

Salt of the Earth

PIGS IN HEAVEN
by Barbara Kingsolver
New York: HarperCollins (1993)

It sounds like a story torn out of recent front-page news: an agonizing custody battle threatening to separate a child from her adoptive mother. Barbara Kingsolver's third novel, *Pigs in Heaven*, brings us into the heart of this conflict but adds another dimension of reality: the profound need for Native Americans to regain their children and to maintain their identity.

Taylor Greer is a spirited, working-class white woman and a gritty single mother who is totally devoted to her 6-year-old adoptive daughter Turtle. Taylor had been handed the child during a trip through Oklahoma three years earlier, with an explanation that the mother had died and the daughter was being badly mistreated. Clearly traumatized by abuse, the child had been given her name because she clung to Taylor like a snapping turtle. The love and rapport they share have worked to start drawing Turtle out of her shell.

Annawake Fourkiller, a bright, young Cherokee attorney who has gone to law school to acquire the tools to defend the human rights and integrity of her nation, grieves from the breakup of her own family under pressures of reservation poverty, alcoholism, and the erosion of traditional values. The keenest loss is her twin brother, Gabriel, who at the age of 10 was adopted out by social workers to a white family.

Unbeknownst to Taylor, her adoption of Turtle wasn't legal. The Indian Child Welfare Act of 1978—a response to the crisis in which a third of Indian children were being adopted out to white families—requires explicit consent by the nation. A series of creative and entertaining events leads to Annawake's discovery of Turtle as an adopted-out Cherokee. The stage is set for a heartrending clash.

> Our tribe [has] been through a holocaust as devastating as what happened to the Jews, and we need to keep what is left of our family together. If you make Turtle leave the only mamma she knows now, you're going to wreck a couple of lives.

While the author presents both sides, she doesn't do so equally. We're emotionally swept into a nifty and vibrant mother-daughter relationship, sharing their struggles for economic survival and partaking of their deep mutual trust. The Native American anguish of physical and cultural genocide is raised more abstractly, and, even then, important aspects—such as wholesale adoptions by whites to build up religious groups and/or family labor supply—are avoided. Nonetheless, the novel slowly introduces us to many of the Cherokee realities, which become a bit more personalized when we hear of the toll that racism has taken on the adopted Gabriel and when we meet Turtle's concerned grandfather.

This isn't a simplistic book of good vs. evil, nor even of the implacable opposition of two antagonists. In this uncharacteristic custody fight, the two camps are able to hear each other, which is further fostered by some improbable small-worldisms. The emerging feeling that something decent will be worked out means that suspense is not the forte of this novel. But what is lost in terms of dramatic tension is more than compensated for in the vividness and empathy with which the characters are drawn.

And Kingsolver can *write*. She has a keen descriptive eye, moves the story along with lively scenes and witty observations, and deliciously revels in the zaniness and zestfulness of human beings. It is refreshing that the romantic subplot involves two individuals nearing 60 and a joy to read about folks who talk back to and eventually execute their television set. While Kingsolver perhaps doesn't feel culturally intimate with her Cherokee characters, she does create a range of people on both sides whom we care about and relish.

We do get at least some suggestions of the values of Cherokee culture. We are taken to a stomp dance, experience the bonds of extended family, hear of the tradition of high literacy with the elegantly curled Cherokee alphabet, learn of the importance placed on being an integral part of the community, and find out why Annawake's grandmother always planted mulberry bushes next to her peach trees (the birds greatly prefer mulberries and therefore leave the peaches alone). The Cherokee meaning behind the title entails more than just the flow of the action to the town of Heaven, Oklahoma, in the heart of their nation. "The Six Pigs in Heaven" is *disihgwa*, the Cherokee constellation of stars (our Pleiades), named from a myth illustrating the problems of greed and of the lack of understanding between parents and children.

Don't read *Pigs in Heaven* if you are looking for gripping suspense or for a politically definitive piece on the rights of either adoptive mothers or native nations. But definitely do read this novel if you're looking for sparkling writing about loveable people that both engages and entertains while examining important real-life dilemmas.

[published in *Metroland*, October 1993]

What Love Does Got to Do with It

OUTLAW CULTURE:
Resisting Representations
by bell hooks
New York: Routledge (1994)

Radical Black feminist and prolific author bell hooks (she uses the lower case) doesn't get the public spotlight lavished on trendy white commentators such as Camille Paglia and Katie Roiphe, who are caricaturing the feminist movement.

But for a few months, the mass media were beating a path to hooks's door, asking her to present the Black feminist viewpoint on gangsta rap. To her eternal credit, she didn't fall for the lure of "15 minutes of fame" in return for providing a media spectacle of Black-on-Black acrimony. After the first phone call, the inquiring producer of each TV or radio show involved never called her back to arrange for an appearance:

> *I suspect they call me, confident that...they will hear the hardcore "feminist" trash of gangsta rap. When they encounter instead the hardcore feminist critique of white supremacist capitalist patriarchy, they lose interest.*

Her incisive piece "Gangsta Culture—Sexism, Misogyny: Who Will Take the Rap?" is in itself worth the price of admission to Outlaw Culture, her latest collection of critical essays and interviews on culture. hook's refusal to play the role of hatchet woman does not mean she is soft on sexism within the Black community. Instead, she understands that the critique must get to the roots.

> *Without a doubt Black males, young and old, must be held politically accountable for their sexism. Yet this critique must always be contextualized. The sexist, misogynist, patriarchal ways of thinking and behaving that are glorified in gangsta rap are a reflection of the prevailing values in our society. More than anything, gangsta rap celebrates the world of the material, the dog-eat-dog world where you do what you gotta do to make it even if it means fucking over folks and taking them out.*

Thus it is but an unvarnished embodiment of the norms of U.S. culture. hooks is also quite conscious of the damage done to young Black males when their rage, produced by vicious racism, is channeled into misogyny:

> *Far from being an expression of their "manhood," it is an expression of their own subjugation and humiliation by more powerful, less visible forces of patriarchal gangsterism... a vision of manhood that can only lead to their destruction.*

The phrase *white supremacist capitalist patriarchy* appears often in this collection that is otherwise mercifully free of argot. But these terms are necessary reference points for the great strength of this Black woman born into a working-class family. She consistently uncovers the connections between the different forms of oppression: racism-sexism-classism-homophobia (her critique of homophobia doesn't come across as centrally but is still unmistakable).

hooks, like this reviewer, is astounded by how often people who fight fiercely against the form of oppression that most impinges on them can at the same time participate in other structures of domination. While her principled stands are fraught with the personal danger of ostracism by all her potential communities of support, she is quite explicit in her critiques of racism within the predominantly white women's movement, sexism within the Black liberation struggle, and class privilege, both among women and within the Black community:

> *Until we are able to accept the interlocking, interdependent nature of systems of domination and recognize specific ways each system is maintained, we will continue to act in ways that undermine our individual quest for freedom and collective liberation struggle.*

Another great strength here is hooks's examination of the internalization of oppression—the toll taken on the self-images of Black people, the poor, women, and gays and lesbians by the negative ways they are treated and portrayed. The book's subtitle underscores the emphasis on internal decolonization—resisting such negative representations and building self-representations that resist the system.

There are a number of weak points, perhaps inevitable in such an iconoclastic and broad-ranging work. One is a standard occupational hazard of cultural criticism: overreaching interpretations. For example, the reasons educed for seeing the early Madonna as a feminist icon and the recent Madonna as a staunch force for patriarchy may make sense intellectually, but still need a reality anchor that recognizes that her political impact on her fans was not so cut-and-dried in either phase.

Similarly, hooks is right that Spike Lee's film—shooting for support from white producers to make a megahit—stripped *Malcolm X* of much of the earthshaking power of his politics, particularly the way he linked racism to colonialism and imperialism. But she misses the great value of bringing a positive, albeit watered-down, glimpse of Malcolm to a new generation of Black youth.

The author goes to excessive, personalistic lengths to impugn the claim of Betty Shabazz, Malcolm X's widow, to having the definitive word on his (evolving) views on the role and rights of women. It would have sufficed for hooks to state her political difference with Shabazz's more conservative politics on feminism.

hooks's critique of how Black middle-class intellectuals are used to control what is presented in the mass media on Black culture is courageous. But leaving it only on the cultural level omits a compelling material reality: it is the Blacks stuck in the impoverished ghettos who are deluged with unemployment, drugs, violence, deteriorating schools, collapsing public health, and AIDS and other preventable epidemics—all together forming a tidal wave of genocidal proportions.

While hooks refers to herself as a revolutionary, she doesn't go much beyond culture and values in terms of grappling with how the oppressed can overturn the current structure of power.

Despite some gaps and miscues, this book offers a great range of thought-provoking analysis. The series of essays on the media-hyped *new feminism* of authors Camille Paglia, Katie Roiphe, and (in some ways) Naomi Wolf is particularly useful. These white, privileged, essentially conservative young women—without any of the history of the struggles of the women's movement—have responded to the market demand by recasting feminism in a way acceptable to patriarchy. They white-out the realities of race and class among women, and at the same time caricature the *old feminism* as anti-sex, anti-men, and pro-censorship (some ammunition is provided them by the strident, narrow anti-pornography focus of the Andrea Dworkin/Catharine MacKinnon wing of the movement). Thus these new critics reduce the value of feminism to only the inclusion of women in the work force, a demand the system has already moved toward accommodating for its own benefit. Two crucial struggles are thus jettisoned: (1) the issues of power and control in domestic relationships, and (2) the interrelationships with class and race.

No wonder that, while radical Black feminist voices can barely be heard, these *new feminists* have been instant successes with the mass media. It is ironic that they cry "censorship" against those who attack the status quo when it is actually the money and power interests who determine which ideas get presented to the public.

A refreshing aspect of hooks's work is her willingness to step beyond the often-staid boundaries of traditional left discourse to look at the role of sex, love, and spirituality. Contrary to the anti-sex stereotype, she asserts:

> *Revolutionary feminism…[denounces] sexual abuse [in order] to transform the space of the erotic so that sexual pleasure can be sustained and ongoing, so that female agency can exist as an inalienable right.*

Within a culture of domination, simple lust becomes a way to violate the other person. In contrast, hooks stresses the value of redemptive love, a way of positively crossing the boundaries that separate people. We don't have to wipe out the differences to achieve a oneness among us. At their heart, love and spirituality call for a mutual interaction and a positive communion with a world beyond the self.

The moment we choose to love we begin to move *Toward Freedom*, to act in ways that liberate ourselves and others. That action is the testimony of love as the practice of freedom.

[published in *Downtown*, June 14, 1995]

Feminizing the Revolution

SANDINO'S DAUGHTERS REVISITED:
Feminism in Nicaragua
by Margaret Randall
New Brunswick: Rutgers University Press (1994)

After the victory of the Sandinista revolution in Nicaragua, Dr. Mirna Cunningham, a Miskito Indian, needed medical care. In December 1981, she and her nurse were two of the earliest victims of kidnap and torture by U.S.-sponsored counterrevolutionaries. "The nurse and I were repeatedly roughed up, hit and raped and they sang religious songs and prayed while they beat and raped us." Surviving this horrible episode, Cunningham persevered in this impoverished and conflict-ridden region. She is presently serving as a senator in the National Assembly.

When FSLN (Sandinista National Liberation Front) guerrillas made their daring 1978 raid on the National Palace, 23-year-old Dora María Téllez was "Commander Two" on that mission. By July 1979, she was part of the Sandinista high command of four women and two men at the decisive battle for León, Nicaragua's second-largest city. Téllez later led some of the revolution's most impressive social accomplishments in her capacity as Minister of Health.

Vidaluz Meneses was born into the upper crust, but her passionate Christian humanism ineluctable drew her to the FSLN. She has lived the harrowing anguish of a family rent by civil war. Her father was a general and a diplomat of the dictatorship and was assassinated by revolutionaries. Somehow this woman has a capacity for love that spans both sides of the chasm: personally for the father she deeply mourns; socially/humanly for the revolution that delights her by bringing health clinics and libraries to people who never had them.

In *Sandino's Daughters Revisited*, we meet 12 extraordinary women who have ridden the tiger of oppression, revolution, and counterrevolution and who thoughtfully analyze those experiences. The title harks back to author Margaret Randall's earlier 1979 collection of interviews with women who had participated in the newly triumphant revolution—*Sandino's Daughters*. (Augusto César Sandino was the leader of the 1927–1934 guerrilla resistance to the U.S. military occupation of Nicaragua. The modern liberation movement was named after him.) This "revisit" is not merely a 1990s reprise of her earlier work. Only two of the prior interviewees appear in this book. As the subtitle indicates, the current focus is on the need for and concepts of feminism in Nicaragua.

The author's informative introduction summarizes the political concerns that propel this new work: while the Sandinistas' vital experiment with popular democracy was undermined primarily by the attacks on it organized by the U.S., the revolution was also internally weakened by its failure to develop a feminist agenda. That means equal say for women in shaping society. Randall argues that feminism also entails creating a new overall process of power that is less hierarchical and more participatory (her own ideas on these themes are presented in her book, *Gathering Rage*).

Given this focus, Randall doesn't attempt to present a cross section of Nicaraguan women. Those interviewed are mainly active Sandinistas from upper- and middle-class backgrounds. They became critical of how power was wielded in the FSLN, and are now in favor of an independent women's movement. In addition, most are still grappling with how the party could have lost the 1990 elections after 10 years in power. A broad consensus emerges on this issue: the people were tired of the terribly costly counterrevolutionary war, which they believed could only be ended by electing a government acceptable to the U.S. Within that context, the Sandinistas as a governing party had slid into elitism and lost some of their previously vital links with the people.

There is also considerable agreement on both the great accomplishments and the undermining weaknesses of the revolution. The gains were tremendous—the literacy campaign, free health care and education, vaccinations for children, women's participation in grassroots politics, their greater access to jobs, and the push to provide child care. The structural flaws proved costly: a reluctance to take on gender-specific issues such as abortion and domestic violence, and an inability to break from a hierarchical model of political power.

Gioconda Belli is clear that the revolution opened up all kinds of new possibilities. "Women participated to an extraordinary degree. The 10 years of Sandinista government offered hope, and it created a tremendous communal energy and sense of collectivity that imbued life with beauty, ethics, heroism." But the advent of power also brought problems. It became difficult to criticize top leadership, and a certain separation from the people set in. While corruption was a relatively small problem, it stood out in sharp contrast to the people's expectations of the Sandinistas. Belli argues that democracy must include an ability to accept differing points of view and a commitment to equality.

While there were a handful of notable exceptions, sexism prevailed among male leaders. Daisy Zamora's experience of it led to her "profound belief that we need a totally different conception of power, one that includes a truly humanist, feminist perspective." Sofia Montenegro asserts, "The essence of feminism is its democratizing character." Active in the FSLN, she resisted what she saw as "its dogmatic, orthodox parochial vision of things. There were nine male leaders (the FSLN national directorate) who took it upon themselves to do the thinking for the rest of us. It's time we women learn for ourselves."

Many of these activists argue that there is a fundamental need for an autonomous women's movement—one that elects its own leadership and defines its own issues. This vision stands in contrast to the old model of an official women's organization (AMNLAE) under the command of the party. Beyond arguing for independent feminism, they've played key roles in its emergence.

In 1987 several women prominent in the revolution came together to form a group that later took on the delectable name "Party of the Erotic Left" (known as the PIE for its initials in Spanish). PIE's program placed an emphasis on land titles for peasant women, the problem of domestic violence, and women's control of their reproductive lives. In 1991 a nonstructured movement of several hundred younger women emerged calling itself "the 52 Percent Majority." In the same period, the lesbian movement became more open and active, working on AIDS outreach and advocacy as well as building opposition to the barbaric "anti-sodomy" law passed by the new pro-U.S. government. By January 1992 a surprise outpouring of 800 women attended the "United in Diversity" meeting hosted by independent feminists.

These interviews are eloquent in expressing the need for feminism to democratize the revolution. There is, however, almost nothing concrete offered on what a different model of power would look like or how it might be implemented. This shortcoming is understandable given that popular movements in general have done so little on these challenging questions. But there is an unfortunately threadbare section in *Sandino's Daughters Revisited*'s otherwise gorgeous tapestry: *class*. While many of the issues mentioned affect working-class and peasant women there is very little presented about their social consciousness and realities.

Diana Espinoza, the one factory laborer who is interviewed, shows awe-inspiring determination. She overcomes the formidable demands on her as a mother of four in a desperate economy to lead her fellow workers in taking over their factory to try to keep it running and to make it into a cooperative. But she doesn't reflect on and isn't asked about the relationship of women in that situation to the formation of a feminist movement.

Perhaps several of the interviewees shied away from the issue of class, because it has traditionally been used by the party as a bludgeon against an autonomous women's movement (that position is represented in this volume by party stalwart and former head of AMNLAE, Doris Tijerino—a woman, incidentally, with an incredibly moving life story). But it would be a serious mistake to cede the class issue to those opposed to independent feminism. The desired feminizing and democratizing of the revolution cannot happen without active participation of peasant and working-class women, something this book needed to engage in a more serious fashion.

This book is not only stimulating for the political ideas and feminist mission it presents, *Sandino's Daughters Revisited* is also a major contribution to framing the challenge for future movements to develop a revolution that is fully four-dimensional—around national liberation, gender, class, and democracy. And, on another level, the book is stunning: it shows the complexity of the revolutionary process and the courage, creativity, commitment, and humanity of 12 very inspiring women. As Randall states without exaggeration in the introduction "there isn't a book big enough for the full history and heroism of Nicaraguan women."

[published in *Downtown*, October 12, 1994]

Chapter 6

No Respect For Human Life: The Criminal Justice System

The War at Home

AGENTS OF REPRESSION
The FBI's Secret War Against the Black Panther
Party and the American Indian Movement
by Ward Churchill and Jim Vander Wall
Boston: South End Press (1988)

A younger generation looking at the terrible social problems of today may well wonder whatever happened to the almost legendary political movement of the '60s. While there is a wide range of contemporary activism, we are missing that sense of overall national power and coherent focus with the potential to radically transform society. There are of course many historical factors in the numerous internal weaknesses of those movements themselves. But few people are aware of another central reason for the decline: the U.S. government's systematic, illegal, and often lethal campaign to destroy all radical opposition.

In 1971, a group of pacifists broke into a small FBI office in Media, Pennsylvania, and came away with a pile of secret documents that revealed "COINTELPRO" (counterintelligence program)—the FBI's strategy for "neutralizing" the New Left and destroying the Black Liberation Movement. For example, a 1968 FBI memo calls on agents to:

> *Prevent the coalition of militant black nationalist groups...prevent militant black nationalist groups and leaders from gaining* **respectability...prevent the rise of a black "messiah" who would unify, and electrify, the militant black nationalist movement. Malcolm X might have been such a "messiah."**
> [original emphasis]

Malcolm X had already been assassinated. The document goes on to cite two other potential "messiahs": Martin Luther King, Jr., who was assassinated later that year, and Stokely Carmichael, who was hounded into exile.

A complete study of COINTELPRO would be a vast undertaking. *Agents of Repression* focuses on two major examples—the campaigns against the Black Panther Party and against the American Indian Movement, with the later account being particularly detailed and useful. Authors Ward Churchill and James Vander Wall begin with an outline of basic COINTELPRO techniques.

Eavesdropping: illegal bugs not just to gather information (often the FBI was most interested in personal tensions and vulnerabilities, for later use in fomenting splits) but also to induce paranoia in the group.

Bogus Mail: fabricating letters, e.g., with one movement person slandering the other, to create tensions between activists.

"Black Propaganda": distributing phony literature under the name of the targeted organization in order to discredit it.

Disinformation: deliberately giving the media false information to depict the target group as violent or corrupt.

Harassment Arrests: several FBI documents talk about arresting targeted activists time and time again, regardless of whether the cases would hold up in court. The multiple arrests totally drained the target's time and meager financial resources.

Snitch-Jacketing: one of the most destructive COINTELPRO tactics was to put out false rumors that someone was a police informant. Not only would this render a dedicated member isolated and ineffective, but it would also create tremendous acrimony and distrust within the organization.

Assassinations: here of course there are no explicit documents. But so many Panther and AIM activists were murdered under circumstances lateracovered up by the authorities that there can be no doubt that political assassination was a major COINTELPRO weapon.

Agents of Repression gives us several examples of how such tactics were used against the Black Panther Party. Promising young leaders Bunchy Carter and Jon Huggins were murdered by "US" (United Slaves) in an interorganizational antagonism fostered by the FBI (the actual triggermen are believed to be police infiltrators of "US"). The FBI was particularly out to get the head of the Los Angeles Panthers, Geronimo Pratt. When a SWAT-Team assault on the Panther office failed to kill Geronimo, he was framed for a random robbery-murder, even though he was under FBI surveillance 400 miles away at the time of the crime. Geronimo is still in prison today [Geronimo finally won a reversal of the conviction and his release from prison on June 10, 1997, after 26 years behind bars].

The most notorious case was the murders of Fred Hampton and Mark Clark. Hampton was the extremely dynamic chairman of the Panthers in Chicago and was also having some success at moving local gangs away from crime and toward social consciousness. Clark was a Panther captain staying at Hampton's at the time. The book describes in some detail the phony pretext for the raid on Hampton's apartment, the role of an FBI informant in setting it up, and how the police massacred the young chairman with a hail of gunfire as he lay sleeping in bed, as well as killing Clark and wounding several Panthers.

These horrors are only a small sampling. While Churchill and Vander Wall don't attempt a total tally—it is hard to know the FBI's precise role in a large flurry of cases—other historians have estimated that, in a five-year period, more than 40 Panthers were murdered as a result of police and FBI action (the total resulted from direct police attacks, the fomenting of antagonisms—e.g., false snitch-jackets—within a movement under such life-and-death pressures, and later police shoot-outs for cadres who'd been forced underground). In the same period, there were over 1,000 arrests on trumped-up charges. Whatever the exact numbers, the organization that had been a leading force in the Black revolution and in electrifying a much wider range of people for social change was reduced to a mere shell by 1972.

COINTELPRO was exposed and officially disbanded in 1971. But the same kind of programs continued under different names. The largest and most deadly of all was conducted against the American Indian Movement (AIM) throughout the '70s—an operation of such scope that it could more accurately be called counterinsurgency warfare.

Two forces converged in 1972 to make the Pine Ridge Reservation a major battleground. First, the traditional resistance of the Oglalas (Sioux) who lived there made Pine Ridge a center of support for resurgent claims to Native rights, sovereignty, and land. Second, although a government secret at the time, satellite photography located an especially rich uranium deposit within the Sheep Mountain area of the reservation. The solution for the U.S. government was Dick Wilson, a former tribal official who had been discredited with corruption. The government and private funding sources provided Wilson with ample funding to run a campaign and organize a GOON (Guardians of the Oglala Nation) squad, securing for him "election" as tribal president. Wilson and his GOONS began systematic harassment of traditionalist Indians and imposed a total ban on AIM-related activists—even speaking—on the reservation. Popular efforts to legally impeach Wilson were physically blocked.

The series of abuses resulted in an AIM-led protest and attempted news conference at Wounded Knee. But the U.S. government quickly sealed them off with massive military force. This created the famous "occupation" of Wounded Knee, from February 27 through May 7, 1973. As one Oglala, who was a combat veteran, stated: "We took more [incoming] bullets in 71 days than I took in two years in Vietnam."

In the three years following the occupation, 69 AIM members and supporters met violent deaths on or around Pine Ridge, and more than 300 were physically assaulted, in many cases shot. Some of the murders were focused political assassinations—such as of those of Pedro Bissonette, head of the Oglala Sioux Civil Rights Organization, and of tribal attorney Byron DeSersa. And the FBI attempted a crude cover-up of the mysterious murder of targeted AIM activist Anna Mae Aquash. Most of the other murders and assaults were part of a more generalized terror campaign against the traditionalist population. In this period, Dick Wilson was "re-elected" tribal president in an election validated by the U.S. Bureau of Indian Affairs despite the U.S. Commission on Civil Rights' documentation of massive intimidation and fraud.

AIM was also under grave attack nationally, with multiple arrests of leaders as well as physical assaults and attempted assassinations. For example, AIM co-chairman Russell Means was subjected to 40 (only one, a minor charge, ever stuck) and two assassination attempts. In such circumstances, AIM became vulnerable to the need for security expertise, and it was in that guise that FBI infiltrator Douglas Durham rose to become AIM's "security director," a position from which he wreaked tremendous havoc. Durham put snitch-jackets on dedicated members, thus causing corrosive distrust and major splits. And it was the FBI's Durham who put out unauthorized statements advocating violence that the FBI then cited as public justification for repressing AIM.

The level of violence against traditionalists on Pine Ridge was so intense (if the murder rate there were projected across the U.S. population, it would come to 400,000 political murders a year) that AIM was forced to organize armed self-defense. On June 20, 1975, the FBI—which had been too "short-handed" to investigate the scores of murders of AIM supporters there—entered Pine Ridge heavily armed, and without a warrant, to arrest a young brave accused of stealing a pair of cowboy boots.

Clearly a pretext to set off a military confrontation, the foray did not go exactly as planned. Two FBI agents were killed in addition to AIM member Joe Stuntz Killsright. The FBI nonetheless accomplished its main purpose: to launch a full military campaign and subsequently decimate AIM.

On the same day that all eyes were turned on this provoked shoot-out, "Tribal President" Dick Wilson was in Washington, D.C. illegally, (with neither approval of the tribal council nor the treaty-required consent of three-quarters of the adults), signing away one-eighth of the reservation—the uranium-rich Sheep Mountain area—to the U.S. Park Service. And today, AIM stalwart Leonard Peltier is still serving a double life sentence for the "murder" of those two FBI agents, despite subsequent proof that the trial evidence against him was fabricated.

AIM and the Black Panther Party were not just two organizations that fought for social justice. They were spearheads for much larger Native American and Black Liberation struggles, respectively. These very strong movements from among the most oppressed people within the U.S. also provide the examples and inspiration that galvanized large numbers of white people into activism. The bloody setbacks and rampant disinformation derailed a much larger movement. COINTELPRO is a reality one ought to have to study and master in order that there be success in the next great wave of social upheavals.

[published in *Downtown*, March 3, 1993]

Prison Culture and National Politics

Below are the two concluding sections of "These Criminals Have No Respect for Human Rights," written for the 20th anniversary of the Attica Rebellion. Unfortunately, the 1991 trends—with the exception of the crack epidemic, which has ebbed—still prevail today. The themes of the first two sections, racism and brutality, and AIDS, are discussed elsewhere in this book. The complete essay appeared in Social Justice, Fall 1991.

Changing Values

Changing values among staff, inmates, and the public respectively put prisons on a frightening collision course for the 1990s. Many younger officers were raised on Charles Bronson and Sylvester Stallone movies. They view prisoners as scum for whom incarceration itself is not sufficient punishment. While the John Wayne movies of the earlier generation were also reactionary, there was at least some pretense that the "good guys" played fair. The more modern action films use only an initial definition of "good" (cops) and "bad" (criminals) as the thinnest veneer to justify the hero's use of the most vicious and criminal forms of violence.

Underpinning the venomous definitions for "good" and "bad" is racism—the basic founding rock of this society. Eighty percent of New York state prisoners are Black or Latino, while the staff is overwhelmingly white. Indeed, prisons could be seen as the state's double-edged sword for dealing with unemployment: take the most rebellious or wildest edge of unemployed youth off the streets of the ghettos and barrios; provide decent-paying jobs for upstate whites in depressed rural communities. As with any situation of oppression, those reaping even small benefits tend to drown their consciences by blaming the victim. Many hassles that characterize the most repressive prisons—like limitations to three showers a week, the obstacles to prisoner-initiated programs, or the absence of any semblance of job or family responsibility—seem to make sense only as an effort to shape prisoners into the "animals" we are accused of being.

This broad view is not to say that every guard is a rabid aggressor. Many just want to put in their hours and collect their paychecks; some even started out with idealistic beliefs about "law" and "corrections"; a few even retain their sense of humanity. Yet a growing number believe that prisoners should be punished more harshly. Though small, this activist core plays a significant role in shaping peer values, since their brother officers feel bound to back them up in any given situation. Further, the daily experience of arbitrary authority over other human beings can readily corrupt the character of even those who started with good intentions.

It is difficult to give outsiders an understanding of how it works. It is not that most prisoners expect violence from the guards on a daily basis, though the possibility is always there, especially in more isolated areas like "the box" and the hospital. More typically, some guards will upbraid and demean an inmate for some minor infraction of the rules (like talking in the halls) in order to polarize his choices between either accepting a humiliation or reacting in a way (like cursing the guards) that will provide the pretext for further punishment. The prisoners most often picked on in this way are those perceived as either weak or "uppity" (usually young and Black). At times, the escalation of these confrontations results in the beating down of the prisoner by the officers. The guards who initiate these regularly attempted humiliations may rationalize them with the concept that inmates need to learn respect for authority. But the experience is far more likely to set off a pecking order of abusive behavior toward those who are "weaker."

The pettiness and arbitrariness in the maximum prisons can drive you crazy. In the halls of one joint, it is fine to have your hands in your pocket, but you'd damn well better have your jacket zipped up. In the next joint, you can have your jacket unzipped, but don't dare put your hands in your pockets. At still another, you'll get yelled at because you didn't take your gloves off before coming inside. An officer yells at you for being out of place even though it is he who misplaced the pass you gave him; even when the pass is found in his pile, it must somehow have been the inmate's fault.

As dull and routinized as prison life can be, it is still impossible to have any reliable schedule or work plan. Times and procedures are shifted without notice and for no apparent reason; you could be prepared to give a presentation at your Alcoholics Anonymous meeting and then be blocked from going because for some reason, or for no reason, your name didn't appear on the evening call-out. The incessant message to the inmate is that you have no control over even the most minute aspect of your life; rather, every little thing you do must be dependent on the decision, or the whim, of those in authority.

The question of changing values among prisoners first requires a demystification of the people involved. Prisoners, by and large, are neither "animals" nor the "noble oppressed." There is a wide range of immediate causes for incarceration, making the category "prisoner" quite a potpourri: from innocent persons convicted due to racist frame-ups and/or lack of economic means, to economic and/or drug crimes, to preying on other sectors of the oppressed, to crimes that go off the deep end of the sexism and power sickness inherent in this society (any serious theory of criminology would have to grapple with the important differences in the types of action involved). There is a broad generalization that does apply: prisoners overwhelmingly come from the oppressed sectors—primarily Third World people, with some poor whites. Also, most criminals hold the predominant values of capitalist society—about making money and being self-centered—but apply them to their own socioeconomic situation.

Like the rest of society, prisoners have been influenced by the deification of greed, individualism, and cynicism of the Reagan-Bush era. Yet there are several other more specific factors.

(1) Almost every leader who stood for more positive values and social advancement for the oppressed communities—from Malcolm X, to Martin Luther King, Jr., to the Black Panthers and the Young Lords—was killed, imprisoned, exiled, or corrupted by the government. This withering attack of the 1960s and 1970s decimated the voices and community hopes for positive and collective social advance. Concomitantly, there is a dearth of anti-racist and progressive white movements to provide a positive example for white prisoners.

(2) Drug abuse is a serious problem throughout society, but the related plagues of widespread violence and wholesale imprisonment affect only the

oppressed communities. There, crack in particular is having a devastating impact on individual values and community cohesion. Many crack addicts will resort to any self-debasement or betrayal of family and friends to obtain the drug they crave so badly.

(3) Prisoners have direct experience that reveals that the ruling authorities' professed morality on the value of human life and upholding of the law is a sham covering a contrary practice. Lacking a social movement, such a recognition can breed cynicism and a "might makes right" mentality.

(4) Simultaneously, prisoners are living under a daily state of repression. Prisoners, more than almost any other social sector, distrust and even hate state authority. Also, most Black and Latino prisoners are very aware of racism in society. The problem is that in the absence of a positive social movement there is an increase in anger, but not in constuctive ways to direct that anger toward social change.

Broadly speaking, prisoners today are less socially conscious and yet angrier than before. In an era of crack and reconsolidation of state power, we are also witnessing a serious erosion in the old convict codes for mutual support and against rape and snitching. On the broadest level, there is less consciousness of the need to deal with racism and surmount racial divisions. But the flagging solidarity can also be seen in many little particulars.

In describing how the change in values is expressed concretely, we must allow for the old-timers' tendency to romanticize the "good old days." Nonetheless, it is clear that significant changes have occurred over the past 15 years. For example, if guards pulled an inmate out of the line in the 1970s, the whole line usually stopped to make sure it didn't become anything more than a frisk. Today, the line will move on as ordered. Or, simply in terms of sense of community, today it is much more common for prisoners to talk loudly from cell to cell at all hours. Most of those loud cell to cell conversations lack a constructive purpose and instead concern matters such as abusing women, which the old-time convict would have at least found embarrassing to broadcast.

Although snitching has always been a problem, its prevalence has reached a qualitatively new level. There was a fairly workable prisoner organizing grapevine in the 1960s and 1970s. Today it seems that anything discussed by more than five inmates will be immediately known to the administration. The current perception among prison activists is that any efforts to develop effective and positive programs will be broken up before they get started. Yet while positive organizing seems impossible, the spontaneous responses of inmates (given the changes in values) in any crisis are very unpredictable and likely to be negative. All in all, it appears that the changing values of prisoners creates greater potential for fruitless violence and offer less prospect for positive social change.

An aware and concerned public is the main hope for avoiding a collision course within the prisons. Here again, however, values have changed for the worse. With the resurgence of open racism and the added frustration with the failure of liberal rhetoric, at best the broader public doesn't give a damn about prisoners and usually tends to support calls for harsher punishment. If the Attica rebellion were to happen today, I believe that the defining public reaction would not be "How could conditions get so bad?" but rather "Why didn't the state kill more of them?"

The public's vindictive attitude, cultivated by politicians and the media, goes to the point of irrationality even in terms of the limited goals of curtailing street crime and tax costs. The whole "get tough" attitude is only an escalation of the dismally failed strategy of repression and more repression throughout the 1980s. As a result, many more young people have been ground through a system that is mainly conducive to producing ex-convicts who are angrier and more violent than before they entered prison. At the same time as the broader public is moving in a reactionary direction, there is now almost no progressive outside movement or activity focusing on prisons.

A Perfect Scapegoat for the 1990s

This article is being written during the post-1991 Iraq War orgy of jingoism. The resurgent enthusiasm for an imperial mission could, over time, lead to other bloody and potentially disastrous interventions. Also, long-mounting contradictions in the economy could come to a head in the 1990s. Capitalism, "triumphant" last year, could very well be capitalism in serious crisis next year (of course, even in the "best of times," capitalism is in a permanent crisis in the Third World, where 40,000 children die each day of malnutrition and easily preventable diseases). When crisis hits the home base of an imperial power, the rulers often create scapegoats to direct mass anger away from themselves and toward a weak and despised group. In certain ways, prisoners are perfect candidates. First, the hatred of prisoners clearly has everything to do with the most fundamental structure and passion in this society—racism—but without the public indelicacy of using explicitly racial terms. Second, such a redirection plugs into a very real frustration and anger that people already have about street crime and drugs. Third, despite the damage done by crime, prisoners are a powerless group. The same public that believes "you can't fight city hall" may feel that it can get some "satisfaction" (more executions and harsher internments) from its rage against prisoners.

The spring of 1991 finds New York State grappling with the first phase of the massive budget crisis. Not surprisingly, the initial round of cutbacks for the prisons focused on the programs seen as "coddling" prisoners—education and visitation—even though these are the only two programs with a proven impact on lowering recidivism. The deepening crisis might also compel the authorities to consider more progressive cost-savers such as alternatives to incarceration for many nonviolent felony offenders. Unfortunately, any such changes are unlikely to be accompanied by the qualitatively increased expenditures on drug treatment, therapy for sex offenders, and job training and opportunity programs needed to break the cycle of crime. Meanwhile, many prisoners fear that the budget crisis will be the juggernaut for accelerating DOCS' long-term strategy of the step-by-step taking back of gains won in the wake of 1971.

The prospects for prisons 20 years after the Attica rebellion are not very bright. Simultaneously, however, the situation presents a challenge for socially conscious people to pose fundamental issues for society: Who perpetrates the colossal crimes that rip off billions of dollars and violently damage millions of lives? Who promotes wars and military interventions? Who presides over the economy of mass starvation in the Third World? Who abets racist violence? Who fiddles while the AIDS virus burns through "despised" populations? Who is responsible for the economic tailspin? Who, in fact, are the real criminals, perpetrating big-time crime, with no respect for human life? Finally, even returning to the very specific problem of street crime, how can we ever make a serious dent in it if those in authority don't set an example by acting according to moral principles, or humane conduct, of abiding by the law?

Those striving for a more humane society need to relate to prison issues—not only because the conditions and terms are unjust, but also because left unattended, prison issues could become key assets for rulers who need scapegoats in times of crisis. This plea is not a parochial call to rank prisons over other burning issues of the day—war and interventions, racist violence, AIDS and homophobia, rising violence against women and children, and economic dislocation. Yet it is a call to recognize that the situation in American prisons is a significant piece in the whole picture and an important place to raise the challenge: Who are the real criminals, and what are humane terms for successfully responding to the crisis and dislocation in this society?

The Criminal Justice System

AMERICA BEHIND BARS:
The International Uses of Incaceration, 1992–1993
by Marc Mauer
Washington, DC: The Sentencing Project (1994)

ACLU FINAL ANAYLSIS OF MAJOR CIVIL
LIBERTIES ABUSES IN THE CRIME BILL
by Nkechi Taifa
American Civil Liberties Union (1994)

CRIME AND PRISONS
by the Prison Law Project of the National Lawyers' Guild
San Francisco: National Lawyers' Guild (1994)

The mega-hypocrisy at the heart of American politics was on particularly garish display in November's election. "Kick those immigrants out of *our* schools and hospitals!" was a rallying cry for descendants of transatlantic immigrants who have grown rich from the brazen theft of the northern half of Mexico (in the War of 1846–1848) and from the merciless exploitation of generations of Mexicano/a labor.

The same forces that sanctimoniously preached "law and order" made Oliver North a viable candidate for U.S. senator and brought in legislation shielding correctional officials who break the law. "Reformers" from both political parties insisted that welfare recipients either work or go hungry—at the same time that the Federal Reserve hiked up interest rates to make sure that unemployment doesn't fall much below 6 percent (by the late 1990s, weakened unions along with the insecurities created by the rise of temporary and contingent jobs meant that the federal government could not let unemployment fall to under 4 percent without major gains in labor's bargaining power).

All the politicians raged about tax money for welfare, with the main program (Aid to Families with Dependent Children) running at $22 billion a year; but not one of them was so impolite as to mention the $200 billion the Savings & Loans bankers are costing us or the $290 billion a year we are paying out—mainly to financial funds and wealthy individuals—just for the interest on a national debt that ballooned out of all proportion while Reagan and Bush played Santa Claus to the super-rich. The Republicans have even resurrected that 1980s sham-and-scam that the new tax cuts for the affluent will somehow bring about greater government revenues.

The plethora of blatant contradictions reveals that these policies are really driven by considerations of class, race, and gender; the ready triumph of such patent irrationality is a tribute to the mesmerizing power of the mass media. But there is an even more dangerous and disturbing trend at the core of this campaign: the response to mass frustration in society is the shameless scapegoating, based in racism, of those with the least power in society—prisoners, welfare mothers and children, and immigrants. This approach, when fully developed, is a defining characteristic of fascism. People who believe in democracy and decency need to analyze this surging offensive in order to be able to mobilize against it.

The lead wave in the rising tide has been the attack on crime and prisoners. This is the one issue that has some actual substance to it; the extent and often random nature of violence constitute a real worry for many citizens, and the despised in this case have often (but not always) done something wrong. At the same time, this concern has been subject to rank manipulation. From 1992 to 1993 the crime rate remained pretty much the same, but the media coverage of it (the number of stories) doubled.

American public opinion followed suit. A *New York Times/CBS News* Poll (NYT, 5/10/94) showed that in mid-1992 less than 2 percent of respondents considered crime the country's most important problem, but by April 1994, it became the number-one choice (24 percent of respondents), eclipsing both health care and the economy (ironically, improvements at the bottom layers of the economy would do far more to reduce crime than all the punitive and costly measures that have flowed from the change of focus). This climate is fraught with the particular danger that precious civil liberties, vital to all members of society, will be sacrificed on the altar of this cultivated hysteria.

There is a monumental fraud at the heart of the current anti-crime campaign: harsher sentences and more lock-ups are fool's gold; they have already been tried and have proven to be dismal failures. Over the past 20 years, the U.S. went on an unprecedented binge of quadrupling the number of persons in prison, along with a vengeful return to the death penalty. This approach hasn't brought any noticeable improvement. The politicians whose main selling point was "it's time for a change" are simply serving up more of the same old sorry soup.

Meanwhile, anyone who offered even a hint of another approach—for example, Surgeon General Joycelyn Elders's suggestion for just a *study* about decriminalizing drugs—has been howled off the public stage. Lesser-known people with valuable experience in programs that actually work—offering opportunities for higher education, strengthening family ties, alternatives to incarceration for non-violent offenders, restorative justice, etc.—can't get heard at all.

Three different reports published in September bring some relevant data and needed elements of rationality into the discussion of criminal justice.

America Behind Bars, by Marc Mauer, was issued by The Sentencing Project, the most authoritative source for international data on incarceration. On a typical day in 1993, America had about 1.3 million persons behind bars. The maintenance costs alone—without even considering expensive prison construction—are about $25.8 billion a year. The prison population doubled from 1980 to 1991. Contrary to the common perception, this wasn't mainly due to rising violence; 84 percent of the increase in new court commitments was for non-violent crimes (drugs, property, and public order offenses).

The current U.S. incarceration rate of 519 persons per 100,000 population (surpassed among major countries only by Russia since its recent economic breakdown) is about five to eight times that of other industrialized nations. While the U.S. does have a lot more violence, our imprisonment rates are also much higher when the crime rates are comparable to other countries, as with many property offenses.

The stark difference in prison population seems to be driven largely by the U.S. penchant for longer sentences. From inside prison I have to wonder whether subjecting so many young men to such dehumanizing conditions for drug and property offenses is, in turn, a significant factor promoting subsequent violence.

As to why some countries are more punitive than others, Mauer cites research that suggests that the greater a society's tolerance of inequality, the more extreme its scale of punishment. In other words, the more pronounced the polarization of wealth and status, the more severe the penalties for those deemed criminals.

The incarceration rate for African Americans is 1,947/100,000, more than six times the rate for whites (Mauer doesn't give any breakdown by income, which is also relevant). Black males in the U.S. are imprisoned at more than four times the rate that Black males were under apartheid in South Africa—3,833 versus 851 per 100,000. One in four young Black men is under some sort of control of the criminal justice system (including probation and parole), while the 583,000 behind bars outnumber the 537,000 enrolled in higher education.

Imprisonment has surprisingly little impact on curbing crime. *America Behind Bars* lists a few of the reasons: (1) only a small percent of crimes are reported and many of those aren't solved; (2) there is a replacement effect, especially with drugs, as new sellers emerge to fill the economic slots that have been vacated; and (3) crime rates are independently and heavily influenced by demographics— i.e., the number of males in the 15-to 18-year-old group.

The Sentencing Project's list of recommendations is very brief and, therefore, superficial. Nonetheless, their indictment of current policies is clear: two decades of steadily increasing rates of incarceration have not resulted in Americans feeling safer from crime; serious reconsideration of such policies is way overdue.

The American Civil Liberties Union (ACLU) is the most prominent and venerable organization devoted to defending our constitutional rights. *The ACLU Final Analysis of Major Civil Liberties Abuses in the Crime Bill*, by Nkechi Taifa, was issued on September 13, 1994, the same day that President Clinton signed this federal bill into law. The report mentions how ACLU lobbying succeeded in modifying or attenuating some of the most harmful proposals. Nonetheless, the final result is "a civil liberties nightmare come true."

Here are some of the more troubling new measures: (1) up to 10 years of additional sentence time are added to certain crimes if committed by a member of a "gang" (defined so broadly that it could be used against political groups accused of anti-government violence); (2) juveniles as young as 13 years old may now be tried as adults for violent crimes; (3) non-permanent resident aliens convicted of aggravated felonies are now to be deported without a hearing, thus eliminating the constitutional right to due process; (4) the severe increase in penalties for passport and visa violations could prove very harmful to those legitimately seeking political asylum; and (5) material support for "terrorist" activities has been criminalized (experience shows that the government is completely subjective and political about which violent actions it labels "terrorist").

A number of new provisions change the rules of evidence and undercut the presumption of innocence for those accused of sexual offenses. The community sorely needs real protection from the terrible damage done by sexual predators. But there is still a problem with provisions that will lead to more convictions of innocent defendants, already a significant reality (when there have been retrospective DNA tests of men *convicted* of rape, one-third were proven innocent). Once installed in this arena, the encroachment on civil liberties may get expanded.

Also, these sensationalist steps geared toward the "sinister stranger" divert attention and resources from the core problem: the vast majority of sexual abuse is committed by family, friends, and acquaintances. The new law provides no funds to expand the now-rare treatment programs, such as the one in Vermont's prisons, with proven success at dramatically reducing repeat offenses.

Thus, this crime law is definitely not about stopping crime. Another example is the elimination of the Pell Grants that funded college education for prisoners—the program with the most striking positive results. Numerous studies have shown that the average of 50 to 70 percent recidivism (repeat offenses after prison) can be reduced to 15 to 30 percent through higher education while incarcerated.

The new law includes the largest expansion ever of the federal death penalty, to more than 50 offenses, including crimes that don't involve murder. Yet, extensive evidence shows that such executions, which are morally and financially costly, offer no deterrence (during the 1980s, death penalty states averaged an annual rate of 7.5 homicides per 100,000 population, while states without the death penalty averaged 7.4). The Racial Justice Act was eliminated from the bill, despite undeniable data that the death penalty is applied in an extremely discriminatory way (and there is a companion, gross disparity based on income level).

Another fulsome example of racism is the staggering 100-to-1 sentencing difference, by weight, between the crack and powder forms of cocaine, where just 5 grams of crack brings the same average six-year sentence as 500 grams of powder cocaine. In 1992, 91.3 percent of those sentenced federally for crack offenses were African American, while only 3 percent were white.

The law's famous "three strikes" provision mandates a sentence of life without parole after three serious felonies (including some non-violent drug offenses). The "truth in sentencing" section makes aid to the state contingent on its ensuring that convicts do more time, with the goal that violent offenders serve at least 85 percent of their sentences.

Of course, these mandates will lead to a mushrooming of prison populations way beyond what the funds for new construction can handle, which forebodes such severe overcrowding as to lead to Dickensian conditions. Perhaps anticipating such prospective horror, this law makes it harder for prisoners to sue for VIIIth Amendment (cruel and unusual punishment) violations, and strips a sizable segment of the courts' jurisdiction over such conditions.

Only a token amount of funds was allocated for "prevention programs," and that pittance is on the chopping block for the next Congress. Overall, the law follows the failed Reagan/Bush approach of investing "scarce resources in more prisons and longer sentences without a concomitant reduction in crime or increase in public safety. These policies have also fostered a criminal justice system devoid of 'justice'—one which is pervaded with racism and class bias, from arrest to imprisonment."

The National Lawyers' Guild, a radical lawyers' organization, offers more in the way of political analysis in its *Crime and Prisons*. Although released in the fall of 1994, this collection comprises essays written over the course of the past few years (unfortunately, the Guild doesn't date them). Steve Whitman's two articles are particularly incisive in exposing the underlying racism. For example, Black people are four times more likely than white people to be arrested for drugs, even though the two groups use illegal drugs at about the same rate. Citing earlier Sentencing Project data that about one in 12 (adult) Black men is behind bars, Whitman goes deeper by raising the devastating impact on the Black community as a whole. He is also clear about how prisons are actually part of the problem, contributing to the crime cycle: "Virtually all experts agree that prisons cause people to become even more embedded in a life of crime. Prisoners rejoin their communities from prisons...where conditions encourage violence and criminality."

Luke Hiken's piece underscores the fact that the skyrocketing increase in incarceration over the past 20 years has accompanied the biggest shift of wealth from the poor to the rich in the history of this country. He, like Whitman, challenges us to look at the definitions of crime. The various banking scandals in high places have cost the public far more than all the property crimes on the streets. The truly destructive acts of denying people health care, housing, and education are rewarded rather than prosecuted. The battering of women by their partners—which happens to about 12 million women a year in the U.S.—is hardly ever considered a crime. As Judy Greenspan's essay points out, when women strike back and kill their batterers, the sentences for murder are often harsher than men's.

Greenspan also calls attention to the alarming, disproportional increase in women prisoners, fueled by mandatory sentencing for drug-related offenses.

We could give countless other examples. How many Americans are aware that 100,000 people die each year from occupational-related diseases, four times the number of murder victims? Where is the public outrage demanding that justice be exacted on the industry and agribusiness executives responsible for those hazards? What about the grand-scale drug trafficking by U.S. intelligence agencies? Or the government's unwillingness to enforce environmental laws against lead pollution because they might impinge on landlords' and urban industrialists' profits? These actions are truly worthy of condemnation. But instead, it is the children most damaged by these policies who will be publicly reviled and brutally punished as "despicable criminals."

As useful as all three of these studies are, none tries to present an overview of the causes and cures for crime. None delves into the prevailing moral values and consumer culture of capitalist society. None mentions how the shortcomings of the '60s "War on Poverty"—which was designed primarily to co-opt and control people rather than empower them—have provided grist for the mill of right-wing attacks against "social programs" (indeed, the direction for real solutions is not in the expansion of government bureaucracy but rather in more power, resources, and initiatives for the oppressed communities themselves).

Finally, none of these short papers takes on the formidable task of formulating an alternative strategy for effective policies against crime. This challenge cannot be met briefly or narrowly. That job would have to start at the foundation: why there is a dearth of positive alternatives for youth in certain neighborhoods; why social resources are poured into lucrative military contracts, into debt payments to the rich, into police and prisons rather than into improving education, providing jobs, and building low-cost housing. Society would have to be awakened that the starting point for any serious anti-crime program must be the strictest standards and enforcement on those with the most power and prestige. The complexity of the drug problem would have to be engaged—why prohibition is a failure (although very profitable for major vested interests); how to take the profit out and also how to stop the promotion of drugs (including ads for tobacco and alcohol); what type of mass education, community initiatives, and individual therapies actually work. For the range of crimes, there would need to be much more thorough study and development of the now-isolated programs that have had significant success in prevention and in reducing recidivism.

Taken together these three reports do, however, provide an illuminating critique of the current political juggernaut, which, while totally counterproductive in terms of its *professed* goal, works brilliantly as a campaign to make "criminals" scapegoats for a failing economy. As Steve Whitman puts it:

> *In reality the "war on crime" and the "war on drugs" have been wars on Black and Latino people. The main purpose of these wars has not been to fight crime (since they could never succeed) but to distract us from fighting against the conditions in society which create and perpetuate crime—racism, sexism, poverty, homelessness, and despair.*

[published in *Downtown*, December 21, 1994]

Capitalism and Crisis: Creating a Jailhouse Nation

LOCKDOWN AMERICA:
Police and Prisons in the Age of Crisis
by Christian Parenti
New York: Verso (1999)

By the time I was captured in 1981, the prologue to a life sentence, I had 20 years of movement experience—both above and underground—under my belt. So I thought I had a good understanding of the race and class basis of prisons. But once actually inside that reality, I was stunned by just how thoroughly racist the criminal justice system is and also by the incessant petty hassles of humiliation and degradation. As political prisoner Mumia Abu-Jamal aptly noted in *Live from Death Row,* there is a "profound horror...in the day-to-day banal occurrences...[the] second-by-second assault on the soul." The 1980s became the intense midpoint of an unprecedented explosion of imprisonment.[1]

Since 1972, the number of inmates in this country, on any given day, has multiplied six-fold to the two million human beings behind bars today.[2] Another four million are being supervised on parole or probation. The U.S. leads the industrialized world in rate of incarceration and death sentences. With just 5 percent of the world's population, we hold 25 percent of the prisoners.

The qualitative political change has been just as stark as the numbers: no politician who hopes to get elected can risk a charge of being soft on crime. Literally thousands of new repressive laws have been passed, and law and order has become the battering ram for a broader right-wing offensive. The political importance of criminal justice is, as we say in prison, "obvious to a duck."

What are far from obvious—in fact purposely obscured—are the real reasons for these dramatic and ultimately very damaging developments. It certainly isn't a rational response to crime. Consider just a couple of the many telling but rarely mentioned facts: Western Europe and Japan, with about 1/7 our incarceration rate, maintain lower levels of violent crime. Throughout 20 years of mushrooming imprisonment here, U.S. crime rates continued to climb. The marked decline in violent offenses didn't start until 1993—along with the fall in unemployment and the lower percent of males in the high-risk 15- to 24-year-old age group. Wholesale repression and incarceration are emphatically not real solutions. However, the political role of these themes makes them burning issues for everyone concerned about social change.

Christian Parenti's *Lockdown America* is an analytical gem, with many facets on key developments—from the advent of computerized, nationwide police files to tower guards shooting down unarmed inmates in California. This book does not take on the complex questions of the causes and cures for crime. Instead, its forte is laying bare the driving forces behind the burgeoning of the criminal justice system. Parenti's starting point might seem far removed from police and prisons, but it proves compelling. It is the serious structural crisis of U.S. and world capitalism that emerged in the late 1960s. To put Parenti's much fuller account into a nutshell, the very success of the post-Second World War glory days of capitalist growth proved to be its undoing. The extraordinary investment opportunities in rebuilding the war-ravaged economies of Europe and Japan resulted in highly productive competitors for U.S. industry. These developments ushered in a period of chronic overproduction, in which capitalism tends to produce more goods and services than can be profitably sold (given the limited purchasing power of most people).

At the same time, capital was hit with political changes within the U.S. The examples of civil rights and anti-war activism inspired growing worker militancy, which resulted in rising labor costs, and a new environmental movement, which led to expensive pollution controls. To summarize a complex international and domestic crunch by how it reads on capital's bottom line, average profit rates fell from a peak of almost 10 percent in 1965 to a low of 4.5 percent in 1974. And there was no prospect for a cyclical upswing out of this pit.

Parenti describes two major phases of capital's counteroffensive. The first was the withering attack on radical movements and insurgent communities, including a counterintelligence program resulting in, among other things, the murders of some 30 members of the Black Panther Party. The real motive behind the law-and-order rallying cry is deftly revealed with a quote from the diary of President Nixon's chief of staff, H. R. Haldeman: "[President Nixon] emphasized that you have to face the fact that the whole problem is really the blacks. The key is to devise a system that recognizes this while not appearing to."

The second stage entailed the sweeping economic restructuring that was kicked off by England's Prime Minister Thatcher in 1979. It became the heart of the Reagan Revolution here and is still going strong today. Here's how Thatcher's chief economic adviser, Alan Budd, put it:

> *Rising unemployment was a very desirable way of reducing the strength of the working classes. What was engineered—in Marxist terms—was a crisis in capitalism which re-created a reserve army of labor, and has allowed capitalists to make high profits ever since.*

This opening salvo was followed by a raft of measures that could best be summarized as successively gutting the Great Society and New Deal social compacts, leaving labor in a weak bargaining position even in subsequent economic expansions.

These changes severely hurt the inner cities. First, capital, now more globally mobile, shifted some manufacturing to low-wage countries and regions within the U.S., eliminating many of the jobs that had provided at least a measure of stability for Blacks and Latinos. The new, poorly paid service jobs more likely went to immigrant workers, who could be intimidated with the threat of deportation. From the point of view of capitalist production, people in the ghettos and barrios became "surplus population" or "social junk." At the same time, these stressed communities, with a history of militancy, were potentially "social dynamite"—a serious threat located near the city center, headquarters of the most profitable sectors of the new economy such as finance, insurance, real estate, and communications. Parenti sees the core of the anti-crime crusade as rooted in capital's acute need to control and contain the ghettos and barrios and to create *cordons sanitaires* around the central business districts. Second, capital's campaign to wrest away many of the last generation's gains for U.S. workers posed a pressing political problem: the need to deflect rising frustration and anger from the rulers. To do so, they recharged their "trusted trope: race spoken through the code of crime and welfare." In short, there is a complete correlation over the past 20 years between the greatest ever recorded shift of wealth from the poor to the rich and our skyrocketing prison population. The dual needs of containment and scapegoating are clearly expressed in the racial character of American justice. For example, African Americans are 13 percent of illegal drug users but 74 percent of drug prisoners. Overall, the ratio of Black to white incarcerations is seven to one. The U.S. now imprisons Black males at four times the rate of South Africa under apartheid.

Lockdown America describes key aspects of the spectacular expansion of repressive powers over the period, in a writing style that combines analytical clarity with striking examples. Below are some of the areas covered:

Police Special Weapons and Tactics (SWAT) teams: Los Angeles created the first SWAT team in 1966. There are 30,000 such units today. SWATs serve as the vanguard of militarizing the police, with weapons such as assault rifles, armored vehicles, attack dogs, and helicopters—all too often accompanied by a commando mentality that makes all Black and Latino people the enemy. While providing some grisly examples of overkill, Parenti emphasizes the broader function of intimidating entire communities.

Anti-crime legislation: *Lockdown America*'s look at just a few provisions of recent federal laws, just a tiny sampling of the spate of state and federal acts, presents a breathtaking cascade of authoritarian measures that greatly expand police powers and stiffen penalties.

Criminalization of immigration: Parenti calls the new level of cooperation among various law enforcement agencies, and at times the military, at the U.S.-Mexican border "the most aggressive and totalizing police enforcement regime the country has ever seen." The racism is patent to anyone who has gone through an immigration checkpoint. Those with white skin are waved right through, while those with brown skin are routinely stopped. The formidable increase in detentions, with people often held under the most wretched conditions, can't begin to stanch the flow of immigration, itself driven by the economic forces of globalization. But the palpable threat of deportation is a powerful cudgel against labor organizing and complaints, while these victims of transnational capital are blamed for the loss of U.S. jobs. So, "politicians get easy scapegoats...employers get docile labor."

Quality of Life: The newest chapter in policing is the highly touted "Quality of Life" and "Zero Tolerance" campaigns. In theory, the thorough crackdowns on minor offenses such as graffiti, open beer cans, and unpaid traffic tickets will nab potential felons and create a climate of compliance with the law. In practice, there have been increased complaints of police brutality as well as widespread ensnaring of young people of color into the justice system. The experiences of abuse and arrest are themselves strong predictors of future felonies. Thus these programs may well generate more crime in the long run, but they are very useful for creating a comfort zone for the higher echelons working in the central business districts.

Each of the above policies leads to more people behind bars. Parenti provides a quality chapter on the growing "prison industrial complex." With about $40 billion per year being spent on building and running prisons, and more than 500,000 full-time corrections employees, crime definitely pays for some sectors.

Perhaps the most chilling example is the California correctional officers' union. It has become the state's second biggest lobbyist, and spends millions on election campaigns. It was the driving force behind "three strikes" and more than 1,000 other anti-crime measures passed in California since the late 1980s. But Parenti wisely avoids economic reductionism. Corrections budgets are nowhere near those for the military industrial complex and don't play the same strategic role of subsidizing research for high-tech industries. Also, despite the impressive initial spurt of the for-profit sectors of private prisons and corporate use of convict labor, these are still a small fraction of the corrections complex, and face major constraints to continued growth. While the pockets of pork-driven prosperity assert some influence, such vested interests are secondary to the needs and strategies of a ruling class responding to structural crisis.

While not attempting a detailed description of prison life, *Lockdown America* spotlights some of its more unsettling aspects, such as gang rivalries and rape. In addition to the horrible direct violence involved, the ever-present dangers and antagonisms prevent inmates from uniting against oppressive conditions, which in turn fuels more frustration and internal violence. The very chaos the institutions create is then used to justify bigger budgets and more repression. The flagship of these trends is the proliferation of supermax prisons and special (or secure) housing units. The rationale is that these are needed for "superpredators," but in practice they are also used against organizers, rebels, and "jailhouse lawyers." These prisons-within-prisons are characterized by 23-hour-a-day lockups, intense electronic surveillance, almost no social interaction or programs, and brutal reprisals against defiant inmates. One couldn't consciously design conditions better suited for fostering mental illness and anti-social, violent behavior.

A lot more could be added about the damage being done: severe HIV and hepatitis C epidemics; the high percentage of women prisoners whose problems started with sexual or physical abuse on the outside and who are then placed under the complete domination of male guards; the impact of sentences on convicts' children, who are more likely than their peers to eventually land in jail.[3] At the same time, correctional programs that greatly reduce recidivism—most notably college education—are being dismantled behind the propaganda myth that our prisons are "country clubs." Meanwhile, the police keep sweeping more young people—whether for "quality of life" misdemeanors or nonviolent drug offenses—into a corrections system primed for chewing up human beings and spitting out violent parolees. While counterproductive, in the long run, against crime, this approach serves capital well. The key, in my view, is the political role of racial scapegoating. Parenti articulates it well:

> As economic contradictions deepen, the racialized class Other— the immigrant, the urban mendicant, the cheats, the dark-skinned, the thieves, and predators—looms larger than ever in the minds of the economically besieged middle and working classes. [Since] the corporate system will not and cannot

> *profitably accommodate the needs of the poor and working majority, [politicians] necessarily turn to crime-baiting and racially coded demonology as a way of inciting, mobilizing, and diverting legitimate political anxieties toward irrelevant enemies.*

The U.S. today is criminalizing an ever-widening range of social problems. The government would rather militarize the police and build prisons than provide quality education, good-paying jobs, and a sound public health response to drug abuse. These trends, while ineffective on crime, serve to aggrandize police power. Even more importantly, the law-and-order mania has become an essential political arena of struggle for the left. Conceding the weight of public opinion to the bandwagon of racial scapegoating would only build the momentum and power of the grand-scale criminals who rule over all of us.

Notes

1 Most of the data cited in this review comes directly from Lockdown America. I've added data based on reports from the U.S. Department of Justice's Bureau of Justice Statistics and from The Sentencing Project.
2 The two million figure is for the number of persons behind bars on a given day. Because many people are in and out of county jails in a matter of months or even days, the number of persons in jail or prison over the course of the year would be several times larger than two million.
3 Ann McDiermert, "Programming for Women Offenders and Their Children," *International Association of Residential and Community Alternatives Journal* 3:4 (September 1990).

[published in *Metroland*, March 2001]

Chapter 7

AIDS in Prison: Global Health

Born on Sunday

Oh that Saturday, that Saturday
why can't we make it go away?
Don't want to believe it—though
It's all too real
Where did our warrior go?

Born on Sunday; died on Saturday;
struggled the whole week through.
Gave "24/7" and more.

As bad as Death is...
no way it could take Kuwasi head on.
No one took Kuwasi head on.
He'd dodged a couple of bullets,
caught a couple too,
always kept moving.
No, Death must have snuck up on him,
to take our warrior away.

Born on Sunday; died on Saturday;
struggled the whole time in between;
Struggled and loved, danced to the beat, laughed,
and then struggled even harder
whole life through, struggled for his people
to be free.

[December 31, 1986]

Dedicated to David's co-defendant Black Liberation Army soldier and New Afrikan anarchist Kuwasi Balagoon, who died in Auburn Prison, New York, on Saturday, December 13, 1986. Kuwasi means "Born on Sunday" and Balagoon means "Warlord."

*Kuwasi and David,
Auburn Prison, 1986*

121

Proposal for a Prisoner Education Project on AIDS

This proposal was the first in the country for a comprehensive prisoners' peer education program on AIDS. Three good friends of Kuwasi Balagoon—Mujahid Farid, Angel Nieves, and I—wrote this in April 1987 and submitted it to the Auburn Correctional Facility administration that June. As brief and simple as this proposal was, 15 years later very few prisons have programs with anything like the scope of outreach proposed here and still so sorely needed.

Background

AIDS is now by far the main cause of death in the New York State prisons. Yet, many prisoners remain woefully uneducated about the true nature of the disease and how it is spread. On one hand, there is periodic panic over forms of contact that don't transmit the disease; on the other hand, high-risk practices continue. The frontline of defense has to be education. For such education to be effective in changing high-risk practices, it must be thorough and ongoing and involve (with proper training and direction) considerable inmate-to-inmate counseling.

Overall Goals

The main purpose is to save lives by providing inmates at Auburn Correctional Facility with health education on how AIDS is spread and how to prevent it. With systematic and qualified prisoner-to-prisoner education, we can significantly curtail the spread of AIDS among inmates as well as to the outside community to which most prisoners eventually return. A related goal would be to provide counseling and support for inmates already afflicted with AIDS.

Specific Goals and Program

a) Have a number of inmates trained as AIDS education counselors.
b) Set up specific and thorough seminars with appropriate groupings of prisoners (e.g., the various inmate organizations).
c) Develop an educational presentation that would become part of the ACF orientation program and thereby eventually reach every inmate at Auburn.
d) Sponsor special educational programs such as movies, slide shows, skits, and speakers.
e) Prepare a special pamphlet that speaks directly to prisoners—about their concerns and in their language.
f) Write articles for the Auburn Program.
g) Establish an information and counseling office.
h) Work with Pre-Release in their efforts to provide information and to encourage a sense of responsibility among released prisoners.
i) Coordinate AIDS educational work with existing substance abuse programs.
j) Provide counseling and support for those inmates already afflicted with AIDS.
k) Fulfill other needs and goals that will emerge from these initial efforts.

Conclusion

Because of the urgency of the situation, we hope that this project can be approved and commenced as soon as humanly possible so that we can stop today's ignorance from sowing tomorrow's death. This proposal is very simply about saving lives.

AIDS Education in Prison

AIDS is now the number one threat to the health and well-being of New York State prisoners. In 1986, 124 state prisoners died from AIDS, while all other causes of death totaled 62 (*New York Times*, March 5, 1987). The number of AIDS deaths has been rising sharply each year.

No one knows exactly how many prisoners are carrying the AIDS virus (HIV) or how fast it is being spread. Official studies indicate that 50 to 60 percent of New York City's intravenous drug users are carrying the virus (*New York Times*, March 5, May 22, and June 4, 1987) and that 50 percent of New York State prisoners have been IV drug users (*Syracuse Herald-Journal*, February 10, 1987). These estimates would suggest, as a ballpark figure, that something like 25 percent of state prisoners may be carrying the virus (prisoners from upstate would lower the percentage while the additional route of sexual transmission would raise it).

The actual spread of the virus in prison cannot be measured precisely. While drugs and sex are officially prohibited, these activities are not uncommon. The conditions of prison mean that those who use hard-to-come-by needles are likely to share them widely and without much access to proper sterilization. Sexual activity is likely to occur without proper safeguards and often with multiple partners. These realities indicate that the ongoing spread of the deadly disease is a very grave problem within New York prisons. Furthermore, in the closely packed and non-voluntary prison community, the rise of the disease is likely to cause increasing fear, panic, and violence.

Given the prevailing political climate, some sectors of the public might just as soon see large numbers of prisoners die-off from AIDS. However, in addition to being inhumane (and thereby promoting criminal-type values), such a vindictive attitude is also self-destructive. The great majority of prisoners eventually return to society; if large numbers of them are carrying the virus and are uneducated about preventive measures, they will unwittingly contribute to the spread of the deadly disease in the outside community. Stopping the spread of AIDS in prison is a problem that concerns all of us. For many reasons, technical as well as social, testing provides no magic panacea. Education has to be the front line of defense.

The New York Department of Correctional Services has made many public statements affirming its commitment to AIDS education (see, for example, *DOCS Today*, I:1). However, those of us behind the walls know that DOCS efforts to date have had almost no impact on the practices and the fears of the inmates of most of the prisons. The little material that DOCS does distribute tends to be sporadic and far too general. More basically, prisoners tend to have a deep distrust for information coming from the state.

AIDS education must go beyond a few general ideas. Rather it requires working with people in a situation of trust and in a thorough and ongoing way in order to change the deeply ingrained high-risk practices. For these reasons, experts emphasize a key role for peer group counseling. These considerations apply doubly to a prison situation, where the very activities that must be discussed—drugs and sex—are punishable under DOCS rules.

There is a burning need for an effective AIDS education program throughout New York's jails and prisons. We see three criteria that distinguish a paper program from one that can really reach prisoners and make a change. Such a prisoner education program must: (1) be sponsored by an outside (of DOCS) organization whose primary work is around AIDS; (2) provide for extensive prisoner-to-prisoner education and counseling; and (3) be ongoing, thorough, and persistent. This issue is not solely for prisoners; the health and humanity of the people of New York are also at stake.

[August 1987]

The Struggle for AIDS Education in Prison

Prisons, although more hidden from public view, are yet another arena where the AIDS epidemic is being allowed to spread because the authorities don't give a fig about human life when it comes to gays, Third World people, and the poor. In 1987, 150 New York State prisoners died of AIDS—two out of every three deaths in a system that holds 40,000 people. The death toll will continue to rise for years to come. Eighty-eight percent of New York State prisoners with AIDS are Latino or Black. AIDS itself is bad enough, and it is heartbreaking to have to face death in prison. But for the prisoner with AIDS, it is triple jeopardy because he or she might be completely isolated even from other prisoners.

The prisoner with AIDS is also likely to have a much shorter survival time. A recent New York State Commission of Correction report shows that, for example, IV drug users with AIDS live for an average of 318 days after diagnosis in New York City but only 159 days in the state prisons. No one has put out a definitive analysis of this stark discrepancy; it is probably a combination of late diagnosis, poor medical treatment, and the depressing emotional atmosphere in prisons. It is shocking that the grim statistic of the short survival time has not produced a public uproar. The deafening silence expresses how little value is placed on prisoners' lives by officials, the media, and sectors of the public.

Continued transmission of AIDS within prisons and to the communities to which most prisoners eventually return is both a dire and an unattended problem. The most realistic estimate of the seropositive rate among New York State prisoners is 25 percent (this figure is arrived at by correlating the percentage of New York City IV drug users who are seropositive with the percentage of prisoners with IV drug histories). Figures for most other states would be considerably lower. Tests of federal prisoners indicate that close to 3 percent are seropositive, and even this figure poses serious epidemiological dangers.

While sex and drugs are officially proscribed in prison, they are far from uncommon. Yet, hard-to-come-by needles are likely to be widely shared, with little access to proper sterilization; condoms are a rarity (condoms, needles, and disinfectants are all contraband in here). There is no question that *there is a grave problem of the continued spread of the epidemic in prison.* Yet the authorities stick by their official position of no "apparent" or "documented" spread. They claim that sharing needles and prison sex are now rare; we prisoners know better.

Quiet as it's kept, there is a way to prevent AIDS: education. The most effective approach is *peer* education. The peer aspect is doubly important in prison, where inmates tend to distrust the authorities and are unlikely to discuss proscribed activities with staff. Some people take the cynical view that "dope fiends" won't change. My experience is that working with people on the basis of respect and trust, in a consistent and day-to-day fashion, can bring significant changes away from high-risk practices. I've seen even more profound, and moving, changes in attitudes toward PWAs; once fears about casual contact are put to rest, people's compassion can bloom.

In June of 1987, at Auburn Correctional Facility, Mujahid Farid, Angel Nieves, and I launched a *Prisoners' Education Project on AIDS* (PEPA). We were spurred into action by the AIDS death of our beloved fellow prisoner, and distinguished Black Liberation Army warrior, Kuwasi Balagoon. We developed our program by applying the example of the successful peer education in the San Francisco gay community to the very different prison context. Of course the Department of Correctional Services rejected our application to form an inmate organization. It rules by maintaining passivity and divisions among prisoners, so the type of initiative and unity intrinsic to a peer counseling program is anathema to the authorities.

We were prepared for their opposition and had developed a good deal of outside support for our program—enough support to force through a compromise of a partial project. What we weren't prepared for was the role of two white male AIDS professionals who became the key to our outside training and sponsorship. They just didn't see prisoners—primarily Third World and poor—as much of a priority, even though we had the highest concentration of seropositive people in their region. Their inordinate delays on promised work gave the prison authorities the space for a war of attrition against our project. These professionals also basically conformed with the administration's position that the program should first be worked out by the professionals and administration, with the prisoners simply the recipients of the final product—some way to develop a "peer" project! Amidst the months of delays and constant hassles, I (the recognized "inmate coordinator" of the project) was suddenly

125

shipped out to the most isolated Max A prison in the state. While several prisoners at Auburn, along with some dedicated outside AIDS volunteers, continue to make a valiant effort, the war of attrition has left a mere shell of the original project.

There is a bitter irony here—bitter with the taste of numerous deaths over time that could have been prevented. Probably the greatest initial obstacle to prisoner involvement was homophobia. Even though most prisoners with AIDS were exposed via needles, AIDS was defined as a "gay disease," and homophobia blocked prisoners from identifying with PWAs and from facing the issues forthrightly. On the other hand, the undoubted basis for how our efforts were undercut by AIDS professionals was their race and class bias. Meanwhile, the crucially needed prisoner peer projects for New York and nationwide continue to be stymied, at great cost to human lives.

My conclusions from this experience: (1) Thorough, consistent, and ongoing peer education can make a big difference in the attitudes and practices of prisoners. (2) The prison authorities will not accede to such programs without strong public pressure to do so. (3) There must be a powerful anti-AIDS movement to push the professionals (or supercede them) to be true to their professed idea and put the fight against AIDS above careerism. To be effective against AIDS, the movement must consciously oppose race, class, gender, and sexual orientation biases.

[This article appeared in *New Studies on the Left*, Spring-Summer, 1989, and also in the anthology of political prisoners' writings, *Cages of Steel*.]

Postscript: AIDS in Prison Today

NYS DOCS's (New York State Department of Correctional Services) own unpublished estimate of the HIV rate in 1987 was very close to my guess of 25 percent. When they took some random samples of incoming male inmates, the actual rate was a lower, but still devastating, 17 percent. The prevalence among women prisoners was probably over 20 percent. By 2000 these rates had come down to 5 percent and 14 percent, respectively.

Yearly AIDS deaths within DOCS peaked at 258 in 1995. Thankfully, New York State prisoners received prompt access to the breakthrough treatment with combinations of highly active anti-virals (outside AIDS activism had led to adequate public funding for such medications. Some other states have not made these anti-virals fully available to their prisoners). Since then, there has been a dramatic 90 percent drop in the yearly number of AIDS deaths, which is a little better than the drop in New York City (DOCS's statistics may be helped by the handful of compassionate medical releases it now allows). The AIDS survival time gap between prisoners and those in the street has undoubtedly been greatly reduced, if not eliminated.

Given the high HIV rates, related illnesses continue to take a serious toll, and major work to prevent new HIV transmissions is still urgently needed. In addition, there is an emerging and potentially bigger epidemic of hepatitis C, which is spread even more readily than HIV via shared needles. Peer education continues to be critical for health and life.

By early 1998, women at Bedford Hills developed the first successful prison peer education program. Their excellent AIDS Counseling and Education (ACE) became a model for several other programs nationwide. Over the years, peer education became widely accepted as the only effective approach and is now endorsed, at least formally, by DOCS. Many New York State prisons have community-based organizations come in to train peer educators. Such programs provide jobs for outside trainers and certificates for peer educators; unfortunately, only a handful affords the crucial component of extensive outreach to and intensive work with the prison population.

I was in Comstock throughout the 1990s. Despite the general hostility to prisoner initiatives, we were able to develop a very strong AIDS education program by 1994. We reached hundreds of people each year, and were able to do major follow-up work with them. The experience was very affirming, even inspiring, in terms of both the peer educators' high quality of work and the population's responsiveness. Despite this program's unblemished record (and mainly due to unrelated bureaucratic factors), our ability to do outreach was severely restricted after 1998.

[March 30, 2002]

ALERT: Danger in Using Bleach to Clean Needles

This alert, sent to every prisoner-oriented publication I knew, is included here to give an example of the practical work. Our policy at Comstock was to be clear about the problems with the bleach method and to stress alternative harm reduction measures. Since this alert was published, studies have shown that the hepatitis C virus is even more difficult than this to kill in needles with bleach.

The standard method to clean injection-drug equipment that has been widely promoted turns out NOT to work. The three squirts in and out with household bleach (10 percent solution) followed by three squirts in and out with water looked promising in the laboratory. But now results have come back from actual use in the field: those injection-drug users (IDUs) saying they used this method all the time had the same high HIV seroconversion rates as those who never used it. The problem is that HIV is a lot harder to kill in human blood, especially with the problem of clotting inside works, than in laboratory cultures. The CDC summarized the research in their report, issued along with the CSAT and NIDA, of April 19, 1993. Current research now suggests using full-strength bleach (100 percent solution) and leaving the bleach inside the needle and syringe when it is filled with pre-bleach wash water, with the bleach, and with the rinse water are also recommended to improve effectiveness. This method does not guarantee sterilization but can play a role in "reducing" the risk of transmission.

Over the past several years, health departments and AIDS service organizations disseminated hundreds of thousands of leaflets teaching the old method that has since proven to be ineffective. It is shocking that there has been so little effort to now publicize these changes, which are of life-and-death importance. Why have the authorities been so lackadaisical about alerting us— are they embarrassed about calling attention to their mistakes? Or are they shrinking from the logical conclusion of the need to push for needle exchanges? Whatever the reasons may be, this appears to be another example of the callous disregard for life that has prevailed throughout the AIDS epidemic.

Most health agencies are now putting out the updated method in their post-1993 literature. But without the needed highlighting that this is a critical change, most IDUs, believing they already know the proper bleach method, won't even look at the new literature. Getting the right concentration of bleach requires a conscious effort, and it will take a lot of work for IDUs to learn to wait the full 30 seconds each time. Because this new method is so complicated and because it still provides no guarantee, much more emphasis and effort should be devoted to not sharing needles/works at all.

In short, it is urgently important to alert all IDUs that: (1) 10 percent bleach solution does NOT work; you must use full-strength, 100 percent bleach; (2) it is important to leave the bleach in for a full 30 seconds each time; either time it with a watch or count from 1 to 100; (3) shaking and tapping the syringe at all phases of cleaning can help; (4) since it is so difficult to sterilize them for sure, your best bet is to never share needles/works.

[November 5, 1994]

Glossary

AIDS: acquired immunodeficiency syndrome

AW: AIDS Weekly

AZT: also known as "Zidovudine" and as "Retrovir," an anti-viral drug often prescribed for AIDS

CAIB: Covert Action Information Bulletin

CBW: chemical and biological warfare

CDC: Centers for Disease Control and Prevention

DNA: deoxyribonucleic acid

E-Z: Edmonston-Zagreb, an experimental measles vaccine

FDA: Food and Drug Administration

HIV: human immunodeficiency virus

IDUs: injection-drug users

NEPs: needle exchange programs

RNA: ribonucleic acid

TB: tuberculosis

WHO: World Health Organization

AIDS Conspiracy Theories: Tracking the Real Genocide

An Almost Perfect Fit

AIDS—which can so heartlessly take people away in their prime of life—is the lethal scourge of our day, and it is still light-years away from being brought under control. This epidemic seems to have an uncanny knack for attacking people that the dominant society considers "undesirable": gays, injection-drug users (IDUs), and prisoners. And AIDS has increasingly become a grim reaper in the Black and Latino communities within the U.S. and among Third World people internationally.

The commonly cited U.S. statistic that Black people have twice the rate of AIDS as white Americans understates the problem because it is based on a cumulative figure (that is, the total number since 1981). But early on in the epidemic a large majority of the diagnosed cases were among white gay men (it is very possible that there were many undiagnosed cases among IDUs— particularly Black and Latino—who lacked access to decent medical care). Looking at new rather than cumulative cases gives us a better picture of what is going on now. In 1992 the rate of new cases for Latinos was 2.5 times higher than for whites.[1] The stark Black:white ratios for the rate of new AIDS cases in 1993 was 5:1 for men and 15:1 for women.[2] By then, AIDS had become the leading cause of death of Black people between the ages of 25 and 44,[3] and it continues to get worse as the AIDS hurricane moves deeper into the ghettos and barrios.

Internationally, the racial disparity is even worse: more than 80 percent of the world's nine million deaths from AIDS through the end of 1995 have occurred in Africa,[4] and this plague has already orphaned over two million children there.[5] In short, there is a powerful correlation between medical epidemiology and social oppression. What is more, that mesh fits—like a tailor-made suit—on the extensive body of the history of chemical and biological warfare (CBW) and medical experiments against people of color, prisoners, and other unsuspecting citizens. Such CBW in North America started when the early European settlers used smallpox-infected blankets as a weapon of genocide against Native Americans. It includes the pre-market testing of birth control pills, before proper dosage was known, on Puerto Rican and Haitian women who were not warned of the potentially severe side effects.

Recent revelations about U.S. human radiation experiments led to a comprehensive review of all government agencies by a Presidential Advisory Committee. It found that there had been at least 4,000 U.S. government-sponsored human radiation experiments, involving as many as 20,000 people, including some children, between 1944 and 1974.[6] It has also been documented that the U.S. Army conducted hundreds of tests releasing "harmless" bacteria, viruses, and other agents in populated areas, including a test to see how a fungal agent thought mainly to affect Black people would spread.[7] (For an excellent summary of U.S. CBW, see Bob Lederer's article in Covert Action Information Bulletin, #28, Summer 1987.)

The most apposite example is the four-decade-long Tuskegee Syphilis study. Starting in 1932, under U.S. Public Health Services auspices, about 400 Black men in rural Alabama were subjects in an experiment on the effects of untreated syphilis. They were never told the nature of their condition or that they could infect their wives and children. Although penicillin, which became available in the 1940s, was the standard of treatment for syphilis by 1951, researchers not only withheld treatment but forbade the men from seeking help elsewhere. This shameful "experiment" was stopped in 1972, only after a federal health worker blew the whistle.[8]

Nor is experimentation on people of color a thing of the past. Beginning in 1989, 1,500 children in West and East Los Angeles and Inglewood were given the experimental Edmonston-Zagreb, or E-Z, measles vaccine as part of a government-sponsored trial. Most of the subjects were Latino or New Afrikan (Black). The parents of these children were never told that they were part of an experiment with an unlicensed drug and thus had a less-than-adequate basis for giving their consent. The E-Z vaccine was also tested in Senegal, Guinea-Bissau, Haiti, Guinea, and more than a dozen other Third World countries. Trials in Los Angeles, conducted with the cooperation of Kaiser Permanente, the Centers for Disease Control, and John Hopkins University, were stopped two years later after questions were raised about the vaccine's relationship to an increased death rate among female infants.[9]

On another level, the drug plague in the ghettos and barrios has the effect of CBW against those communities. The government's role in this scourge is probably much more direct than the obvious stupidity and corruption. There has been considerable evidence, going back to the 1960s, of CIA involvement in international drug trafficking in order to raise money to finance anti-Communist guerrilla forces in Vietnam, Afghanistan, and Nicaragua.

A new bombshell has just hit with the August 18–20, 1996 series of articles by Gary Webb in the San Jose *Mercury News*. Based on recently declassified documents, court testimony, and personal interviews, Webb describes how a CIA operation was instrumental in the new influx of cheap cocaine into Black communities in the early 1980s, paving the way for the emergence of the devastating crack epidemic. The CIA set up and ran the "Contras," a terrorist force fighting to overthrow the leftist Sandinista government in Nicaragua. Starting in 1982, two key Contra fundraisers (Norwin Meneses and Danilo Blandón), enjoying obvious protection from investigation and prosecution, brought the first large-scale and cheap supplies of cocaine into South-Central Los Angeles.

Once we move beyond specific health issues into the political realm, government plots to prevent or destroy Black liberation are a continual and central feature of U.S. history. The most relevant example for today's dire political situation is the FBI's "COINTELPRO" (counterintelligence program), which peaked (but undoubtedly didn't end) in the late 1960s and early 1970s. This secret but extensive sabotage campaign against Black liberation and other movements of oppressed people, as well as against white radical groups allied with them, was exposed only after activists broke into an FBI office and found some of the documents. For example, a 1968 FBI memo calls on agents to

> *prevent the coalition of militant black nationalist groups...prevent militant black nationalist groups and leaders from gaining* **respectability**... *prevent the* **rise of a black "messiah" who would unify and electrify the militant black nationalist movement. Malcolm X might have been such a "messiah"**...
> [emphasis from the original document]

The program included a devilish array of dirty tricks and disruptions. While of course none of the documents explicitly discusses assassinations, about 40 Black Panthers were murdered over this five-year period, and the Panthers were hit more than 1,000 arrests on trumped-up charges. Another grisly example is what was done to the Native American movement. In the three years following their 1973 occupation of Wounded Knee, at least 69 American Indian Movement members and supporters met violent deaths. (For more detail on COINTELPRO, see Ward Churchill and Jim Vander Wall, *Agents of Repression*, Boston: South End Press, 1990.)

The violent plots against these movements have everything to do with the terrible setbacks in power and conditions for oppressed peoples today. In light of all the documented horrors, there are good reasons why so many prisoners as well as a significant portion of the New Afrikan community believe that government scientists deliberately created AIDS as a tool of genocide.

There is only one problem with this almost-perfect fit: It is not true. The theories on how HIV—the virus that causes AIDS—was purposely spliced together in the laboratory wilt under scientific scrutiny. Moreover, these conspiracy theories divert energy from the work that must be done in the trenches if marginalized communities are to survive this epidemic: grassroots education and mobilizations for AIDS prevention and better care for people living with HIV.

Dangerous to Your Health

It is this dangerous diversion from focusing on the preventive measures so urgently needed to save lives that makes the rash of conspiracy theories so disturbing. That's the concern that compelled the writing of this paper. I've been doing AIDS education in prison since early 1987; these conspiracy myths have proven to be the main internal obstacle—in terms of prisoners' consciousness—to concentrating on thorough and detailed work on risk reduction. What's the use, believers ask, of making all the hard choices to avoid spreading or contracting the disease if the government is going to find a way to infect people anyway? And what's the point of all the hassles of safer sex, or all the inconvenience of not sharing needles, if HIV can be spread, as many conspiracy theorists claim, by casual contact such as sneezing or handling dishes?

The core of the mind-set that undermines prevention efforts is "denial." People whose activities have put them at risk are often so petrified that they don't even want to think about it. Conspiracy theories serve up a hip and seemingly militant rationale for not confronting one's own risk practices. At the same time, such theories provide an apparently simple and satisfying alternative to the complex challenge of dealing with the myriad of social, behavioral, and medical factors that propel the epidemic.

In addition to my extensive personal experience, a recent study out of the University of North Carolina at Chapel Hill found that New Afrikans who believe in the conspiracy theories were significantly less likely to use condoms or to get tested for HIV.[10] To put it bluntly: The false conspiracy theories are themselves a contributing factor to the terrible toll of unnecessary AIDS deaths among people of color.

While convinced by scientists I know that humans did not design HIV, my main concern here is not to disprove the conspiracy theories. Neither do I attempt to solve the problem of the origins of AIDS or even review the many different theories and approaches to that question. The origin of this disease, as of many others, is likely to remain unsolved for years to come. Various theories of AIDS origins include a virus that jumped species, an accidental by-product of biological warfare experiments on animals, a new viral mutation, and a virus that lived in an isolated ecological niche until new social conditions facilitated the explosion of an epidemic. There is also a set of theories based on the now highly dubious proposition that HIV is not the cause of AIDS (for excellent discussions of HIV's likely history and the social factors that facilitated the explosion of the epidemic, see Gabriel Rotello, "The Birth of AIDS," OUT, April 1994, and Laurie Garrett, The Coming Plague, pp. 281–390).

Instead this article examines the validity of one set of theories being widely propagated to prisoners and to New Afrikan communities: that HIV was deliberately spliced together in the lab as a weapon of genocide. These theories have had important public health and political implications. My urgent, life-and-death purpose is to refocus attention on AIDS prevention and care and, more broadly, on the struggle against the racist and profit-driven character of a public health system that is causing tens of thousands of unnecessary deaths.

Readers not interested in a detailed critique of the conspiracy theories are invited to skip right to the last four sections of this essay, starting with "The Real Genocide." Hopefully, that is also where all readers will concentrate their attention.

Scientific Unraveling

When first introduced to a conspiracy theory in 1987, I believed it because of the sordid history of U.S. CBW. The version I saw then was based on the work of two East German scientists, Jakob and Lilli Segal, and was published by the Soviet news agency Tass on March 30, 1987. They claimed that HIV couldn't possibly have evolved naturally, and that it was obviously an artificial splice between visna virus (a retrovirus that infects the nervous system of sheep) and

HTLV-1 (the first retrovirus known to infect humans). They argued that the splice was created at the notorious CBW lab at Fort Detrick, Maryland, and then tested on prisoners in the area.

Upon receiving and believing this article, I immediately sent it to Janet Stavnezer, a professor of molecular genetics and microbiology (now at the University of Massachusetts Medical School), who specializes in immunology. My friendship with Janet goes back to the 1960s and her support for civil rights and the anti-war movement. While that does not make her analysis infallible, there is certainly no way she could be a conscious part of a conspiracy against oppressed people. Stavnezer's response to the article I had found so politically credible was unequivocal: the splice theory that the Segals posit is scientifically impossible (all references in this paper to Stavnezer's analysis, as well as to her colleague at U. Mass. who specializes in virology— Dr. Carel Mulder, professor of molecular genetics and microbiology—come from personal correspondence and discussions).

A couple of years later, the Soviet Union withdrew the Segals' charges. But it is open to interpretation whether it did so because the "science" involved is so demonstrably dishonest or because with *Perestroika* they were now cultivating diplomatic favor with the U.S. In any case, there are other fatal flaws in the Segals' theory. First, in an obvious error of U.S. geography, they speculated that Maryland prisoners, once released, congregated in New York City to become the seedbed of the epidemic; but most Maryland prisoners would return to Baltimore or Washington, D.C., and neither of those cities was an early center of AIDS. Second, they posit sophisticated forms of genetic engineering and cloning that hadn't yet been invented in 1977. [11]

Since the Segals, there have been a number of related theories that HIV was man-made. One posits a splice of visna virus and equine infectious anemia virus; another, a splice of visna virus and bovine leukemia virus. One sets the date at Fort Detrick back to 1967; another implicates the World Health Organization (WHO), starting in 1972. Most of these other theorists (such as Robert Strecker, John Seale, and William Douglass) come from the far right politically and charge that—whether it was engineered at Fort Detrick and/or by WHO—the AIDS virus is a Soviet biological warfare assault on the Western world.

I sent these various splice theories to Stavnezer and Mulder for review; none of them holds water scientifically. The method for analyzing the relationship of different viruses is to compare the base pairs of nucleic acids that constitute the DNA. None of the viruses posited in the various splice theories has nearly enough similarity (or homology) with HIV to be one of its parents.

At the same time as my 1987 inquiry, another, and far more exhaustive, study independently came to a similar conclusion: the various genetic engineering theories were fundamentally flawed. Investigative journalist Bob Lederer researched the topic for *Covert Action Information Bulletin* (CAIB), a publication that has been outstanding at exposing CIA and related operations. Lederer, an anti-imperialist and an AIDS activist, also started out with a political predisposition for believing the government could well have created AIDS. His in-depth research led him to conclude that HIV splice theories were false. One of his prime sources was Dr. David Dubnau, a longtime activist against CBW, who was emphatic: the HIV splice theorists "are simply wrong." This movement scientist independently offered the same explanation as Stavnezer and Mulder: HIV does not have any nearly sufficient sector of homology with the proposed parent viruses.[12]

Needing a vehicle for the deliberate dissemination of the allegedly spliced virus, the conspiracy theorists also characterize various vaccination programs (against smallpox in Africa, hepatitis-B among gay men in the U.S., and polio in various places) as examples of CBW campaigns. While vaccination programs with inadequate controls for contamination may have contributed to the spread of infection, they could not have been a prime cause: The geography of the vaccination campaigns does not correspond with the locations of early centers of AIDS[13]—and retrospective tests have not found any such contamination.[14]

Meanwhile, such unsubstantiated rumors can dangerously discourage people here and in the Third World from getting the same protections for their children that have done so much to stop diseases among more-privileged whites. The danger is illustrated by the unnecessary and serious 1989-1991 outbreak of measles among children within the U.S. More-privileged children had routinely been protected by a safe and effective vaccine (*not* the later, experimental E-Z variety) in use since 1963. The tragic result of the public health system's failure to carry out thorough vaccination campaigns in poor, primarily Black and Latino, communities was 27,000 cases of measles and 100 deaths in 1990 alone.[15]

There is another major problem with the splice theories—timing. Why in the world would scientists searching for a weapon of genocide in the early 1970s plunge into the then, completely, uncharted territory of human retroviruses when there were already many known and available lethal agents? Marburg virus, for example, discovered in 1967, would have made an excellent candidate.[16] On the other hand, scientists had no reason to even consider the class of viruses to which HIV belongs as possible CBW agents to destroy the human immune system.

The first human retrovirus (HTLV-1) was not discovered until 1977, and even then it could not immediately be linked to any disease. Yet the epidemiological evidence shows that AIDS had already appeared in several countries by 1978.[17] For full-blown AIDS cases to already be so geographically dispersed, HIV (a virus with a long incubation period) had to have existed at least several years before that.

And it is probably considerably older. Retrospective tests on blood taken in 1971–1972 from 238 IDUs across the U.S. found that 14 of the 1,129 samples—or 1.2 percent—were HIV antibody positive.[18] There are also a number of known cases of patients who died of AIDS-defining diseases decades ago. These include a teenager who died in St. Louis in 1968 with four different opportunistic infections; a Norwegian sailor, his wife, and a child in the late 1960s; and a sailor in England in 1959. Preserved tissue and blood samples from all of these cases later tested HIV antibody positive, although when the more difficult direct test was tried in two of these cases they could not recover HIV itself.[19]

Medical case histories going back to the 1930s—the earliest period in which accurate records were kept—show isolated cases with all the earmarks of AIDS. Various analyses of the DNA sequences—a technique used for broad assessment of a species' age—have provided estimates for the age of HIV that range from 30-900 years.[20]

Whenever HIV first arose, and however long it may have subsisted at a low level in isolated populations, there is no mystery as to why its spread would take off in the mid-1970s. There was a host of new social conditions to serve as powerful amplifiers for any infectious agent: international jet travel flourished; a sexual revolution provided many more opportunities for multiple sexual partners; injection-drug use greatly accelerated; there was a revolution in the use of a range of blood products, including multiple-donor blood-clotting factors for hemophiliacs; and there was the scandalous practice, born of poverty, of multiple re-use of syringes for legitimate medical practices in Third World countries. The travel, sex, drug, and blood products revolutions all combined by the mid 1970s to create powerful amplifiers for the rapid global spread of infectious diseases.[21] Far from being an anomaly, AIDS is a harbinger of other pandemics to come if humanity doesn't radically change its approach to worldwide public health.

In brief, the lack of knowledge of any human retroviruses before the late 1970s and the compelling evidence for the earlier genesis of HIV virtually eliminate the possibility that scientists deliberately designed such a germ to destroy the human immune system. More specifically, and decisively, Stavnezer and Dubnau independently confirm that all the alleged splices are in fact impossible because HIV does not have nearly enough genetic similarity with any of the proposed parent viruses.

Shyster Science

The most common article on the alleged conspiracy theory circulating in New York State prisons is "WHO Murdered Africa," by William Campbell Douglass, M.D., which appeared in *Health Freedom News*, September 1987 ("WHO" stands for the World Health Organization). Douglass has developed these themes at book length in *AIDS: The End of Civilization* (Brooklyn: A & B Books, 1992). His work deserves careful scrutiny because he has become a prime source for many Black community militants and prisoners who embrace the conspiracy theory out of a sincere desire to fight genocide. Douglass, however, who is white, expresses little concern for Black lives. Instead his avowed purpose is the defense of Western civilization, and he describes his politics as "conservative"— which turns out to be quite an understatement for his ultra-right-wing political agenda.

The authorities' response to the AIDS crisis has been disastrously inadequate, and establishment science has tended to be arrogant and glib. Their quick pronouncement of the African green monkey theory of the origins of HIV and their intense promotion of AZT as the main medical response to AIDS were particularly suspect. This experience makes people prone to embrace any attacks on establishment science. But the crisis we face demands that we think critically rather than simply becoming reactionary.

Douglass is clearly opposed to mainstream science, but what he offers instead is a bizarre cocktail of half-truths, distortions, and lies. He may be an M.D., but he obviously has little or no background in genetics, virology, or epidemiology. On page 171 (all page references are to his book), he confuses the most basic distinction in epidemiology between the cause of AIDS (a virus) and a means of transmission (dirty needles). He evidently thinks (p. 230) that all RNA viruses are retroviruses, which is like thinking all fruits are citrus. In fact his whole discussion there and in his article as to the possibility of transmission by insects displays a fundamental ignorance of the science involved.[22] There is also something radically wrong with his statistics, as he offers five very different figures for the number of HIV infections in the U.S. (p. 53, 60, 63, 168, 170) without making any effort to reconcile the variations. Douglass "proves" that HIV is a splice of two other viruses by comparing the shapes of the viruses as depicted in his own crude and inaccurate sketches of them (p. 231). But the scientific method for determining the degree of relatedness of different viruses is by detailed comparison of the sequence of base pairs of nucleic acid in the DNA. Such an analysis in fact disproves the splice theory. Douglass also promotes a strange cure for numerous ailments—photoluminescence—in which small amounts of blood are drawn, irradiated with ultraviolet light, and reinjected (p. 251–52). Treatment at his Clayton, Georgia, clinic can span several weeks and cost thousands of dollars.[23]

Disinformation

Douglass goes beyond such misconceptions and distortions to perpetrating fraud. His "smoking guns" to prove the conspiracy are two key articles, one from *Bulletin of the World Health Organization*, the other from *Science*. If you take the time to read the actual articles, they don't say anything like what he claims they do. Douglass must be consciously promoting a disinformation campaign.

His centerpiece is that WHO actually called for engineering a retrovirus to cause AIDS. He "proves" this by citing a 1972 article in the WHO *Bulletin* (A. Allison et al., "Virus-Associated Immunopathology: Animal Models and Implications for Human Disease," 47:1, p. 257-64). Douglass is emphatic: WHO is talking about *retroviruses* and is calling for scientists to "attempt to make a hybrid virus that would be deadly to humans." As Douglass sums it up:

> That's AIDS. What the WHO is saying in plain English is "Let's cook up a virus that selectively destroys the T-cell system of man, an acquired immune deficiency."
>
> (from Douglass's *Who Murdered Africa*. He presents an almost identical description in his book, p. 80)

On the surface, it is astonishing that any conspirators would reveal themselves by openly publishing a call for such an evil project. If one takes the time to find and read the WHO article in question, it becomes totally obvious that Douglass completely flipped the whole meaning and intent. The article in question (1) is NOT primarily about retroviruses, (2) is NOT at all about engineering new viruses, (3) NEVER discusses making hybrids, and (4) is absolutely NOT about making a virus to destroy the human immune system.

Instead, the article is all about a number of viruses already known at the time that cause various illnesses (in humans and other mammals). Evidence was emerging by 1972 that some of these known viruses, in addition to their direct damage, worked in part by selective effects on the immune system—in some cases by impairing and in other cases by overstimulating immune responses. There is a call to study these secondary effects. The article is simply a legitimate inquiry into existing diseases and has absolutely nothing to do with creating some new virus to cripple the immune system.

Douglass offers only one quote from the original article. Not only does he completely change the context, he also makes a crucial deletion from the quote: the list of viruses they are studying (*Bulletin*, op. cit., at p. 259). All the listed viruses were related to already recognized illnesses; most are not retroviruses; none is a retrovirus that affects humans; and none is suspect in any of the proposed scenarios for HIV splicing. Douglass has created a bogeyman out of thin air.

The other key and verifiable fraud is Douglass's oft-repeated claim that "seventy-five million Africans became infected, practically simultaneously" [his emphasis] (p. 83 of his book). The citation offered for this figure is an article by T.C. Quinn, J.M. Mann et al. in *Science* 234, p. 955. But this 1986 article never mentions 75 million people infected or anything like that, not on the page Douglass cites, not anywhere else. The authors, who've done very valuable work on AIDS in Africa, didn't offer a specific figure because not enough was known at the time. But they did cite, on p. 962, "estimates of several [i.e. two to 10] million infected in Africa." Incidentally, Douglass never mentions that this same *Science* article presents strong evidence contradicting his allegations that HIV can be transmitted by mosquitoes and that HIV was spread by vaccinations.

AIDS Holocaust in Africa

Douglass's citation of 75 million Africans infected practically simultaneously is a far cry from the actual discussion of between two and 10 million between 1981 and 1986. But the actual numbers are a true horror, and have continued to rise over the years. By flaunting blatantly phony figures, Douglass makes a cruel mockery of the real AIDS conflagration consuming Africa. He would have us write Africa off as a lost cause, making AIDS medical care and prevention there already beyond hope. This direction is the exact opposite of what is needed: to fight fiercely for world health resources for this most pressing human need (see my articles on the AIDS holocaust in *Downtown* [November 10, 1993], and in *Toward Freedom* [August 1996]).

Awareness of the real and horrendous human toll must serve as a rallying cry to promote the urgently needed measures that can stem the current march of death. WHO's official estimates of the worldwide toll reached by the beginning of 1995 was 18.5 million HIV infections, 6 million cumulative cases of AIDS, 4.5 million AIDS deaths. About two-thirds of these HIV infections and three-quarters of those AIDS cases occurred in Africa.[24] The Global AIDS Policy Coalition offers figures that are somewhat higher and probably more accurate. It estimates that 1.3 million Africans died of AIDS in 1995 alone, bringing the cumulative death toll there to 7.6 million.[25]

The lies about a WHO conspiracy serve as a diversion from attacking the real causes of this tragedy: the way imperialism and neo-colonialism have drained and crippled Africa. As Dr. Pierre M'pele, director of Congo's Anti-AIDS Program, puts it: "It is undeniable that AIDS is a disease that comes with poverty."[26]

Here are some of the ways the exploitation of Africa and the resulting poverty have blown the dangerous spark of HIV into a raging AIDS forest fire:

- some 300,000 Africans are becoming infected with HIV each year from blood transfusions alone[27] because those plundered nations don't have the money to screen their blood supply.

- HIV is also being spread because many health clinics cannot afford disposable needles and have to reuse old ones. For example, a mission hospital in rural Zaire had just five syringes to use for its 300 to 600 daily patients.[28]

- one of the most powerful factors in the sexual transmission of HIV is untreated sexually transmitted diseases (STDs). A recent pilot project in rural Tanzania showed that proper treatment for STDs can reduce HIV transmission by 42 percent.[29] The high rate of untreated STDs in Africa is a direct result of the lack of the most basic public health resources.

At the same time, the prevailing poverty means that many Africans with AIDS don't have even the most basic medication—such as an aspirin to relieve pain or a lotion for itches that can have them scratching until bloody.[30]

These conditions result not only from the history of exploitation but also from current programs imposed by the World Bank and International Monetary Fund that force these governments to spend money on debt payments to banks rather than on health care for people. Uganda is typical; it spends just $3 per person a year on health care compared to $17 per person on debt payments.[31] But in another way Uganda is atypical. Despite the poverty, community initiatives and government education on prevention have resulted in a major decline in new HIV infections.[32] Given this courageous start by people in Uganda, think what they could accomplish with a workable public health budget.

Overall, the world has failed to marshal even one-tenth of the $2.5 billion a year that WHO says is needed to mount an effective prevention campaign throughout the Third World. Compare that paltry but unattainable sum to the more than $40 billion a year these same countries lose in debt payments to banks in the U.S., Europe, and Japan. The phony charges about WHO actually serve to reinforce the prevailing and deadly neo-colonialism. The U.S.'s failure to pay any of its 1995 assessment of $104 million—one-quarter of WHO's budget[33]—has gutted that agency's already grossly inadequate program of assistance to vulnerable and impoverished countries. Meanwhile more than 2.7 million human beings worldwide are becoming newly infected with HIV every year.[34]

The crimes around AIDS are just one part of a global economic order where 14 million children die from hunger and easily preventable diseases each year, where 2 billion people are illiterate, and where 1.5 billion people have little or no access to health care.[35]

Douglass would have us believe that Africa was essentially already murdered by 1981 and have us off chasing the WHO bogeyman. In contrast the urgent need is to stop the murders *in progress*, to save lives in Africa, by attacking the real source of the problem—global exploitation and the misuse of resources.

Deadly Lies

Douglass's disinformation becomes a deadly threat when he discredits the very prevention measures needed to save lives:

> *It is possible that even the government propaganda concerning intravenous drug use is a red herring. If the intravenous route is the easiest way to catch AIDS, why does it take as long as five to seven years for some recipients of contaminated blood to come down with AIDS?* (p. 171)

Here he seems to forget the well-established incubation period between infection with HIV and the onset of AIDS, although he manages to remember it later when he refers to a "latency" period of 10 years. (p. 245) And arguing that there isn't a perfect correlation between the number of acts of intercourse and infection, he declares, "AIDS is not a sexually transmitted disease." (p. 243)

Then, after sabotaging prevention efforts by disparaging the well-established danger of needle sharing and unprotected sex, Douglass fuels hysteria with claims that AIDS can be contracted by casual contact. In his article he says, "The common cold is a virus. Have you ever had a cold? How did you catch it?" By failing to differentiate between airborne and bloodborne viruses, he is conjuring up a scare tactic as scientific as a warning that your hand will be chopped off if you put it in a goldfish bowl because, after all, a shark is a fish. He also asserts, citing no evidence, that "the AIDS virus can live for as long as 10 days on a dry plate," and then asks, "so, are you worried about your salad in a restaurant that employs homosexuals?"

While people are understandably skeptical of government reassurances on any matter, we can turn instead to the experiences of families of people with

AIDS and of grassroots AIDS activists: There are hundreds of thousands of us who have worked closely with infected people for years without catching the virus. The unwarranted fears about casual contact deter sorely needed support for our brothers and sisters living with HIV infection and divert attention from the most common means of transmission: unprotected sex and shared drug injection equipment.

Reactionary Politics

Despite the apparent irrationality, there is a coherence to Douglass's distortions and fabrications. They are driven by an ultra-right-wing political agenda that, as research by Terry Allen of *Covert Action Quarterly* shows, goes back to the 1960s. Douglass, a member of the John Birch Society, ran a phoneline spouting a 90-second "patriotic message." In it, he railed against the Civil Rights Movement and denounced the National Council of Churches and three presidents as part of a "Communist conspiracy." Among the nuggets he offered callers in at least 30 U.S. cities was the likelihood "that those three civil rights workers [presumably Schwerner, Chaney, and Goodman] in Mississippi were kidnapped and murdered by their own kind to drum up sympathy for their cause." In another he predicted that "the Civil Rights Act will turn America into a Fascist state practically overnight."[36]

Two decades later he was blaming gays for AIDS in *The Spotlight*, the organ of the ultra-right Liberty Lobby, for which he wrote regularly and in which he ran advertisements for "The Douglass Protocol," his cure-all medical clinics. In 1987, he wrote, "Some have suggested that the FDA [Food and Drug Administration] is waiting for the majority of the homosexuals to die off before releasing ribavirin," a drug he was at the time promoting as a miracle cure for AIDS. Douglass, however, opposed withholding a "suppressed" cure, "although I feel very resentful of the homosexuals because of the holocaust they have brought us." [37]

The political heart of *AIDS: The End of Civilization* is quite explicit: AIDS is part of the "entire mosaic of the current attack against western [sic] civilization." (p. 14) The term "western" is a thinly veiled way of saying "white."

Douglass sees AIDS as a diabolical plot perpetrated by WHO, which "is run by the Soviets." (p. 118) He weaves an elaborate and intricate plot for how the Communists—much like an invading virus—took over the machinery of the U.S. Army CBW labs at Fort Detrick and the U.S. National Institutes of Health in order to use them to create and propagate AIDS.

Douglass is so deeply into the tradition of the Communist bogeyman that he doesn't bother to revise this scenario for his 1992 edition—after the collapse of the Soviet Union. Nor does he explain how such an involved and extensive plot would not get exposed now that there is no Soviet loyalty and coercion to prevent past operatives from talking about it. He even goes so far as to charge that a Soviet functionary named Dr. Sergei Litivinov was the head of WHO's AIDS control program in the late 1980s. But it is a matter of indisputable record that the American Jonathan Mann, whose writings Douglass cites favorably, was the director from the founding of the program in 1986 until 1990—when he was replaced by another American, physician Michael Merson.[38]

Historically, one important function of generating anti-Communist hysteria has been to use it as a political cover to mobilize Americans against Third World people's efforts to achieve control over their own land, labor, and resources. The Vietnam War is one of many examples. Many of us who are anti-racist are very critical of WHO because it is Western-controlled and offers such a pitifully inadequate response to the health needs of the world's majority. But self-avowed rightists like Douglass hate the UN and WHO because of the little bit of say that Third World nations have there. Rather than put this in explicitly racist terms, they rationalize the issue as "Soviet control"—even to the degree of misstating who was the director of WHO's AIDS control program and even after the Soviet bloc had collapsed.

In the guise of a program against AIDS, Douglass proposes a basketful of traditional ultra-right and neo-Nazi political policies:

- Support and strengthen the powers of local law enforcement. (p. 139)
- Make preemptive military strikes against Russia. (p. 138)
- Abolish the UN and WHO. (p. 120)
- Stop all illegal Mexican immigration into the U.S. (p. 253)

Then there are a number of other proposals more directly about AIDS:

- Mandatory testing for HIV. (p. 66)
- Quarantine of all those with HIV. (pp. 165-6)
- Removal of HIV-positive children from school. (p. 161)
- Incarceration, castration, and even execution to stop prostitution. (p. 158)

While these may have some visceral appeal to people's fears, a wealth of public health and activist experience has shown that such repressive measures are counterproductive in practice. Discrimination and repression drive those with HIV and risk activities underground, making people unreachable for prevention, contact notification, and care. But while completely negative in terms of public health, such proposals are very useful for furthering the right-wing's police state agenda.

Douglass fans fears about casual transmission in order to promote a political platform. He argues that if we don't overcome a tradition "where civil rights are more revered than civil responsibility," hundreds of millions will die. (p. 165) And here is the final appeal in his book:

> *It appears that regulation of social behavior, as much as we hate it in an egalitarian society such as ours, may be necessary for the survival of civilization.* (p. 256)

A Sign of the Times

As bizarre, self-contradictory, and refutable as his pronouncements are, Douglass is not an isolated crackpot. Not only does his material readily get published, but it has also been widely propagated among Black prisoners. In addition, his program is in perfect harmony with the politics of Lyndon LaRouche, a notorious neo-Nazi with documented links to U.S. intelligence agencies. Somehow, for 28 years now, LaRouche has always had plenty of money for a host of slick publications and for a series of front organizations that operate on a national and international scale.[39]

LaRouche's National Democratic Party Committee organized the intensely homophobic campaign in 1986 for Proposition 64 in California, which would have mandated an AIDS quarantine (fortunately voters rejected this measure). The "scientific" source the LaRouchites used for their reactionary campaign was Robert Strecker, MD. Douglass has worked closely with Strecker, considers him a mentor, and dedicates *AIDS: The End of Civilization* to him.

We live in a strange and dangerous period when the attractive mantle of "militant anti-government movement" has been bestowed on ultra-right-wing, white supremacist groups. The only reason they can get away with such a farce is that their big brother—the police state—did such an effective job in the blood-soaked repression of the genuine opposition, such as the Black Panthers, rooted in the needs and aspirations of oppressed people. With people's movements silenced, the right has co-opted the critique of big government and big business to achieve new credibility.

The resurgence of the ultra-right is based on growing discontent. The previous guarantee of economic security and significant privileges for a wide range of middle- and working-class white people has become threatened by global capital's relentless quest to boost profits. The right-wing, however, portrays the threat as primarily coming from the inroads made by women, immigrants, and people of color. Thus their vehemence and militancy springs from the same legacy of white supremacy and violence that is the basis of the government they criticize, and their program is in essence a call for a return to the pioneer days' ethos that any white male had the right and power to lay a violent claim to Native American land, New Afrikan labor, and female subservience. In short, while capitalizing on legitimate anger against the establishment, the far right's logic leads only to an intensification of white supremacy and violent repression.

Michael Novick reported in *White Lies/White Power* (p. 309) that within the far right, "[t]he LaRouche groups are particularly dangerous because, despite their fascist orientation, they have been attempting to recruit from Black groups for some time." Another source for AIDS conspiracy theorists is the political analysis of Bo Gritz, head of the Populist Party.[40] As Novick's book shows, the "Populists" use anti-business rhetoric to try to recruit among the left, but the organization has clear roots in the Klan and definite ties to the extremely white supremacist "Christian Identity" movement.

When such forces propagate AIDS conspiracy theories among New Afrikans, one result is to divert people from the grassroots mobilization around prevention and education that could serve to foster greater cohesion, initiative, and strength within the Black community. At the same time, the right fans the flames of homophobia, which has combined with racism within the predominantly white gay and lesbian movement to prevent the forging of a powerful alliance of the communities being decimated by the government's negligence and inaction on AIDS.

Whatever the right's motives are, the practical consequences are clear: there is a definite correlation between believing these myths and a failure to take proven, life-saving preventive measures. To put it in three words: *these lies kill.*

The Real Genocide

The *New York Times* ran a series of articles in May 1992 expressing alarm that many Black people believe in various conspiracies—with AIDS as a prime example. In its editorial of May 12, 1992, the *Times* could only understand this as "paranoia." Educated white folks, to the degree that they are aware of such matters, tend to be "amazed" by such beliefs among Blacks. But what is actually amazing is that so many white people are so out of touch with the systematic attack by the government-medical-media establishment on the health and lives of New Afrikans. Indeed the problem is far more powerful and pervasive than any narrow conspiracy theory can capture.

The health horror this society imposes on New Afrikans is not at all made into a "mainstream" public issue, but Black people know what they are experiencing. That may explain why some people become very vested in a plot scenario that seems to crystallize, in an unmistakable way, the damage being done. The bitter twist, though, is that those conspiracy theories are serving as a red herring that can divert people from tracking down and confronting the real genocide.

There was a radical gap between the life expectancies of New Afrikans and white Americans even before AIDS burst onto the scene. A Department of Health and Human Services report showed that "excess deaths" among Black people for 1980—the number of Black people who died that year who would not have if they had had the same mortality rate as whites—was 60,000. That figure marks more unnecessary deaths in one year alone than the total of U.S. troops killed during the entire Vietnam War.

The New Afrikan body count is a direct result of overwhelming Black/white differences in living conditions, public health resources, and medical care. The infant mortality rate—a good indication of basic nutrition and health care—is more than twice as high for Black babies, and Black women die in childbirth at three times the rate of white women. There are also major differences in terms of prevention, detection, treatment, and mortality for a host of other illnesses, such as high blood pressure, pneumonia, and appendicitis (the summary in this paragraph and the preceding one is based on "Black Health in Critical Condition," by Steve Whitman and Vicki Legion, *Guardian*, February 20, 1991). The comparisons are even starker when you look at class as well as race, and, of course, the health status of both Latinos and poor whites is worse than that of the more well-to-do whites.

The situation has worsened since 1980 with the advent of AIDS and the new wave of tuberculosis (TB). TB, long considered under control in the U.S., began to resurge in 1985. One big factor was the greater susceptibility of HIV-infected people. But TB is an important example for another reason: it has always been closely linked to poverty. Crowded tenements, homeless shelters, jails, inadequate ventilation, and poor nutrition all facilitate the spread of this serious disease. Given the distribution of wealth and privilege, it is not surprising that the rate of TB for New Afrikans is twice that for white Americans.

In addition to disease, the tragedy of the high rate of Black-on-Black homicide—a secondary but particularly painful source of needless deaths—is in its own way a corollary of the frustration and misdirected anger bred by oppression. Black people are also assailed by a range of problems such as high stress, poor nutrition, and environmental hazards. One telling example of environmental hazards is the excessive blood levels of lead in children—a condition with proven links to lowered academic performance and to behavioral disorders. For the latest survey, in 1991, harmful levels of lead were found in 21 percent of Black children compared to 8.9 percent for all children.[41]

The public health history makes it clear: Far from being a mysterious new development with AIDS, it is all too common for epidemics and other health hazards to flow along the contours of social oppression.

While government plots such as the Tuskegee and the secret radiation experiments do in fact exist, the brutal damage they've done is small-time compared to the high human costs of the everyday functioning of a two-tiered public health system—the malign neglect of denying people basic means of prevention and treatment.

Overall, the conditions for people of color within the U.S. can best be described as a concatenation of epidemics cascading down on the ghettos and barrios: AIDS-TB-STDs; unemployment, deteriorating schools, homelessness; drugs, internal violence, police brutality, wholesale incarcerations; violence against women, teen pregnancies, declining support structures for raising children; environmental hazards. All of these mutually reinforcing crises very much flow from the decisions made by government and business on social priorities and the allocation of economic resources (the numerous public health essays of Rodrick and Deborah Wallace provide excellent analysis of the sources and effects of this series of epidemics).

When governmental policies have such a disparate impact on survival according to race, that fits the crime of genocide as defined under international law. Whatever term one uses, the cruelty of tens of thousands of preventable deaths is unconscionable. This reality is the basis for the scream of a people that "mainstream" society seems unable or unwilling to hear. These conditions are the real genocide in progress that must be confronted.

STDs and Drugs

There are two particular ways in which the racist structure of U.S. society fosters the spread of HIV: the public health system fails to stem the spread of sexually transmitted diseases (STDs), and the legal system seeks only to punish drug abusers rather than to treating them or ameliorating the underlying social and economic causes.

A major risk factor for HIV transmission is untreated STDs. These infections can concentrate HIV-laden blood cells in the genital tract, and can also cause genital sores, which are easier points of entry for HIV.[42] Although some STDs can be readily contained by responsible public health programs, rates began to soar for Blacks in the mid-1980s, with, for example, a doubling of the syphilis rate for Blacks from 1985 to 1990. At the same time, the rate remained stable for whites. This grave racial difference probably results from the lack of adequate STD clinics and the failings of public health education, along with the more general breakdown in social cohesion and values that can affect communities under intense stress.

Drugs, along with the violence and police repression that accompany them, constitute a plague in their own right for the ghettos and barrios. However, the public perception that illicit drug use is more prevalent among non-whites is wrong. Household surveys conducted by the National Institute of Drug Abuse show that New Afrikans, 12 percent of the U.S. population, comprise 13 percent of illicit drug users. Where there is a tremendous difference, though, is in incarceration. Seventy percent of the people in prison for drug possession are New Afrikans.[43]

There is also a major disparity in terms of drug-related infection by HIV. Some studies indicate an HIV rate (seroprevalence) among Black IDUs five time higher than among white IDUs.[44] While this is partially a result of which drugs are used and how they are used, there is certainly a big and deadly difference in who has access to new (sterile) needles and syringes through either pharmacies or personal networks. Also, on the street, police are much more likely to stop and search Blacks and Latinos. This practice deters injection-drug users of color from carrying personal sets of works (in states where they are illegal) and pushes them instead to share needles at shooting galleries.

Criminal Negligence

Many people are now aware, from books like *And the Band Played On* by Randy Shilts, of how the government and medical establishment shamefully fiddled while the early AIDS flames began sweeping through the gay community. But there is almost no public discussion of today's deplorable failures around AIDS prevention, which continue to wreak havoc in the ghettos and barrios.

The latest example is hardly known beyond the immediate circles of AIDS workers. Health agencies and AIDS service organizations distributed hundreds of thousands of leaflets over the years teaching a quick bleach method for sterilizing needles and syringes. It involved shooting a 10 percent solution of bleach in and out three times and then thoroughly rinsing with water. The method looked good when tested in the laboratory, and it made sense to try to get the information out quickly and widely. But when actual studies in the field were completed in 1993, the results were a very high rate of transmission,[45] revealing that the method was useless on a practical level.

Health authorities analyzed what went wrong and developed a new—more thorough and complicated—bleach method that should work well if the user takes the time to conscientiously carry out all steps. Literature published after 1993 describes this new, more effective method. But there has been no wide-scale effort to publicize—to sound an urgently needed alarm—about the error of the old method that was disseminated to perhaps hundreds of thousands of people. As I know from my work in the field, most IDUs don't even bother to look at new literature because they're sure they already "know" the bleach method. At the same time, there's been no serious effort to find ways to teach IDUs, who may be impatient to get high, practical methods to assure that they complete the cleaning process properly. Studies indicate that 80 percent of drug users do not clean their equipment for the more than 30 seconds that is required.[46]

A main reason the authorities haven't trumpeted the warnings about the problems with bleach—the failure of the old method and the difficulty of getting IDUs to take the time to do the new method correctly—may well be to avoid pressure for programs that provide users with new, sterile needles and syringes. In fact the government initially suppressed the report on a study the government itself had commissioned on "needle exchange programs" (NEPs). The report, which concluded that NEPs are highly effective, was eventually leaked to the press.

The main resistance comes from politicians who don't want to risk being labeled "soft on drugs." Drugs are indeed incredibly destructive to oppressed communities, but the phony posturing of politicians is no part of the solution. Instead of creating decent ways to make a decent living, the politicians dish out poverty and despair; instead of providing drug treatment centers and programs to build community cohesion, they proceed with wholesale incarceration of the youth; instead of seeing the need for self-determination in the Black and Latino communities, the politicians use the drug crisis as a rationale to catapult us toward a police state. The vehement opposition to NEPs follows this same failed pattern. It does nothing to stop drugs but rather sows pain and death for people of color.

The study that the government commissioned and then tried to suppress involved a comprehensive review of all known needle exchange programs and experiments in the U.S. and Canada. The authors found no evidence that the NEPs led to any increased drug use.[47] (And of course such programs could even help reduce drug use if they served as a form of outreach for involving users in drug treatment programs—except that the "anti-drug" politicians aren't providing the funding for treatment). While it doesn't increase drug use, providing sterile equipment is highly effective in reducing transmission of HIV and hepatitis C. In one telling example the study found the rate of HIV among IDUs to be five times higher in states where needles are proscribed compared to states where they are legal.[48] A recent open letter from 32 AIDS prevention researchers declared that, after extensive research, experts are virtually unanimous that NEPs are highly effective in reducing HIV transmission without leading to increased drug use. Yet there is still a ban on any federal AIDS funds for such programs, and many states still outlaw possession of needles.[49]

Tens of thousands of IDUs, their lovers, and their children have been condemned to die because health agencies won't advertise their mistake and because politicians won't risk being labeled "soft on drugs."

Shared needles is just one of the areas for risk reduction. For overall prevention work, the far and away most effective method for sharply reducing HIV transmission is peer education.[50] Homeboys and homegirls with appropriate training in HIV/AIDS information speak the same language, live in the same situations, and can work with the people in their communities in the detailed, consistent, caring, ongoing way needed to achieve concrete changes away from risky behavior. In fact, such peer programs are the only approach proven to work.

Prisons are not only a locale of some of the highest HIV rates in the U.S., they are also places where people who might have been constantly on the move in the street are stationary and collected—a perfect setting for peer education. And the vast majority of prisoners eventually return to their outside communities— where they can spread AIDS awareness, or they can spread AIDS. But prison administrations have generally been hostile to peer-led HIV-AIDS education; only a pitiful handful of such programs exist, and many of those are hamstrung by bureaucratic restrictions.

Allowing misinformation about cleaning needles to persist, blocking needle exchange programs, failing to treat STDs, and thwarting prison peer programs are major examples of the current criminal negligence on AIDS—and in particular of how this plague has been allowed to expand in the ghettos and barrios.

Fight the Power/Fight the Plague

Waiting for the government to stop AIDS would be suicidal. We have to step up to the problem by taking responsibility for ourselves, our families, and our communities. And the peer education model shows us that we do have the ability to make a big difference through our own grassroots efforts.

At the same time, communities that take the initiative to help themselves can ally to demand socially beneficial use of social resources. Our tax money that goes to corporate welfare—the $2.5 billion, for example, for one unnecessary Sea Wolf submarine being produced simply to keep the companies afloat or the hundreds of billions of dollars to pay for the savings and loan scandal—could instead be spent on public health and other human needs, both nationally and internationally.

What we don't need is Dr. Douglass and the like convincing people that HIV is not spread through sex and drugs. Instead, we need to engage youth in detailed and sensible education on sexuality and responsibility, and we need to make measures available to move IDUs away from needle sharing. We don't need hysteria about casual contact to generate cruelty toward people with AIDS and to foster support for police state repression. Instead, we need to support and learn from our brothers and sisters with HIV, and we need more open and democratic dialogue throughout our communities. Finally, we don't need to be led on a wild goose chase searching for the little men in white coats in a secret lab—which we will never find—which only leads us away from confronting the colossal crimes of malign neglect that are right in front of our faces, that can be documented, that are completely rooted in racism, homophobia, and profiteering.

Once we see the real nature of the problem, we can step to it with programs of proven effectiveness against AIDS that also strengthen oppressed communities. Grassroots public health education and mobilization that includes and fights for

- extensive peer-led programs in prisons, schools, and communities;
- thorough and responsible sex education in the homes, schools, and other institutional settings for youth, along with more and accessible STD clinics; and
- general access to NEPs and much more intensive and culturally relevant anti-drug education and treatment.

At the same time we need movements that fight:

- to make the resources of society, now being lavishly squandered on the superrich, available in order to (a) stop lethal public health and environmental conditions with programs that respond to initiative and leadership within the Black, Latino, and poor communities; (b) make medicine and social services for survival needs universally available; and (c) put qualitatively more effort and focus into treatment and research for AIDS and the host of other health problems causing tens of thousands of unnecessary deaths, and

- for international solidarity with the people of Africa, including putting an end to the debt payments, along with returning reparations back to them, so that they can mount the health campaigns needed against the scourges now threatening to take millions of souls.

It's time to stop the real genocide.

[A shorter version of this first appeared in *Covert Action Information Bulletin* 58 (Fall 1996) and was later published by Cooperative Distribution Services, 1997. It was then published in pamphlet form by Abraham Guillen Press and Arm the Spirit in 2002.]

Notes

1   Centers for Disease Control and Prevention (CDC) report, March 1993.
2   CDC figures reported in the *New York Times* (NYT), September 9, 1994.
3   *NYT*, September 19, 1994.
4   Figures are based on correlating the August 1994 report (at the World Conference on AIDS in Japan) by the Global AIDS Policy Coalition and the update of their figures cited in J. Osborne, "The Unbeliever," *New York Times Book Review*, April 7, 1996, p. 8. Global Coalition estimates are somewhat higher—and in my opinion probably more accurate—than official figures from the World Health Organization.
5   J. Mann, D. Tarantola, and T. Netter, eds., *AIDS in the World* (Cambridge: Harvard University Press, 1992), p. 90, gives an estimate of 1.3 million by 1992. The death toll has more than doubled since then.
6   *The Final Reports White House Advisory Committee on Human Radiation Experiments* (Washington, D.C.: U.S. Government Printing Office, 1995, 925 pp).
7   L. Cole, "OpEd" pieces, *NYT*, January 25, 1994, and March 23, 1995.
8   S. B. Thomas and S. C. Quinn, "The Tuskegee Syphilis Study, 1932 to 1972: Implications for HIV Education and AIDS Risk Reduction Programs in the Black Community," ... *American Journal of Public Health*, 81:11, November 1991, p. 1501. For an in-depth discussion, see J. Jones, *Bad Blood: The Tuskegee Syphilis Experiment* (New York: The Free Press, 1981).
9   M. Cimmons, "CDC Says It Erred in Measles Study," *Los Angeles Times*, June 17, 1996.
10 *AIDS Weekly* (AW), November 13, 1995.
11 L. Garrett, *The Coming Plague: Newly Emerging Diseases in a World Out of Balance* (New York: Penguin, 1995), p. 362.
12 B. Lederer, "Origins and Spread of AIDS," *Covert Action Information Bulletin (CAIB)*, 28 (Summer 1987), p. 47.
13 T. Quinn, et al., "AIDS in Africa: An Epidemiologic Paradigm," *Science*, November 21, 1986, p. 959.
14 Garrett, op. cit., p. 381.
15 Ibid., pp. 510–11.
16 See the description in Ibid., pp. 53–59.
17 Ibid., pp. 291, 297, 350, 381, and Lederer, op. cit., p. 47.
18 Garrett, op. cit., p. 363.
19 Ibid., pp. 364-65, 380.
20 For a fuller discussion, see G. Rotello, "The Birth of AIDS," *Out*, April 1994.
21 For an in-depth discussion of these revolutions and their role, see Ibid., and Garrett, op. cit., pp. 281-390.
22 For an explanation of the actual factors involved, see "Can Mosquitoes Transmit AIDS?" *Natural History*, July 1992, p. 54.
23 G. Garelick, "Desperately Seeking Solutions: Chronic Fatigue Syndrome," *American Health*, May 1992.
24 *Aids Weekly (AW)*, December 25, 1995.
25 Cited in J. Osborne, op. cit.
26 *AW*, December 4, 1995, p. 26.
27 Ibid.
28 Garrett, op. cit., p. 129.
29 H. Grosskurth et al., "Impact of Improved Treatment for Sexually Transmitted Diseases in Rural Tanzania," *The Lancet*, 346:530–36, August 1995.
30 *AW*, January 29, 1996.
31 *NYT*, March 16, 1996.
32 *NYT*, April 7, 1996.
33 *NYT*, March 11, 1996.
34 Estimate by the UN Joint Programs on HIV/AIDS, cited in *NYT*, June 7, 1996. They give the figure in the form of 7,500 new HIV infections per day.

35   F. Castro, speech at "Summit for Social Development," Copenhagen, March 11, 1995.
36   L. Peirez, "The Telephone Hate Network," *ADL Bulletin*, September 1965.
37   W. C. Douglass, MD, "New AIDS Scandal Brews," *Spotlight*, October 5, 1987.
38   For an account of the founding and development of WHO's Global Program on AIDS, see Garrett, op. cit., pp. 360, 459–81.
39   For more on LaRouche, see B. Lederer, "Origins and Spread of AIDS" (Part II), CAIB 29 (Winter 1988), p. 56–57; and M. Novick, *White Lies/White Power* (Monroe, ME: Common Courage Press, 1995).
40   E.g., a speech by Gritz is included as an appendix in T. Jackson's *AIDS/HIV is Not a Death Sentence* (New York: Akasa Press, 1992).
41   *NYT*, February 7, 1996.
42   J. Wasserheit of the CDC, "Heterogeneity of Heterosexual Transmission: The Roles of Other STDs." Presentation at the XI International Conference on AIDS, Vancouver, July 10, 1996; Abstract We.C.453.
43   M. Mauer and T. Huling, *Young Black Americans and the Criminal Justice System: Five Years Later* (Washington: The Sentencing Project, 1995), pp. 5, 12.
44   My calculations based on the several studies on drug use, race, and HIV summarized in *Justicia*, December 1995.
45   CDC et al., "HIV/AIDS Prevention Bulletin," U.S. Department of Health and Human Services, March 31, 1993; and *Medical Alert*, October 11, 1993.
46   *Medical Alert*, October 11, 1993.
47   P. Laurie, A.L. Reingold, B. Bowser, et al., *The Public Health Impact of Needle Exchange Programs in the U.S. and Abroad: Summary, Conclusions and Recommendations, School of Public Health*, U.C. Berkeley, and Institute for Health Policy Studies, U.C. San Francisco (Wash. D.C.: U.S. Dept. of Health and Human Services, 1993), p. 18.
48   Ibid., p. 5.
49   *AW*, January 29, 1996.
50   There is virtual unanimity on this point in studies presented at the various "AIDS in the World" conferences and in the studies of the National Academy of Science.

AIDS Holocaust in Africa

Sadly, AIDS in the World's dire 1992 projections were on the mark. In 2001 alone, 3 million people worldwide died of AIDS, while another 5 million became newly infected with HIV. This review is included (1) to show that Jonathan Mann and colleagues sounded the alarm at a time when concerted action could have averted such a massive tragedy, (2) to indicate some of the resources and programs that are needed, and (3) to stress this voracious plague's centrality to contemporary human and social reality. Giant strides could be made with just a small fraction of the money Third World countries are spending on debt payments, yet today's global response remains woefully inadequate. The AIDS holocaust, which was preventable, continues as a callous and colossal crime against humanity.

AIDS IN THE WORLD:
A Global Report
edited by Jonathan Mann, Daniel J.M. Tarantola, and Thomas W. Netter
Cambridge: Harvard University Press (1992)

As terrible as the AIDS plague and the inadequacy of the response to it have been in the U.S., the situation is excruciatingly worse in the Third World. Several African countries have astronomically high rates of HIV (the AIDS virus) infection, on top of wrecked economies and decimated public health systems. And debilitation and death of so many citizens in their prime productive years will in turn further cripple development efforts. In the West, an eerie silence prevails about this incalculable human toll and social devastation.

Jonathan Mann, the former director of the World Health Organization Global Program on AIDS and currently a professor at the Harvard University School of Public Health, and his two colleagues, Daniel J.M. Tarantola and Thomas W. Netter, have performed an invaluable service in drawing together a global overview of the AIDS pandemic (the word "pandemic" is used to mean everywhere because AIDS is now present in 164 countries, on all inhabited continents, and in the Pacific Islands). They open their inquiry with a stark question: "Is the pandemic now out of control?" Their main conclusion, 841 pages later: "The pace of the pandemic is fast outgrowing the pace of the response, and the gap is widening rapidly and dangerously."

It is not a simple matter to chart even the current scope of the pandemic, let alone to project its future course. Official figures for AIDS are notoriously low because many cases are never reported. The much larger number of people with HIV (most of whom won't be visibly sick) can only be estimated from fragmentary blood sampling of various populations. A prognosis entails taking this imperfect data and then assessing the likely rate of progression. *AIDS in the World (AIW)* produced a very thorough, careful, and reasonable compilation of the data and future projections. Mann et al. provides an appendix that explains the basis for their model, which was developed between 1988 and 1990. Actual surveys from 1991–1992 show that AIW's projections were conservative.

By early 1992, there were cumulatively 12.9 million persons worldwide who had been infected with HIV, of whom 2.7 million had developed AIDS, of whom 2.5 million had died. Sub-Saharan Africa, with 10 percent of the world's population, has 68 percent of the total HIV infections, 8.8 million persons, and 72.8 percent of the AIDS cases, or 1.9 million persons. Pregnant women provide a good indication of the overall adult infection rate. In the capital cities (the problem is the worst in urban areas) of Uganda, Zambia, and Malawi, 20 percent of pregnant women are HIV positive.

AIW also cites a study indicating a nationwide infection rate of 5 percent in Uganda (other studies have come up with even higher estimates). There are already some 1.3 million African children orphaned by AIDS. Many areas of Africa don't even have the means to consistently screen blood, which means that HIV is still being transmitted through blood transfusions, and very few medicines or social services are available for persons with AIDS.

By 1995, there will be 6.4 million cumulative cases of AIDS worldwide; that is to say that the new cases from 1992–1995 will outstrip the entire previous history of this plague. Eighty-four percent of these cases will be in the Third World. Africa will have suffered 4.6 million cases of AIDS, eight times the U.S. total.

Without dramatic changes to stanch the pandemic, we can expect cumulative totals by the year 2000 of up to 110 million HIV infections, 25 million AIDS cases, and 20 million deaths worldwide. There will be something like 10 million orphaned children in Africa alone. Currently, the U.S. is spending an inadequate $2.75 per capita on prevention efforts. For sub-Saharan Africa the figure is seven cents; for Latin America, three cents. For some of the African countries hit hardest by AIDS, their entire national health budget is equal only to that of a large hospital in the U.S.

AIW's great contribution is in providing this statistical overview with all-too-rare attention to the Third World. The editors then go on, with a collection of essays by various experts, to try to provide a comprehensive report on all aspects of the worldwide AIDS crisis. In this respect, their efforts are uneven, and the studies tend to be broad and survey-like rather than trenchant and critical. They would have served us better with a shorter, more focused work on prevalence, prevention, and public health in the Third World. Perhaps their promised annual editions will do so.

There are nonetheless a number of particularly valuable points included that are worth underscoring. One is AIDS' mutually reinforcing relationship (synergy) with other diseases, particularly tuberculosis (TB) and certain sexually transmitted infections (STIs) like syphilis. TB, although long considered under control in the industrialized world, is the leading infectious killer worldwide. One-third of the world's population, 1.7 billion people, carries the TB bacterium, but most healthy persons keep it in check and it just lies dormant. With AIDS, and the breakdown of the immune system, many more persons are progressing to active TB, and they in turn can transmit this airborne bacterium to others.

Right now there are an estimated 4.6 million persons worldwide carrying both the TB and HIV infections. In sub-Saharan Africa, there's been a doubling of the active TB cases over the past five years. Also, new drug-resistant strains of TB have now been found in the U.S. Synergy also occurs with various sexually transmitted infections because they leave people much more vulnerable to catching HIV; yet many of the 250 million new such infections per year go untreated because of the public health crisis in the Third World...and within Third World communities in the U.S.

AIW goes beyond a static view to analyze where there is dangerous vulnerability for the future spread of HIV. It sounds a badly needed alarm about the densely populated countries of Southeast Asia, where the incidence of AIDS is still low but where many factors point to a rapid burgeoning of the epidemic if concerted measures are not taken immediately.

This book is also clear, contrary to the prevailing cynicism, in arguing that prevention efforts, if done right, can work. Not only has there been a dramatic reduction in the rate of transmission in the gay communities of San Francisco and New York City, but also a number of needle exchange programs, reviewed in a useful essay by Don Des Jarlais and Patricia Case, have had significant success in reducing HIV transmissions among injection-drug users. There is a deadly irony in the current prevention efforts. The method proven to be the most effective in raising consciousness and initiating behavior changes in the various communities—*peer support*—was the approach least in use by the national AIDS programs that were surveyed.

Finally, to its credit, *AIW* makes at least a formal statement about the costs of bigotry: "Societal discrimination in all its forms creates increased vulnerability to HIV infection. Therefore, efforts to protect human rights and to promote human dignity are extremely important for protecting public health in the HIV/AIDS pandemic."

This tone also has a number of problems, big and small. In covering such a broad area, there are bound to be gaps and inadequacies. For example, the serious problem of detecting TB infection in those with HIV is considerably understated, and the effort to measure the important equity gap between rich and poor nations is distorted by using only the expensive and problematical drug AZT, rather than focusing on the very effective preventive medications for PCP (*pneumocystis carinii* pneumonia) and treatments for opportunistic infections.

A broader weakness is that so much of the assessment is based on collecting data by surveying governments. Many of these statistics are worthless because statements about priorities and allocation of funds tell us next to nothing about what is actually getting done in the field. The assurance regarding prisons, for example, that "there has been real progress in bringing information on AIDS and risk behaviors to...prisoners" is rubbish because what is mainly measured is output of government literature—pamphlets that prisoners don't read, by officials they don't trust, in a language they don't understand, with no engagement of specific risk factors in prison.

The biggest problem is the social perspective of the editors and many of the authors. Despite the general statement against discrimination, there is virtually nothing on the forms of oppression that have been so central to the course of the pandemic—the disdain for gays, drug users, and Third World people that was behind the initial criminal negligence that allowed the infection to mushroom and that continues today in the lack of adequate focus on resources on this mass killer.

Thus, there is no critique or even analysis of homophobia in *AIW*; instead, the reference is to the subjective state of the victims: "Some gay communities... feared stigmatization." There are rhetorical references to the need for "peer" support and "empowerment" of those affected, but very little in actual voices from the grassroots, concrete studies of peer projects or developed examples of organizing in the affected communities. In short, *AIW* misses just how much AIDS has been a *social* epidemic and can't be stemmed without conscious mobilization against the structures of oppression and neglect.

The clearest example is in Chapter Six, on the cascading social and economic impact of this plague in Africa, a matter that should be at the very heart of this book. This essay, written by two analysts with the World Bank, does list some of the factors involved: loss of productive labor, decline of agriculture, strain on family structure, and overloading of an already stressed public health system.

But this is a soulless exposition with little feeling for the harrowing human tragedy in progress.

One must wonder what Africans will make of this dispassionate discussion of AIDS' effect on demographics given the World Bank's emphasis on limiting population growth there. Most fundamentally, this chapter says nothing on the reasons these countries are such economic basket cases in the first place—nothing on the incredible toll taken on Africa by the history of the Western imposed-slave trade, colonialism, and continued hemorrhaging under the auspices of the world market. Inexcusably, it says nothing about the "structural adjustment programs" (mentioned only once, in passing, in another section of the book) currently being imposed on these countries by the World Bank that have devastated the public sector. To assess sub-Saharan Africa's ability to respond to the AIDS scourge, it's important to know, for example, that per capita food production there fell 9 percent over the course of the 1980s and that average gross domestic production was declining by 2.9 percent a year.

This studied obliviousness to social reality also undermines *AIW*'s subsequent righteous appeal for a transfer of funds to the poorer nations. Without mention of the history and structures of exploitation, such request sounds like a plea for charity, which will not receive much sympathy in these days of "tight budgets." In truth, a transfer of resources is a profound obligation as reparations to begin to meet human needs. Being honest about such institutions as the World Bank would also underscore why the best programs, the best use for resources, will be generated by the affected nations and communities themselves.

Despite the elitist perspective of much of the book, there are important exceptions such as an insert on the role of ACT-UP (AIDS Coalition to Unleash Power) activism in speeding drug development, a strong essay by Elizabeth Reid on the impact of women's social status, and a useful survey by Jeff O'Malley on the cutting-edge role of non-governmental AIDS service organizations.

AIW, with its predominantly top-down perspective and excessive reliance on surveys of governmental programs, could be fairly characterized as "bureaucratic." But, to be fair, it is an unusually *enlightened* bureaucratic approach—not only because of the awareness of such concepts as anti-discrimination, peer support, and empowerment, but most particularly for its clarion call about the mounting conflagration in Africa and the ominous vulnerability in Southeast Asia. In this regard those of us who have been involved in AIDS and/or anti-racist activism have to be very self-critical that we haven't been screaming bloody murder about this unconscionable and preventable human tragedy. The urgent task remains to raise consciousness and fight for adequate resources and programs for the *global* AIDS pandemic.

The last chapter of *AIW* reminds us how much we live in one world. Laurie Garrett argues that a future viral epidemic is almost inevitable given present policies. Many viruses lie dormant and localized, especially in viral-rich tropical areas. Terrible health conditions such as malnutrition and poor sanitation make populations in those areas much more vulnerable to succumbing to disease; impoverished public health surveillance systems mean that serious new pathogens may well not be detected until they become widespread; modern transportation and sexual intercourse mean that such infections can rapidly spread to other parts of the world. "From a microbial point of view, the global village of the 1990s is miniscule. Never has it been so obvious that poor health care and surveillance in one corner of the planet can imperil every person on earth, rich, as well as poor."

As with problems of the environment, AIDS shows us just how much the fate of all humankind is interlinked. It is not just right and more fully human to respond to the plight and struggles of the oppressed, but there is also no way the destruction and misery won't rebound to the point where they will eventually threaten the coherent functioning of society and any chance for a decent future for our children. Unfortunately, the social structures and psychology of privilege are so entrenched that those who are presently comfortable don't seem capable of deeply identifying with the oppressed. The outlook for a timely and adequate response to the crisis is not bright.

[published in *Downtown*, November 10, 1993]

The Global Village for Microbes

THE COMING PLAGUE:
Newly Emerging Diseases in a World out of Balance
by Laurie Garrett
New York: Penguin Books (1995)

> *Unequal development in different countries in the promotion of*
> *health and control of disease... is a common danger.*
> — Constitution of the World Health Organization, July 22, 1946

A man walked into the missionary hospital in Yambuka, on the edge of the dense rain forest of northern Zaire, with a searing headache and a high fever. The Belgian Sisters naturally assumed he had malaria, but the quinine injections they administered did no good at all. Within a few days, Mabalo Lokela was vomiting and had such acute diarrhea that dehydration left his skin pale and parched. Soon, his fever spiked and he became delirious; he bled profusely from his nose and gums, and his vomit and diarrhea were laced with blood. After a few more days of agony, Lokela died, on September 8, 1976. That was the first recorded case of what was later called "Ebola" virus, named after the local river.

Soon this previously unknown disease swept through both the hospital staff and the nearby villages. By November 6, there had been 358 cases, and 325 of those people had died. Ebola virus thus had the second-highest lethality rate of any known microbe (untreated rabies is 100 percent fatal).

Fortunately, in part because of how fast it kills, Ebola has not (yet) become a major epidemic. But it set off a frightening, if largely unheeded, alarm: today's global conditions facilitate both new exposures to deadly microbes and the means for them to spread. AIDS is that nightmare warning come true, and other such deadly pandemics are likely to follow if humanity doesn't radically change its approach to worldwide public health.

The sensational coverage of the Ebola outbreak highlighted the role of tribal traditions—where relatives clean out the intestines of the deceased before burial—in spreading this blood-borne virus. But what was completely muted in the Western media's account was the even more telling role of the mission hospital itself, where 70 percent of the primary, and most lethal, infections occurred. The problem is that indigent medical facilities in Africa cannot even afford disposable syringes. Each morning the hospital clinic issued five syringes to be used and reused for the 300 to 600 patients who came in daily. The dire problem of the reuse of syringes throughout Africa is a major reason for the AIDS holocaust there today.

Laurie Garrett's *The Coming Plague* provides a detailed account not only of Ebola but also of outbreaks of Machupo fever, Marburg virus, Lassa fever, Legionnaires' disease, toxic shock syndrome, Hanta virus, drug-resistant tuberculosis, new resurgences of malaria and cholera...and so much more. There is a 109-page chapter on AIDS alone.

Garrett writes with the clarity of a quality reporter (she is the health and science reporter for *New York Newsday*) and researches with the depth of a serious scholar (she has an advanced degree and was a fellow at the Harvard School of Public Health). The result is a magisterial work of 750 pages and more than 1,300 footnotes. Many of the chapters read like adventure stories, as we travel with epidemiologists who face great danger to fly into isolated tropical areas to find the source and the means of control of a rampaging disease before it becomes a widespread epidemic. But this book builds off of the drama and the fascinating detail to offer a broader and more trenchant analysis of the exigent public health challenges for humanity today.

Garrett shows how our contemporary world has created ideal conditions for new, lethal microbes to emerge and then to spread rapidly. A key concept is what she calls "amplifiers"—factors that promote the ready transmission of germs. There have been a host of global amplifiers that has burgeoned over the last three decades. One is jet travel. In 1950 there were two million passengers on international commercial flights; in 1990 there were 280 million. Another major force (and the jet plane gives it an international dimension) is the sexual revolution with the much greater opportunities for multiple sexual partners, whether gay or heterosexual, to pass along the host of sexually transmitted infections.

Shared injection-drug equipment is an extremely efficient way to pass along blood-borne microbes. Illegal injection-drug use greatly accelerated in the 1970s as the Vietnam War led to a big increase in both users and supply. The number of heroin addicts in the U.S. rose from 55,000 in 1955 to 1,500,000 in 1987. The 1970s was also the time when "disposable" syringes became widely available in medicine—and were pilfered and used and reused by addicts. At the same time, reuse of syringes for legitimate medical purposes, as the Ebola outbreak illustrates, began to be a big amplifier throughout the Third World and in Eastern Europe. There was also a blood-products revolution, as their use doubled in the U.S. in the 1970s due to more surgery being performed and the development of clotting factors VIII and IX. A hemophiliac could receive needed coagulants made up from thousands of different donors—and any undetected blood-borne pathogen any one of them might have. In short, the travel, sex, drug, medical, and blood-products revolutions over the past 30 years have created powerful amplifiers for the rapid worldwide spread of infectious diseases.

At the same time, many social and economic developments put human beings in new contact with lethal microbes. A major threat, which is behind many of the outbreaks Garrett examines, comes from microbes that live in a "reservoir" species within a once-isolated ecological niche. A virus may have been endemic in a species of monkeys for many years without doing them any harm. But if such a virus jumps to a new species that has not developed any immunity, it can be devastating. For example, when human beings encroach into the rain forests to cut them down for the timber industry, or to clear them for cattle ranchers, they risk virgin contact with such pathogens.

Human action itself can also create more virulent microbes in a number of ways. One such blunder is the careless use of antibiotics, which can result in breeding drug-resistant bacteria—which has already happened with strains of tuberculosis, gonorrhea, "staph" (staphylococcus), and many others. Another grave danger comes from environmental damage and pollution. The former can eliminate natural predators that keep disease carriers such as mosquitoes and rats in check. The latter, especially with human waste and industrial chemicals in water, can create new and rich breeding grounds for viruses, bacteria, and parasites.

The amplifiers and the new microbes surge together in a most explosive mix in the abject poverty of the Third World (and the growing Third World conditions within the U.S.). The majority of people in the world still suffer from diseases caused by unclean water, and more than half the people in underdeveloped and moderately developed countries lack sanitary toilet and sewage facilities. One-third of city dwellers in the Third World don't even have garbage collection. Hundreds of millions of people suffer from malnutrition, which seriously weakens their immune systems, enabling microbes not only to take hold but also to multiply and mutate into more powerful strains.

Yet it is precisely among the destitute that vaccination campaigns and other preventive measures are scandalously lacking. Meanwhile the Third World countries lack not only the means to treat diseases but even the surveillance systems to spot new outbreaks before they get picked up and broadcast widely by global amplifiers. As long as our sisters and brothers in the Third World are condemned to the hell of poverty and medical neglect, we are all at risk.

Garrett does not want simply to scare her readers. Her last chapter begins to explore solutions. She emphasizes two main areas. First there is a series of measures to stop or at least mute the main amplifiers: sensible and extensive safer sex education; complete availability of disposable syringes for medical use worldwide; needle exchange programs or legal syringes for drug users; and much more attention to eliminating sources of transmission such as vermin, water contamination, and overcrowded housing. Her second area is to develop much more extensive and better-equipped disease surveillance systems around the world. This proposal, however, requires a change in priorities and expenditures that goes completely against today's political grain. Even within the relatively affluent U.S., regional and local disease surveillance systems were hit by crippling budget cutbacks in the 1980s and 1990s. Garrett doesn't really tackle proposals for the more colossal problems that make humankind so vulnerable: a world rife with widespread and debilitating poverty right alongside the most decadent misuse of wealth and resources. But the implications are clear when the book summarizes the conclusions of epidemiologist Joe McCormick while he was fighting an outbreak of Ebola in the Sudan in 1979:

> *Dangerous diseases would continue to haunt the most impoverished communities on earth, constantly threatening to explode into epidemics, some of which might some day lap at the shores of the planet's richest nations.*

The point is made most succinctly with this quote from journalist I. F. Stone at the end of *The Coming Plague*: "Either we learn to live together or we die together."

[published in *Aquarian Weekly*, October 9, 1996]

Chapter 8

Global Lords of Poverty: The Nature of Imperialism

Naming the System

Resistance in Brooklyn (RnB): You refer to "the system" and "imperialism." In current radical discourse, it is more common to talk of various systems of oppression. How do you define imperialism?

David Gilbert: Imperialism is built on and incorporates the structures of patriarchy and capitalism. And it is important—whatever name we use—to recognize the fullness of all modes of oppression: class exploitation, male supremacy and the related homophobia, white supremacy, and the host of other ways human beings are demeaned and limited.

But I think it all comes together in a more or less coherent social structure, with a range of sophisticated and brutal methods for a ruling class to maintain power. The value of the term "imperialism" is that it emphasizes the importance of a global system: the crucial polarization of wealth and power between a few rich and controlling "centers" (in Western Europe, the U.S., and Japan) and the impoverished "periphery" of the Third World. The wealth of one pole is totally connected with the abject poverty of the other; the human and natural resources of the Third World have been ruthlessly exploited to build up the developed economies. Thus, "imperialism" speaks most directly to the oppression of three-quarters of humankind.

That vantage point helps us see why Third World struggles have been so central in the modern world. And there is the added resonance with the foundation of the U.S. on the internal colonization of Native Americans, New Afrikans (Blacks), Mexicano/as, and Puertoriqueño/as. Those structures help to explain the depths of racism within this country, and why racism has so often corroded potentially radical movements among white people. "Imperialism" is a summary word meant both to include all those elements author bell hooks underscores with the phrase "white supremacist capitalist patriarchy" and to emphasize the importance of solidarity with Third World struggles.

[Excerpted from an interview by the Resistance in Brooklyn collective (RnB) with David Gilbert, Laura Whitehorn, and Marilyn Buck. An edited version of the interview first appeared in the now-defunct revolutionary anarchist newspaper Love & Rage as *Enemies of the State*. The entire interview was published in pamphlet form in 1998 by RnB. A new edition was published in 2002 by Abraham Guillen Press and Arm The Spirit.]

Revolution in Africa

HOW EUROPE UNDERDEVELOPED AFRICA
by Walter Rodney
Washington, D.C.: Howard University Press (1982)

> *White racist notions are so deep-rooted within capitalist society
> that the failure of African agriculture to advance was put down
> to the inherent inferiority of the African. It would be much truer
> to say that it was due to the white intruders, although the basic
> explanation is to be found not in the personal ill-will of the
> colonialists or in their racial origins, but rather in the organized
> viciousness of the capitalist/colonialist system.*

— Walter Rodney, *How Europe Underdeveloped Africa*

The horror of mass starvation in Africa is a reality whose images we now see daily. Charity is the officially sanctioned form, the readily available channel, for a humanitarian response. Even on the level of charity, we must ask—when the U.S. government spends $250 billion per year, involving some of the world's best technical resources, on the military, and when billions of dollars are paid to farmers to not grow food in order to keep prices high—why anyone in the world should die from want of food?

But there is a much more fundamental question behind the current violent assault, through hunger, on millions of African people: why can't Africa, with a land abundant in resources and a people rich in labor and genius, produce enough to meet all the basic needs of her people? Charity involves a condescension expressing unequal power. The only long-term solution is to change power relations so that each people can produce to meet its own needs and determine its own future.

The Western media are not above exploiting the most heartrending human tragedy for their own cynical political purposes. One common mechanism is to select surface images without providing any understanding of historical development and underlying relationships. To the degree that they present any explanation of the causes of famines, they are laid to the drought and the inefficiency of the African governments. The "Science" section of the *New York Times* (January 8, 1985) goes a little "deeper": it points out that long-term soil exhaustion and desertification have been caused by human overexploitation of lands; and, it explains, "such overexploitation is generally caused by population growth."

The critique of inefficient government and of population growth puts the primary blame on African people themselves for their plight. The subliminal message being pounded into mass consciousness is that African people are just not capable of governing themselves. But there is something wrong with all these explanations. The developed countries have dealt with periods of extreme weather conditions without suffering famine; the population density in many well-fed European nations is much greater than that of Africa; the basic underlying assumption of the incapacity of African people is just one more cruel example of the centuries of racist myths used to justify oppression.

The ugly truth hidden behind the media mask of hand-wringing and arrogant condescension is that poverty and hunger in Africa are direct results of brutal exploitation by the West. Indeed the wealth from such plunder is one reason that the Western media now have the power to trumpet, around the world, their own interpretation of famines.

Rodney provides us with an outstanding study of the history and relationships behind African economic backwardness ("underdevelopment"). He was not only a brilliant analyst of society but also a revolutionary activist in his native Guyana. He was assassinated by government henchmen on June 18, 1980. His book does not provide a specific analysis of the current crisis. It was written in 1972, and only goes up to the end of the colonial period, 25 years ago; it covers but is not a specialized study on agriculture. What this book does provide, however, is an indispensable basis for understanding the current crisis by revealing the structure of exploitation and the resulting economic devastation of Africa by Europe.

The contemporary economic gap between Africa and the West is completely obvious. To take just one indication, per capita income in the U.S. is about 25 times higher than in Africa [since Rodney wrote, 30 years ago, this ratio of inequality has skyrocketed to 60 to 1]. What is less known, in fact, what has been purposely obscured, is that the economic gap between developed and underdeveloped countries has grown 15 to 20 times over the last 150 years. This situation does not express independent history but rather reflects a relationship; the wealth and development of one sector have been based on the impoverishment of the other. When Europe and Africa first commenced regular contact, the gap between the two societies was not great at all. In 1500, the developed areas of Africa compared favorably with Europe. The slave trade began the process of bleeding Africa for the benefit of Europe and America. For all of the horror of slavery, the period of colonialism was far more devastating in economic impact on Africa.

Rodney provides us with a solid summary of the pre-1500 state of development of African societies. He clearly refutes the racist myths without in any way lapsing into romanticization of the history. He recognizes the class nature of the ancient empire. Africa in 1500 contained communal societies, fairly developed feudal societies, and many societies in transition between the two. There were developed trade routes within Africa; high-quality leather, cloth, copper, and iron were being produced on a small scale; agricultural methods while not yet involving a systematic application of science did reflect an understanding of the particular local ecological conditions. Not only were many African societies at a comparable level to Europe, but, more importantly, there was also a process of development within Africa.

One key difference between feudal Africa and Europe was that the latter was

163

at the threshold of capitalism. Rodney deals only cursorily with the issue of why capitalism first arose in Europe, which is quite an involved topic in itself. Suffice it to say that there were material, historical reasons that have nothing to do with later racist justifications. In fact, in some ways, features of European backwardness in earlier phases of development provided the impetus toward its initiation of capitalism. The initially small threshold gap provided Europeans with an edge in three key areas—navigation, weapons, and political organization—that provided the means to turn trade with Africa to European advantage.

The slave trade had a major impact on both continents. In Africa, the export of tens of millions of slaves—perhaps more than 100 million—meant a depletion of some of the most vigorous workers. Further, it meant that Africa's overall population did not grow at all between 1650 and 1850 (in the same period, Europe's population more than doubled, an important pressure for increasing productivity as well as a source of growing markets for manufactured goods). Beyond labor depletion and population stagnation, the slave trade was the basis for very destructive internal conflicts within Africa as warfare intensified, both within and between different societies, in order to capture slaves for the European trade. Europe was interested almost solely in slaves, rather than goods, for trade; this distorted African development away from production.

These relationships also impacted the areas of Africa not directly involved in the slave trade, for they radically changed the terms of the previously developing trade and the motion toward greater integration within Africa (internal trade and integration into nation-states had been critical to Europe's reaching the threshold of capitalist development).

While the slave trade was profoundly destructive to African development, it was a key to Europe's advance. The vast profits from the slave trade and from slave labor on plantations in the Americas were major sources of the capital necessary for England's highly touted industrial revolution. Slavery together with the British looting of India undoubtedly provided much more of the needed capital than what was generated within England. The Caribbean slave plantations were probably the most profitable part of the whole British economic domain (for more detail than Rodney provides, see a book that he cites: Eric Williams, *Capitalism and Slavery*). The great manufacturing centers first arose in the ports like Liverpool that were already centers for the slave trade. And many of the big names in finance today—like Barclay and Lloyd—got their start in the very lucrative traffic in human flesh.

While it is not his main focus, Rodney soundly refutes the standard racist rationalizations that shift responsibility for slavery: "there were already slaves in Africa"; "it was Africans who sold their own people." The pre-European slavery in Africa was very small scale and characteristically did not entail hereditary bondage—quite different from the massive chattel slavery organized from Europe. Rodney does not excuse those Africans who collaborated, but clearly it was the European traders who provided the overwhelming impetus, set the context, and reaped the lion's share of the profits from the slave trade. In fact, in those instances where African empires tried to withdraw from the trade, they were soon forced by a combination of European military pressure and economic payments to resume. The massive profiting from human flesh was very much the European slave trade. The indescribable horror of probably more than 100 million people kidnapped and killed, and internal wars as a result of the slave trade, provided vast capital for the industrialization of Europe while it meant social and economic stagnation, and destruction in Africa.

As damaging as the 350 years of the slave trade were to Africa, the 70 years of colonialism were far more devastating to its economic development. The preceding centuries of slavery provided a major basis of European development to the point where the now-giant slave trade industry had to organize production and expand investment on a world scale. As Rodney tells us, the "penetration of foreign capitalism on a world-wide scale from the late 19th century on is what we call *imperialism.*" (p. 136) Africa's greatest value to Europe at the beginning of the imperialist era was as a source of raw materials —e.g., palm products, groundnuts, cotton, and rubber—needed for Europe's expanded production. While slavery had involved a trade relationship—no matter how unequal and inhumane—investment and guaranteed access to raw materials mandated direct control over African territory. Also, Europe had developed to the point where it now had the power to exercise direct control over African societies. Meanwhile, the slave trade had fostered the internal divisions that made Africa vulnerable to conquest. In 1885, the imperialist powers met in Berlin to agree on how to divide Africa among themselves.

Colonialism was so much more damaging because the complete takeover of those societies killed the internal political development and cultural self-definition that were still occurring. Also, by now, virtually all African economic activity was organized by and oriented toward the colonizing powers. There was much more economic integration with the "mother countries" in Europe than with African societies right next door.

Political conquest was the basis of enforcing wages for African workers that were a tiny fraction of those paid to Europeans; Rodney gives several examples of 10 to 1 and greater wage ratios. So not only were raw materials guaranteed but they were also cheap for European industry, while the colonial mines and plantations made fabulous profits. Another form of exploitation was the unequal exchange in trade between European manufactured goods and raw materials produced by African peasants. For example, by 1939 there was a 40 percent drop, compared to pre-colonial times, in the amount of manufactured goods that could be purchased by a given quantity of African raw materials.

Rodney doesn't examine the non-colonized countries—Liberia and Ethiopia—in depth. But he indicates that the these basic economic terms set by Europe predominated for these nations, too. There was no independently developing Africa to provide any other context and relationship for those two. Similarly, while Rodney doesn't examine the post-colonial period, he indicates that the same economic patterns have continued and even accelerated up to the present time.

Europe also got more from Africa than raw materials and profitable investments. Rodney traces a series of indirect effects such as the growth of the economic scale, greater national integration, capital for scientific research and advance—all lubricated by wealth extracted from Africa. Africans, meanwhile, suffered not only slave wages and unequal trade but also economic and political structures completely externally determined and oriented. This meant that economic activity had the opposite impact from national integration and self-propelled development. "The mining that went on in Africa left holes in the ground, and the pattern of agricultural production left African soils impoverished; but, in Europe, agricultural and mineral imports built a massive industrial complex." (p. 180)

The overall patterns of exploitation and underdevelopment also had specific expression in the destruction of agriculture. The European slave trade began the negative consequences. Slavery not only drained labor but also impaired the remaining population from effectively engaging in agriculture. Many potential producers instead became professional slave hunters and warriors, while communities under attack had to put more resources into defense. Formerly stable conditions for agriculture became unsettled. Areas like Dahomey, which had been a food exporter in the 16th century, were suffering from famine in the 19th century.

But colonialism meant a qualitative transformation of the use of African land. European industry needed raw materials; this meant replacing African food production with cash crops. One method was the outright seizure of African land to create European plantations. For example, the British declared the Kenya highlands "Crown lands" and then gave Lord Delamere 100,000 of the best acres at a penny-a-piece. Then there was a whole series of techniques to force peasant producers into either growing cash crops for export or losing their land to the plantations. The colonialists imposed taxes that had to be paid in cash, and also created dependency on imported manufactured goods; thus, the peasants had to grow crops that would earn cash. When there was a bad crop, peasants had to borrow money at exorbitant rates. If they fell too far behind on payments, they losed their land altogether. When these tax and market forces didn't do the job, the colonialists resorted to laws and military force to impose the growing of cash crops. This all occurred in the context of the long-term drop in the relative price of raw materials on the imperialist-controlled world market.

Many of the cash crops were very demanding on the soil. Their steady cultivation and the abandonment of traditional methods that had been more attuned to the local ecology meant widespread soil impoverishment and also encroachment of the desert in countries like Senegal, Niger, and Chad. At the same time, the Europeans, with control of cheap African labor, invested very little in advancing the technology of agriculture. Rodney cites the systematic studies of Brazilian scientist de Castro to show that the pre-colonial diet of Africans was much more varied and nutritional. The few contemporary tribal groups that have been able to maintain old food patterns are actually models of good health frequently studied by Western scientists.

A great variety of foods was grown in the pre-colonial economy. Diversified agriculture was part of the African tradition; monoculture (the growth of a single cash crop) was a colonial invention. The replacement of diversified food crops with monoculture and the related soil exhaustion laid the basis for chronic malnutrition and periodic famine in Africa. In addition to the destruction of food agriculture, the long-term decline in the relative price of African exports greatly constricted African's ability to import food. "Colonialism created conditions which led not just to periodic famine but to chronic undernourishment, malnutrition, and deterioration in the physique of the African people." (p. 236)

For those of us committed to building a revolutionary movement within the imperial nation, the impact of this history on our own society is of critical importance. This is not a subject of Rodney's study, but he does make some helpful references. Racism, which developed as a justification for the slave trade and then colonialism, came to play a pervasive and vicious role beyond the immediate economic functions that spawned it. European and North American societies were called "democracies" but were actually based on racism and the oppression of workers. All classes in the imperial nations, including the working class, benefited (to varying degrees) from colonialism—for example, through the availability of cheap consumer goods. However, "European workers have paid a great price for the few material benefits which accrued to them as crumbs from the colonial table." (p. 199) In explaining this position, Rodney considerably understates, in my opinion, the scope of material benefits and relative privileges that have historically tied such workers to imperialism, and he makes capitalist class rule too much a question of control of information. But the broadest point Rodney makes is crucial to our revolutionary mission: the most important result of imperialism for our working class is how it has immeasurably strengthened the rule of the capitalist exploiters.

How Europe Underdeveloped Africa provides brief sketches of several important themes that I won't attempt to summarize here. Rodney looks at the status of women in both traditional and colonialized Africa. While not romanticizing the former, he shows how colonialism intensified the oppression of women. For a fuller essay on this subject, see Frantz Fanon's "Algeria Unveiled" in *Studies in a Dying Colonialism*. Rodney also shows how the modern problem of tribal conflicts in Africa has been very much fostered and exacerbated by imperialism. For both of these important themes, Rodney provides a really good outline; one only wishes that he had treated these subjects more fully.

Rodney also provides a sketch of the forces that led to the successful independence movements in Africa with particular emphasis on colonial denial of educational opportunity. Here, I found his brief sketch useful but inadequate, especially in its discussion of the development of different classes within colonial society. Class analysis within Africa has proven to be a problematical and complicated task of great importance (see, for example, Amilcar Cabral's detailed study of the class structure of Guinea-Bissau).

It is only fair to warn the reader that I found the writing dry and at times hard to follow. For me, at least, it was very slow reading. An accompanying map would also have been helpful. But this book is well worth the effort. It provides the necessary and fundamental analysis of the structure of Africa's relationships with imperialism without which none of the contemporary developments there can be understood.

This book will not provide you with all the specifics relevant to today's famine. To complete that understanding also requires study of more recent economic data for imperialism and more specific analysis of agriculture. *But How Europe Underdeveloped Africa* provides us with the foundation. Poverty in Africa does not come from a curse of nature and certainly not from the incapacity of the African people. Rather it is the result of systematic exploitation for the benefit of Western capital. When oppression is so destructive to human life and so thoroughly maintained, revolution becomes a necessity. Walter Rodney provides us with direction both through his analysis and in how he led his life.

suggestions for further reading:
Kwame Nkrumah, *Neo-Colonialism: the Highest Stage of Imperialism*
Fidel Castro, *The World Economy and Social Crisis*
Frances Moore Lappé, *Food First*

[published Spring 1985]

Night-Vision

NIGHT-VISION:
Illuminating War & Class on the Neo-Colonial Terrain
By Butch Lee and Red Rover
New York: Vagabond Press (1993)

Today's world is wracked by a proliferation of bitter and bloody conflicts, as divisions and hatreds crack open around a multitude of national, ethnic, religious, and tribal fault lines. In addition to intolerable pain and suffering, it becomes hard to see where any of it can lead except to planting the seeds for unending generations of strife. Many activists of the '60s have grown nostalgic for that decade, when there seemed to be real hope that the oppressed—and particularly the national liberation struggles—were reshaping the world by creating more humane societies. Now, in so many situations, we don't even know who to root for, let alone how to take constructive action.

Nostalgia, however, is not an answer to social problems. Instead of lamenting the failure of world developments to follow our aspirations, we need to develop an analysis that comes to grips with current realities. "Butch Lee" and "Red Rover" attempt to start us down this road with *Night-Vision*, saying, "Today's revolutionary need is to de-tox ourselves from the old, stereotyped political formulas from 20 or 30 years ago." They don't claim to have the answers for new strategies and programs—that will have to emerge from grassroots movements themselves—but they certainly raise some penetrating points about a rapidly changing world system.

The preface is exciting because it is so bold in stating both the dynamic of a voracious capitalism and our own need for a new, creative thinking: "Capitalism is again ripping apart and reconstructing the world and nothing will be the same. Not race, not nation, not gender, and certainly not whatever culture you used to have." The paradigm of change from colonialism to neo-colonialism provides important insights but also leaves many gaps and loose ends. *Night-Vision* does not provide a definitive overview of our new world, but it is a wonderfully thought-provoking book that begins to thaw some of the ice blocks of our old conceptions.

The writing assumes a familiarity with left analysis and terms—using, for example "New Afrika" (to denote the colonization of Black people within the U.S.). without first defining it. The authors also display a caustic sarcasm toward those they see as sell-out elements of various oppressed groups. The use of pen names blurs the authors' own race, class, and gender standing to take such swipes, but they do use the term "we" when referring to white women. Of course, ultimately the value of the book rests on the validity of its analysis.

The concept of neo-colonialism was first promulgated by the great African independence leader Kwame Nkrumah to describe imperialism's shift after World War II from direct to indirect rule of the Third World. Formal independence was granted, but local elites were used to maintain imperialism's essential economic and political control.

Lee and Rover move from this initial definition to use neo-colonialism to stand for the system as a whole, including important developments within the industrialized countries. Moreover they focus on the shifts in methods in world rule since 1975—after the U.S. military defeat in Vietnam and the emergence of a globally integrated economy. The modern dynamic of neo-colonialism is to create vertical class structures, producing capitalist forces tied to imperialism within and among the range of oppressed groups—racial minorities, white women, gays and lesbians, and workers as well as the once-colonized peoples. This dynamic is transforming the struggles of these groups and necessitates an anti-capitalist strategy for all of them.

Not surprisingly, Lee and Rover are clearest where the greatest body of material already exists. The rule over the former colonies has shifted *from* an era of imperialist rivalries (World Wars I and II) over monopoly control of directly ruled colonies *to* one of multinational corporations, managed world trade, a common interest in keeping the Third World open for a range of exploitation via the market, and the co-opting of native petty bourgeoisies into maintaining imperialist rule.

There's been a parallel change in the role of New Afrika, from white America's chief economic asset for 400 years (with riches reaped from slave and near slave labor) to a liability in the national consciousness; and resistance has become an obstacle to the smooth functioning of the system. The strategy has become a form of de-colonization by adopting a few New Afrikans into middle-class

America while having a policy of genocide toward the rest. This analysis helps explain today's apparently contradictory reality of an increasing number of Black individuals in positions of wealth and prestige while the masses in the inner cities have been relegated to the devastation of cascading epidemics of unemployment, drugs, incarceration, homelessness, AIDS, and tuberculosis. The old slogan "Black unity" is not adequate if it entails unity with elements— from drug pushers to Supreme Court justices—participating in the genocide.

The section on the political economy of neo-colonialism, particularly pages 93-113, is a tour de force. If you want to see if this book is worth reading, start by checking out these 20 pages, which provide an unvarnished view of the vicious parasitism of the world economy.

> *Just as slave labor was the greatest source of profits for early capitalism, Third World women and children have become the most important commodity today, to be violently used up and discarded at a pace of exploitation so rapid that it is even cheaper than chattel slavery was. They are the main ones forced into the arduous and deleterious manufacturing jobs that pay as little as $.07 an hour. Such slave wages are also the piston pressing many women into prostitution, which, with the advent of sex tourism, has become a major hard currency industry in the Third World. Women also provide the bulk of crucial unwaged labor in growing food and raising families.*

> *Narcotics production and distribution has become a major industry, much bigger than steel. It is driven by the desperation of traditional agriculture in the Third World, and many governments are actively complicit in the trade.*

> *Imperialism has totally restructured world agriculture so that impoverished countries are exporting crops to the West while their own people starve (the issue isn't one of our "charity" to give food to Africa but rather of the $ billions in forced tribute to the West it continues to extract from them). The paradox [is] the more food, the more deaths from the lack of food. Despite abundant productivity, something like 35 million persons worldwide, most of them children, die from hunger-related illnesses each year, and 700 million other people are malnourished.*

As brilliant and searing as this analysis is, the authors seem to accede to the common left myth that the export of manufacture to the Third World is taking jobs away from U.S. workers. Of course, there is a shift from production to white-collar jobs. But as the book's own example shows—the Nike "Air Jordan" sneakers cost $30 to make in Asia but sell for $130 here—the super-exploitation of Third World labor supports many nonproductive advertising, sales, finance, and management jobs here. At the same time, the export of production actually causes unemployment in the Third World, as traditional handicrafts and peasant agriculture are destroyed there. The reason that unemployment has become so bad throughout most of the world is based on deeper problems of capitalist stagnation and irrationality. These conditions in turn lead capitalism to treat increasing numbers of Third World people as "surplus population" relegated to genocide.

The value of *Night-Vision* is its emphasis on what is new and changing. One central development is how much the process of production has become internationalized. Behind the vaunted German engineering of Mercedes Benz, for example, are the chromium metal alloys mined by African workers, assembly lines manned by Turkish immigrants, and a major investment of Kuwaiti capital. This helps us see why the ruling class, now so focused on global profits, has become increasingly indifferent to the decline of the national infrastructure. At the same time, the need to defuse national liberation and to make use of a range of talents and faces explains the growing number of women and Third World people in management positions—at the same time that the conditions of life gravely deteriorate in the inner cities.

Lee and Rover argue that the very ascension of the global economy is the cause for the disturbing surge of ethnic and national antagonisms, as players below the world ruling-class level frantically scramble to control pieces of territory in order to have some arena of power (while this insight is helpful, it is not adequate because it doesn't explain why these forces won't ally in order to enhance their power). There's been a shift from a bipolar world of colonizer vs. colonized to a more fluid, chaotic world of transnational capital on top of a range of fragmented subgroups let loose to fight out their sectional needs. The resulting social conflicts are not moral issues to the ruling class but simply matters of the maximization of profit for capital. They are perfectly willing to let these subgroups fight it out for position—and then make use of the victors against the losers and of the conflict itself to maintain social control from above.

Night-Vision takes the forceful position that it is *class* changes that are being manifest in struggles that appear to be about race, nation, and gender. On one hand, there are now significant capitalist strata within each of those groups; on the other, neo-colonialism subsumes those old social categories to create a highly exploited proletariat, now consisting first and foremost of Third World women. As suggestive as Lee and Rover's broad strokes are in this regard, they leave a lot of room for oversimplification of collapsing race, class, and gender.

For example, (some) Third World men are used to controlling "their" woman, but many of these men are also highly exploited by imperialism. Nor should white women's gains around abortion rights, even if achieved without armed struggle, be totally reduced to a convenience for neo-colonialism. Similarly, the emergence of a multinational labor force and the breakdown of protected monopoly markets may well mean that capital is no longer willing to pay for the high standard of living given in return for the loyalty of whites: "Capitalism is now demanding that white workers start to live low like workers" (this analysis does help explain the growing anti-U.S. government tendency among white supremacist groups). But the continued and crucial political role of a loyal, and even angry, home base should not be lightly dismissed. Race, gender, nation, and class still have their own interrelated histories and deep social realities. A big part of any revolutionary strategy is to correlate the needs and aspirations of various oppressed groups, under the leadership of the most oppressed, toward a universalist project of liberation.

Night-Vision doesn't turn the prevailing darkness into radiant sunlight, but it has sent up some very useful tracers that provide streaks of illumination and expose critical targets. We all need our very best analytical fire.

[published in *Downtown*, December 8, 1983]

Technological Advance and Social Decline

THE INFORMATIONAL CITY:
Information Technology, Economic Restructuring,
and the Urban-Regional Process
by Manuel Castells
Cambridge: Blackwell Publishers (1989, reprint 1993)

You've heard the pet phrases of the pundits a thousand times: we live in a post-industrial society; manufacturing jobs are fleeing to runaway shops abroad, leaving us with a service economy at home; the locus of economic power within the country has shifted from the rust belt to the sun belt, and from the city to the suburbs.

As with many clichés, each one of these contains elements of reality. But the commentators and futurologists simply project such trends ahead on a straight trajectory without any consideration of possible countertendencies or of underlying causes with more telling ultimate effects on economic and social changes.

Manuel Castells provides a fruitful effort at a deeper analysis. His *The Informational City*, first published in 1989, was reprinted in 1993, and continues to be relevant in explaining current developments. This book can be tough reading (e.g., "structural dualism manifests itself in the transformation of bipolar dialectics into dual dichotomies"), but behind the at-times obtuse language is a complex and varied analysis of considerable force. This work provides a particular focus on the geographic, or spatial, impact of economic changes and what they mean for our modern cities.

Castells argues that the terms "post-industrial" and "service economy" don't tell us much about the driving forces of economic change. What is more definitive is that we have moved into an "informational mode of development," within what is still an overall capitalist structure. In the old industrial capitalism, the source of increasing output and profit was the introduction of new energy sources and their application in more advanced machinery. For today's economy, the key source of productivity lies in the quality of knowledge and its application not only to producing goods but also to the process of generating still higher levels of knowledge itself. The key industries in this informational revolution have been semiconductors, computers, software, telecommunications, and—in a very different field that is in its own way based on control of informational processes—bioengineering.

This new mode of development creates the possibility of much greater flexibility (as computers permit reprogramming production for very specific markets and needs) and of an expansive geographic sprawl of production (since it can all still be coordinated through sophisticated and instantaneous global telecommunications). The specific locations of different aspects of production can be tailored either to access to a key market or to where the labor force is most favorable for the employer. For example, a U.S. semiconductor company may center its research and development in Silicon Valley (California), perform the skilled production of wafer fabrication in Scotland, locate the semiskilled testing functions in Singapore, and send the low-skill but labor-intensive assembly work to the Philippines.

But Castells is far from being a technological determinist. The new technology could be applied in a range of ways—including automation—to eliminate drudgeries combined with an upgrading of education to prepare people for more creative jobs. The way the informational mode has been applied has been shaped by the restructuring of capitalism of the past 20 years. In the '70s, U.S. capital found a markedly decreasing proportion of national wealth going to profits. This decline resulted from both the surge of nationalism in the Third World and the growing government expenditures to respond to social demands at home. Castells offers a complex outline of the interrelated restructuring measures through which capital moved to hike up its rate of return (although, curiously, he omits dealing with the brutal ratcheting down of prices of Third World raw materials).

One major aspect of the restructuring process has been the shift from the welfare state to the warfare state. The government has moved away from its role as legitimating capitalism by redistributing some resources to the poorest sectors and is placing fuller emphasis on reducing social costs, assuring U.S. global power, and focusing domestic spending on areas that promote high technology and that service the social needs of the elite.

The new priorities of the state entailed breaking the social compacts with labor (the New Deal of the 1930s) and with minorities and the poor (the Great Society of the 1960s). As Castells puts it, this change "is instituted by the state which abandons the spaces of destitution to their own decline, while concentrating resources in and targeting policies on the preserved spaces of functional management and upgraded consumption." (He would add that there is a sad irony: White production workers who were mobilized on a racist basis to attack welfare helped capital build the momentum to undermine the unions that had

173

protected the relatively high pay and security of those same workers).

Capitalism's ability to readily break the old social compacts was largely predicated on another aspect of restructuring: the conscious use of the new technology to fragment and weaken the workforce. The changes in job structure correlate with but aren't nearly as simple as the media-touted postindustrial trends.

There has been a dramatic rate of growth in the technical and scientific elite (but, starting from a small base, these still constitute a small percent of total jobs). These are jobs that require advanced education, that afford high pay and benefits, and that are overwhelmingly filled by white males. The dynamic areas for the informational economy develop in what Castells calls "milieux of innovation." These often start around a center for high-quality engineers (Stanford University for the Silicon Valley and MIT for the Rte. 128 area around Boston) that collects the scientists and innovators. Despite all the wonders of modern communication, direct, personal interaction is often important for developing new ideas and diffusing their application to industry. Once such a center is established, the quality of labor it attracts and the advantages of accumulated knowledge for generating new knowledge frequently keep it in the lead.

Similarly, the new technology also leads to an intensified concentration of top corporate management personnel in the central business centers of cities like New York, Los Angeles, Chicago, Boston, and San Francisco. Even if a lot of production has spread out to other areas, the command centers require the most advanced telecommunications systems, which generally radiate out from the old industrial cities. For similar reasons, these central business districts now play the lead role as the hubs for the high-powered and frenetic flows of capital in the world financial markets. So the importance of these central business districts hasn't evaporated with the decline of their cities' manufacturing activities—far from it. What we have now is a more concentrated and commanding elite, whose members are globally connected to each other through sophisticated communications but increasingly severed from day-to-day interaction, and any social accountability to those living around them.

Below the financial and corporate command centers and the professional and technical elite, the job structure has become highly fragmented and often degraded. Much of the more labor-intensive work requiring fairly educated laborers—for example, the "back office" record-keeping for big insurance companies or some of the advanced and security-conscious defense production—has been moved out to the suburbs, in particular to take advantage of educated but traditionally underpaid women. There has been a relative decline of the traditional, well-paid blue-collar jobs, as manufacture has not been a growth area and some of it has been shifted abroad (there are, however, some significant countertrends to the runaway shops).

The bulk of new employment has come in the service sector of the economy. But "service" is an analytical potpourri ranging from high-powered financial analyst to the kid flipping hamburgers at McDonalds. The major growth has come in the low-skilled and low-paid end. Even though more dynamic sectors like information technology power economic growth, those areas are also marked by rising efficiency. The growth of the GNP, including a growing, fast-paced elite more than willing to spend money to save time, spawns the growth of areas like personal service that are not as amenable to gains in labor productivity. These low-end service jobs tend to be filled by uneducated women, immigrants, and some minorities—the populations most vulnerable to low wages and hazardous work conditions. These same groups are also the basis for the growing informal economy (outside of state regulation and protection) from garment sweatshops to gypsy cab drivers.

Overall, then, there has been a powerful polarization of the work force: (1) dynamic growth and enhanced privilege for the elite (predominantly white educated male) in high-tech and advanced services; (2) a relative decline in high-paid production jobs, accompanied by some shift to educated but underpaid white women; and (3) the bulk of jobs in increasingly low-end services that, along with the informal economy, are mainly staffed by uneducated women, immigrants, and some minorities. At the same time, the decline of traditional manufacture in the cities has removed the best source of decent jobs for Black males.

Within the polarization there has been a tremendous fragmentation. Not only are the work areas and their roles in the economy spread out spatially, but these different components of the workforce also have little contact and little in common culturally, making it very difficult to organize them effectively, even among the most exploited sections. "The recycling, downgrading and conditions of labor lead to the configuration of territorially segregated, culturally segmented, socially discriminated communities that *cannot constitute a class* because of their extremely different positions in the new production relationships, reflected and amplified in their territorial differentiation in the city."

These trends are intensified by the now-preeminent importance of international finance, with colossal flows of capital moving around the world at a dizzying pace. The amounts and speed involved are way beyond the capability of any national government to control such operations, and yet they have the power to dramatically change the fate of local economies: "The mobility of [international] capital has now embraced in its uncontrollable spiral the heartland of America."

Castells gives only brief attention to the social implications of his analysis. He underscores the stark bifurcation of the cities into highly privileged sectors of economic control and abandoned zones of people who are powerless in the new economy. He also briefly limns some suggestive ideas about the impact on social struggles.

With the replacement of spatially clustered corporations and economically accountable governments by a system run by a flow of information among global networks, "there is no tangible oppression, no identifiable enemy, no center of power that can be held responsible for specific social issues. But, people still do

175

resent what is being done to them and struggle to affirm their identity."

While there is some positive potential here for political struggle, the fragmented territorial and cultural space makes such self-assertion easily prone to forms of cultural fundamentalism (hostile to other oppressed groups). "The historical outcome of this process could be the ushering in of an era characterized by an uneasy coexistence of extraordinary human achievements and the disintegration of large segments of society, along with the widespread prevalence of senseless violence."

Castells is terribly remiss in failing to highlight the devastating implications of these trends for the urban Black and Latino populations. He does mention that the decline of urban manufacturing leaves many Black males as "surplus population" from the point of view of capital. Poor public education systems mean that these people don't get the skills needed for high-tech and advanced service jobs. But quality education is not a prerequisite for the bulk of new urban jobs in services. In my view, capital's preference for immigrant labor over native Blacks has to due with the latter's history of social struggle and rebellion, which would portend a greater resistance to the highly exploitative work conditions imposed.

The notion of "surplus population" is consistent with the terrible neglect of these sections of the cities—for example, the devastating collapses in both public health and education. But contemporary racism may be driven by more than disregard and perceived "superfluity." Castells never mentions the potential threat to the invaluable command centers of management and finance in the central business districts that is posed by the juxtaposition with such abandoned and resentful populations. This problem could be the impetus for capital to take a more active and pernicious role to keep such communities crippled and demobilized.

While it is hard to know where neglect ends and conscious strategies begin, such a decimation of these communities is certainly the end result of the drug plague along with the related criminalization and violence. There is a possible parallel in the conscious use of such areas as "sacrifice zones" for the disposal of toxic waste. Predatory capital could well perceive an interest in plunging these communities into a permanent agony of powerlessness.

The gruesome conditions for the Third World people within our cities is at the heart of an overall problem for those with an interest in humane social change. The key has always been to unite and mobilize all the oppressed, with the needs of the most oppressed leading the way. With the high-level and sophisticated flow of information on the one hand and the drastic fragmentation of working and "surplus" populations on the other, the need and challenge for creative new strategies to build such unity has never been greater.

[published in *Downtown*, April 13, 1994]

The Collapse of Communism

Resistance in Brooklyn (RnB): Does the collapse of communism spell the end of revolutionary potential for this era?

David Gilbert: It has certainly been the most visible, dramatic turnaround, and it has contributed to the general sense of global decline of the left. But to me it is not at all the primary issue. Overwhelmingly, the main problem has been the series of defeats since 1979 suffered by the national liberation movements in the Third World. These movements—mass-based uprisings of the most oppressed—created the best hope for defeating imperialism and remaking the world on a humane basis. The Soviet bloc countries, on the other hand, were never models of socialism; their progressive contribution in the post-World War II era was in the material aid they provided national liberation. My critical view here is not some latter-day wisdom. A main reason we called ourselves the New Left was to emphasize our break from the Soviet bloc and the old-line Communist parties. Perhaps our stance was wrongly tinged with some of the anti-communism with which we were raised, but the main points of our critique were on target: Bureaucratic state control is emphatically not socialism, which instead means social and economic control by the working and oppressed classes themselves. That can only be accomplished through active and participatory democracy on all levels of society. Most of the East European countries had the contradiction in terms of "revolution from above." Even in Russia, where there was a real and heroic revolution based in the working class, they failed to bring the majority, the peasants, into the process. That was the basis for some of Stalin's worst atrocities. This is not to say that the people in Eastern Europe are now better off with the fool's gold of "the free market." They are losing the highly developed version of the welfare state that was the most important internal achievement of the Soviet period. But the bureaucratic welfare state did not entail the popular participation and power that are essential to socialism. The New Left critique did not mean that we saw the Soviet bloc as a main enemy. Overwhelmingly, the primary oppressor and destroyer of human life and potential was—and still is—U.S.-led imperialism. But the East European countries certainly weren't our leadership or our model for an alternative. Some new leftists came around to a more favorable view of the Soviet bloc because of the importance of its aid to struggles such as Vietnam, Cuba, and Angola. But for me, and for many of us, that never spilled over into seeing them as "socialist."

The great inspiration and hope for the New Left were the national liberation movements, both internationally and within the U.S. These movements were all-important in two ways: First, the linchpin of imperialism's economic survival is the riches it extracts—via cheap labor and raw materials—from its economic control of the Third World. A series of victories for national liberation—"the domino effect"—could fatally weaken imperialism. In fact, I would argue that even the obsessive anti-communism of the cold war was more about the support that bloc could offer the struggles of the all-important exploitation zones of the

Third World, trying to break from imperialist control. Second, these revolutions involved the most desperately oppressed people and represented the vast majority in the world. Most had some sense that women's liberation is essential. Also, they stood for a complete overthrow of the old order. So the exhilarating hope was that the rising of the oppressed, the world's majority, could finally reshape society in a humane way.

Therefore, the political definition of this period comes from the setbacks to national liberation after 1979, starting 10 years before the collapse of the Soviet bloc. I don't know of a definitive analysis of what happened or of current prospects. The high point was Vietnam's victory in 1975 and the wave of liberation through 1979. But even though Vietnam heroically won the war, the economic and social devastation was overwhelming. In Angola, Mozambique, and Nicaragua, imperialism showed that it could use a combination of economic and "low-intensity" military warfare to bleed such small countries to the point that the social gains of the revolutions were obliterated, with heartbreaking human suffering. The alternative approach to such costly confrontation was the negotiated agreements—such as in Zimbabwe and South Africa—that left most of the old basic economic structures in place. With both sets of movements, internal political weaknesses became very telling under such pressures. And we also have major responsibility for not building—especially since the early 1970s—strong and effective solidarity movements within the imperial nations.

Even Cuba, whose revolutionary accomplishments and resolve have been exemplary, is now having a terribly rough time with the combination of U.S. economic embargo and the collapse of Soviet aid. But, in a way, the most discouraging example to me is China, because it has the size and was well enough established to not be as vulnerable to external destabilization. And it had also made the breakthrough of deep roots in the peasantry. So the reality that China—with all its monumental achievements—moved in a bureaucratic, repressive, and capitalist direction is particularly telling. There is a series of historic questions posed by today's crisis for the left—or, more importantly, crisis for oppressed people: What is the world balance of forces between imperialism and national liberation? What level of economic development and/or international cooperation is a prerequisite for revolution to be viable? How can the internal dynamics leading toward state bureaucracy and/or capitalism be overcome? What will it take to build a revolutionary movement and effective solidarity within the imperial nations?

To try to put it in a nutshell: The Soviet bloc was neither socialist nor the main opposition to imperialism. Its collapse—which followed in the wake of the setbacks to national liberation—is most significant for the loss of vital aid to those movements. The real revolution and hope of the post-World War II era has been the rising of the most oppressed, the world's vast majority, in the Third World. So the burning questions of the day involve what happened to those movements and what the prospects are for a new period of revolution.

[from *Enemies of the State*]

Global Lords of Poverty

DARK VICTORY:
The United States, Structural Adjustment and Global Poverty
by Walden Bello, with Shea Cunningham and Bill Rau
Oakland: Food First (1994)

You've probably been taught about systems of debt peonage that prevailed in more sinister eras or lands. The sharecropper or laborer was forced to work to pay off perpetual debt to the landlord or the company—who of course set the prices and kept the accounts. This system was nothing but a thinly disguised form of slavery, with the peons in bondage and worked to the bone to enrich the overlords.

What you'll never be told in any mainstream textbook or news report is that today's world economy has evolved into a colossal system of debt peonage, with some 70 nations and billions of human beings in its cruel thrall. It's a system that brings unprecedented wealth to the superrich while, quite literally, squeezing the lifeblood out of the people who can least afford it.

Over the past 20 years, a ruthless economic restructuring has been imposed by means of the "Third World debt crisis." After the sudden jump in oil prices in 1973, the big banks in the developed countries found themselves with a surplus of deposited "petrodollars." To expand their moneymaking opportunities, they hawked loans to underdeveloped countries—often for ill-conceived projects that benefited only the elites of those countries and that financed costly imports from transnational corporations (TNCs) allied to the banks. By the late '70s, interest rates started to climb while the prices on raw materials exported by Third World countries began to plummet. Thus, the payments owed on the debt soared while the means to pay crashed.

By 1982 this situation definitely entailed a crisis for the many big banks that had a large portion of their money tied up in loans headed for default. Spearheaded by the U.S. government (which certainly won't be bound by its platitudes about the "free market" when the interests of big business are at stake), the leading world financial institutions—the World Bank (WB) and the International Monetary Fund (IMF), both run by the U.S. and other wealthy nations—stepped in to design and enforce strategies to resolve the crisis. A key component has been to impose "structural adjustment programs" (SAPs) on the debtor nations so that more foreign exchange earnings can go to debt repayment. The U.N. Economic Commission for Africa recently estimated that six million children die in the Third World each year as a result of these WB/IMF "austerity" measures.

There is probably no dynamic in motion in the world today that has more devastating impact on more lives than these SAPs, yet it is a non-issue to the U.S. media, which prefers whipping up a frenzy about street crime or demonizing (only) those Third World tyrants who don't completely toe the U.S. line.

Walden Bello and associates perform an invaluable service by offering *Dark Victory*, a short and readable book that examines the SAPs along with quick looks at the changes for the newly industrialized countries and at restructuring within the U.S.

Bello is the executive director of Food First, an institute with an outstanding record of analysis of world hunger and related problems. As he sees it, the collapse of centralized socialism in Eastern Europe shifted the primary axis of world conflict from West/East to North/South—between the have and the have-not nations. (My view is a little different: economic control of the Third World was always the top priority, the very lifeblood of modern imperialism; a major reason the East was seen as such a threat was the alternative model and material aid it often offered the national liberation movements). A decisive weapon in the contemporary global war raging between rich and poor is the SAP.

While specific details vary for each country, Bello et al. provides us with a summary of the SAP's general features. The debtor governments are required to (1) radically reduce government spending and subsidies, (2) cut or restrain workers' wages, (3) remove barriers to imports and foreign investments, (4) devalue the local currency (thus making the country's exports cheaper on the world market), and (5) privatize state enterprises and remove regulations on business. These are the typical steps required to get the new loans and debt rescheduling without which the debtor could fall into a default with consequent economic reprisals.

Since these conditions determine the parameters of major social policy, the WB and IMF, without ever winning an election, have become the hegemonic political force in scores of nations, in effect recolonizing the Third World. The theory behind these measures is that they will make production more efficient and prices much lower on the world market, thus stimulating the country's exports and earning it more foreign exchange for debt payment and for stimulating the domestic economy as well.

Dark Victory makes a convincing case that after 13 years of relentless application these programs are a resounding failure in terms of their stated goals. Bello et al. summarize several comprehensive analyses, including one done by the IMF itself, that show that economic conditions deteriorated in the vast majority of nations subjected to SAPs.

For example, a UNICEF study of 24 such African countries showed that capital accumulation slowed in 20 of them, manufacture declined or stagnated in 18, and even the total dollar value of exports declined in the majority. Bello et al. goes further by doing a more detailed analysis of some prime examples of proclaimed "success stories" such as Ghana and Mexico; he shows serious weakening of the internal economies and stark intensification of already terribly unequal distribution of wealth, all along with accelerated degradation of the environment.

One reason for the dismal results is that many of the measures—such as slashing government expenditures, tight money policies, and opening up to more imports—severely contract the domestic economy. In addition, a howling fallacy lies at the core of WB/IMF logic. The driving force, the thrust of each and every specific measure, is to expand production and lower prices on exports. For any particular country, lower prices should mean a competitive advantage, resulting in expanded sales and income. But the kicker is that the WB and IMF are imposing these same changes on a number of Third World countries producing the same commodities.

So, as WB/IMF economists surely must have known, individual competitive advantage evaporates as a number of different countries simultaneously flood the market—which further and drastically depresses prices. For example, Ghana's enormous boost in cocoa production was accompanied by a 48 percent decline in the world price between 1986 and 1989; Ghana's current accounts deteriorated, and its external debt grew over the period. Overall, the SAPs failed on even the narrowest stated goal of debt reduction: the total Third World external debt, $785 billion in 1982, climbed to a staggering $1.3 trillion by 1992.

But in other terms the Draconian campaign has been a tremendous success: (1) The loans and rescheduling have effected a shift in the risk on outstanding debts from private banks to public (and taxpayer-supported) financial institutions. The Third World debt crisis has been publicly declared as "over" because the dire threat to the private banks' solvency has been removed. (2) Various restructuring measures have torn Third World countries wide open for greater penetration by foreign business investments and imports. (3) Debt repayment has forced a gush of capital flow from the poor to the rich nations.

Between 1982 and 1986, Third World countries paid the private banks $183 billion more in interest and amortization than they received in new bank loans, and the hemorrhaging continues to get worse. "Not since the conquistadores plundered Latin America has the world experienced [such] a flow in the direction we see today."

A fourth major economic result is implicit in the discussion of why export incomes didn't rise, but it is unfortunately not spelled out in this part of *Dark Victory*. Every single condition set, as well as the even greater impact of the sum of the different SAPs, serves to ratchet down prices on Third World exports (terms of trade for the Third World fell by a whopping 16 percent between 1980 and 1988). Many of these exports are the raw materials and assembly components used by the TNCs based in the North. The rock-bottom prices mean big savings and thereby higher profits for the corporations. This collapse of raw material prices is, in my opinion, a significant piece for solving the apparent economic puzzle of how the U.S. could pump up its economy through colossal debt expansion throughout the 1980s without setting off extreme inflation.

What have been the human costs of these policies? Here, *Dark Victory* can only suggest what would take volumes to adequately chronicle. The already brutal poverty in these areas escalated sharply. Per capita income in Africa has plunged to '60s levels, and that of Latin America has fallen to the level of the late '70s, while the gap between the North and the South has widened, with an average per capita income of $12,500 and $710, respectively. (And recent data show that more than one billion people now live in the netherworld meeting the dire standards for "absolute poverty," almost double the number of a decade ago.)

Overall an estimated 13–18 million persons worldwide, mostly children, die of hunger and poverty each year. At the same time, forced cuts in government spending have decimated public health, as AIDS runs rampant and easily prevented killers such as TB and cholera are resurgent in these areas. (The world hasn't even been able to marshal one-tenth of the $2.5 billion a year needed to mount an effective AIDS prevention program throughout the Third World. Compare this paltry but unattainable sum to the more than $40 billion per year these countries are now paying out to the Northern banks.) Further, the SAPs' frenzy to generate exports has been a major force behind destruction of local food agriculture as well as for causing widespread deforestation and environmental degradation.

Dark Victory devotes a chapter to sketching a parallel, or at least companion, "adjusting" of America over the last 14 years. The broad strokes include a record increase in maldistribution of wealth, a hollowing out of the domestic economy as some manufacture moves abroad, a war against labor unions and social programs, declining real wages and sinking real welfare benefits, and a dire reduction of public funds to the cities. Over the course of the '80s, the income of the top 1 percent of families grew by 63 percent; they now earn 14.1 percent of the income and own 38.3 percent of the total wealth, while 20 million Americans are experiencing hunger.

This book, trying to cover extensive territory in a thin volume, has a number of problems. One area is statistics. It's not always clear what time span Bello et al. is covering nor do they explain which changes might reflect cyclical swings more than structural change. More importantly, not enough is done to give a human face and passion to what the statistics mean.

Dark Victory never analyzes the role of the elites within the Third World—their class interests and the benefits they accrue—so their continued support for SAPs seems to be a mystery mainly explained by the hegemony of Northern economic theories. Similarly, the book never says why default on the debt is considered unthinkable and never considers whether default could be a radical alternative.

Bello et al.'s model for what is driving the changes is superficial, emphasizing the competition among national capitalisms in the North without adequately accounting for their clear common interests against the South or for the heady trends toward globalization, nor do they indicate deeper contradictions causing stagnation in the world economy. Further, in their haste to spotlight the damage SAPs have wreaked, they slips into romanticizing the preceding period, with only token mention of its intolerable poverty. It is almost as though Bello et al. have no analysis of the underlying structures of imperialism, but instead see the more enlightened ideology of Keynesianism being overwhelmed by a corporate-driven free market zealotry.

Dark Victory extols the New Deal social contract without admitting that it entailed big labor's collusion with imperial exploitation of the Third World. The book then slides over the qualitative differences in standards of living ("this process has brought home to workers in both North and South their common condition as workers....") and thus is much too facile about what it takes to achieve the laudable goal of unity. However, while there is no developed strategy for change, the book's mention of movements for "sustainable" and "people-centered" development is at least suggestive and does offer some encouraging prospects for future struggle.

The bloody dismemberment of the Third World with the usurer's blade is the life-and-death emergency of the day. *Dark Victory*, short and readable, is not an adequate treatment of the issues, but it is a great place to start.

> *The material misery that capitalism implies for 3/4 of humanity... is the principal problem of our time.*
>
> —Samir Amin

[published in *Downtown*, August 24, 1994]

50 YEARS IS ENOUGH:
*The Case Against the World Bank
and the International Monetary Fund*
edited by Kevin Danaher
Boston: South End Press (1994)

The end of World War II ushered in an unprecedented 25 years of economic growth, a kind of golden age, for capitalism. Of course it wasn't so glorious for the world's majority who continued to suffer back-breaking labor and stomach-wracking poverty. Still, world capitalism could boast an average growth rate of 5 percent a year over the period, which provided enough cushion to bring large sectors of the working classes of the developed countries into the consumer society and the "welfare state."

Much of the credit for this euphoric period of expansion was given to enlightened Keynesian economics and to the international economic structures set up at the Bretton Woods (New Hampshire) conference of July 1944, for which John Maynard Keynes himself was one of the prime movers. The two key institutions that emerged were the International Monetary Fund (IMF) and the International Bank for Reconstruction and Development ("World Bank"). The IMF created a reserve of funds to be loaned to countries experiencing temporary balance of payment problems to enable them to continue to participate in world trade without interruption. The World Bank (WB) was responsible for making loans for infrastructure projects (e.g., roads, utilities) needed for capitalist development and for backing and supporting private investment.

Whatever the genius of these policies and institutions, they were not the main basis for the 1944–1970 boom. In reality there was a much more fundamental set of historical factors resulting from the war's destruction of much of Europe's and Japan's productive capacity. This situation alleviated the typical problems of "overproduction" and competition that in the past had saturated world capitalist markets. These advanced countries in rubble offered grand opportunities for new productive investment. At the same time, U.S. hegemony provided a new, neo-colonial framework for all developed nations (the North) to share in the plunder of the Third World (the South).

By 1970 those historical circumstances had been played out, and world capitalism entered a new period of stagnation and structural readjustments that continues to produce economic difficulties and political instability today. From 1973 to 1988, the average world economic growth fell to 2.5 percent a year, or one-half the rate of the preceding 25-year period. The main response has been to squeeze even more out of the poorest and most vulnerable. By 1990 the gap between rich and poor nations in per-person gross national product had risen to 17:1, and the polarization of wealth within each set of countries had also greatly intensified.

The once highly feted Keynesianism is now widely reviled, mainly for its faint implication that the public sector should slightly bolster the purchasing power of the working classes. But despite all the tumultuous changes in economic policies, the IMF and WB are still revered pillars of world capitalism. However, without any fanfare and without missing a beat, they have made a big shift from their charter functions to a completely different role: imposing structural adjustment programs (SAPs)—in reality draconian austerity measures designed to extract debt payments to the Northern banks—on the impoverished countries of the South. Kevin Danaher, editor of *50 Years Is Enough*, aptly summarizes it as a form of financial warfare being waged by the rich on the poor.

This collection of 36 very short essays on the WB and IMF leaves a lot to be desired. *50 Years Is Enough* does not provide much of an overall analysis on how the WB and IMF fit into a broader world capitalist strategy (Walden Bello's *Dark Victory* does a much better job in this regard). Without that context, a few of the authors lapse into the fantasy that these institutions can be "reformed" to serve the poor. Similarly, there are some anomalies such as citing a WB internal report on project failure rates without examining the criteria it uses or as projecting the Japanese model of capitalism as a qualitative alternative to the SAP prescriptions. At the same time there is not enough detail in any particular area, especially in giving the reader a sense of the lives of specific human beings. But this book does introduce the reader to a range of key authors and activist organizations on this most important of topics, and its section on the impact of SAPs on women, tribal peoples, and the environment is particularly valuable.

That section opens with an exposé of an internal memo written by the WB's chief economist, Lawrence Summers. This "expert" lauds the economic logic of "dumping...toxic waste in the lowest wage countries" and of "encouraging more migration of dirty industries to the LDCs [lesser-developed countries]." Vandana Shiva makes good analytical use of this document to show how WB policies promote a global system of environmental apartheid, in which *the last resources of the poor are taken over by the rich, and the poor are pushed into "pollution reservations" to live with waste. They themselves are treated as waste, to be dispensed with either through poisoning and pollution...or through population control and denial of health care to children....*

Another essay discusses the extremely negative environmental impact from how SAPs force Third World countries to shift from local food production to soil-exhausting cash crops and to earn further foreign exchange through deforestation and other depletions of natural resources for export. "[T]he lack of a just resolution to the debt problem is the single most important cause of environmental destruction and poverty."

One particularly graphic example is presented by Nilufar Ahmad's work with grassroots organizations of rural women in Bangladesh. The WB and collaborating local elites imposed a plan to cultivate shrimp for export to rich countries. This project entailed flooding coastal areas with salt water, thus destroying much of Bangladesh's prime grain-growing land. Meanwhile the women who work harvesting the shrimp are suffering serious damage to their health due to the lime mixed in with the salt water. The foreign exchange earned from shrimp exports goes into the pockets of a few rich people...while some 25 million people in Bangladesh are dying of hunger. Ahmad also provides one of the few hopeful stories as she describes how local women took over a vacant delta island to grow grain and then physically defended their precious harvest from a raid by the landlords' police.

The overall result of the SAPs that emerges from these essays, as also demonstrated in Bello's *Dark Victory*, is the intensification of poverty and polarization of wealth. In today's world 1.2 billion persons live in the dire conditions of "absolute poverty." In sub-Saharan Africa, one-half of the children are malnourished and starving. The SAP-imposed slashing of health and education budgets not only makes the impact of such poverty worse, but also cannibalizes these countries' potential human resources for future growth.

The WB and IMF also serve to undermine democracy. Key social policies are imposed by their functionaries—who are not subject to any popular elections—through plans that are negotiated in secret with local elites.

Meanwhile the SAPs have failed on even the narrowest of economic grounds. The outstanding external debt of the Third World has climbed from $785 billion in 1982 to $1.5 trillion today, and Africa's external debt increased by a factor of 2.5 during the 1980s. The overall growth rates for countries following SAPs tend to be lower than for those that rely more on the public sector.

Economic growth in the South is strangled by the relentless transfer of capital to the North. The total flow—the amount of interest and principal paid minus all the new loans coming in—is running at $45 billion a year. The other side of this multibillion-dollar coin is the real success story of the WB and IMF: securing the solvency and profits of Northern commercial banks. The SAPs have also been brutally effective at decimating the prices for Third World exports used by Northern industry.

Historically the plunder of the South has been tacitly condoned by broad sectors in the North. Access to the comforts of the consumer culture tends to blind people to the long-term cost—to our souls and ultimately to our survival—of such wanton destruction of human beings and of the global environment. Now, capital is beginning to apply at home some of the weapons it so ruthlessly developed to loot the Third World: the slashing of social and environmental programs, the maintenance of high unemployment to drive down wages, and the undermining of labor unions and social movements.

As middle- and working-class whites experience the erosion of the economic security they once took for granted, the orchestrated, and so far loudest, response has been a frightening surge in the politics of racist scapegoating and hatred. Their fears and anxiety have been diverted to attacks on people of color and the disenfranchised. Anger spewed out at Third World immigrants shields the transnational corporations and banks that have wrecked those people's home economies. Scorn heaped upon people who need public assistance protects the business planners who consciously create unemployment. The demonization of street crime justifies the awesome repressive apparatus that can be turned against any radical challenge to the elite. All the screaming about the costs of social programs means that not even a whisper is heard about the burden to 99 percent of the population of the one percent of the U.S. population that owns 40 percent of the wealth.

In these dangerous times, we desperately need an activist movement that dramatically shines the spotlight on the real sources of the problems: the lion's share of public welfare that goes to the rich via staggering interest payments on government debt, bank bailouts, and pork-barrel military contracts, etc.; the unaccountable big bureaucracies run by the handful of corporate executives who determine the life choices of the vast majority of people; and the growth of big government in its most virulent form—prisons, police, military might, and the concomitant attacks on civil liberties.

The demagogy that prevails today serves only to further the concentration of wealth for the superrich, to stimulate the cancerous growth of white supremacy, and to build the trends toward a police state—thus strengthening the very forces that are the source of the crisis. The only real solution lies in the completely opposite direction: people's movements representing and uniting the interests of the most oppressed and combining local activism with a consciousness of global solidarity. This requisite alternative has to be all about the humane use of social resources, controlled by grassroots organizations within the communities—like the seeds that were sown, for example, by those rural women in Bangladesh who courageously reclaimed land to grow life-sustaining grain.

[published in *Downtown*, August 23, 1995]

Chapter 9

*But Today We Say ENOUGH!: Popular Struggles
and Human Rights Internationally*

The Palestinians are consistently depicted as the aggressor in U.S. media coverage and political discourse on the Middle East. To maintain this image, the dominant narrative obliterates two colossal facts that are central to understanding the conflict: (1) it is Israel that is occupying Palestine, and (2) Israelis have killed far more Palestinian civilians than vice versa. The review below gives a glimpse of the realities of the occupation. As bad as these conditions were, they pale in comparison to Israel's spring 2002 invasion and reoccupation of the West Bank. The third piece in this section assesses civilian casualties in the 1990s. The subsequent second Intifada, with its highly publicized suicide bombings, has modified somewhat but not at all inverted these figures. Since September 2000, there's been about a 5 to 2 ratio of Palestinians to Israelis killed. From September 2000 to April 18, 2003, according to statistics from the Palestine Red Crescent Society (PRCS) there have been 2,252 deaths and 22,541 other casualties, including 5,648 persons injured by live ammunition, and another 5,645 injured by rubber bullets. These statistics are considered lower than the actual deaths and other casualties because of the interference of the PRCS's work by the Israeli occupation forces, which includes delaying and shooting at ambulances. For up-to-date statistics, visit the PRCS's website at http://prcs.intellinetinc.com

Gaza: A Military Occupation

GAZA: A YEAR IN THE INTIFADA
A Personal Account from an Occupied Land
by Gloria Emerson
New York: The Atlantic Monthly Press (1991)

What is it like to live under a military occupation? What would you do if, for example, your child became seriously ill? When Mohammed's four-and-a-half-year-old daughter had bad stomach pains and a high fever, the worried father decided she needed to see a doctor—but it was well after the 8 pm curfew. Spotting a Red Cross car, he ventured outside with the girl: "Suddenly an Israeli jeep stopped in front of me. I raised the child up with my right arm, as a sign of peace. I tried to tell him why I was out, but he fired five times. I was hit by a plastic bullet at close range." Mohammed ended up in the hospital with multiple fractures of his left leg. The girl, who had been frightened, was still shy and withdrawn weeks after the incident.

Gloria Emerson's *Gaza* presents the voices of many Palestinians who are living under military occupation of this small strip of land bordered by Egypt, the Mediterranean, and Israel. We meet, for example, a 13-year-old girl who lost her right eye when shot at close range with a "non-lethal" rubber bullet. We listen to an interview with human rights attorney Raji Sourani, who describes his own arrest, interrogation, and torture and how he was held for a year without charges in administrative detention. We learn of the seven-year-old boy, in shock and unable to speak even his name after being severely beaten by Israeli soldiers. We hear Dr. Zakari Aga, fired from his hospital and arrested after expressing too much sympathy for two students who were killed, emphasize that he is not at all against Jewish people but only against Israel's negation of Palestinian rights. We're told the story of Naela Zaquot, who suffered a painful miscarriage under harsh interrogation in jail—"You must talk if you want a doctor." We see Yusra Barbari, the elderly head of the Palestinian Women's Union, hauled into military courts four times for such "crimes" as displaying the Palestinian flag.

It is all too rare in the U.S. to read anything that recognizes the Palestinians as human beings and that details the systematic abuse of their human rights. This book is invaluable even if not terribly well written. Emerson, a reporter for many years with the *New York Times*, often interweaves the personal accounts with how and when the story was told to Emerson, which can make the actual sequence of events hard to follow. Useful bits of factual background are scattered into the text in a way that is hard to assimilate. It would work much better to let those interviewed tell their stories more directly, without the intercuts and author's reflections, and to separately consolidate reportorial summaries of relevant data.

Also, we are not provided an in-depth view of the Intifada. (Intifada literally means "shaking off" and refers to the mass uprising, continuing since December 1987, against the Israeli occupation of the West Bank and the Gaza Strip.) Emerson does present a sense of how deep and determined longing for independence is among the people. She provides glimpses of the role of the clandestine leaflets from the Unified Leadership and the functions of the Popular Committees. There are scattered references to youths throwing rocks at Israeli troops. But we are not provided with a real sense of the mass energy, action, and organizing that have sustained militant protests and numerous strikes for so long despite the draconian repression. Regardless of these shortcomings, *Gaza* is well worth reading for the numerous personal stories that provide such a graphic, human account of the occupation. Many important general theses emerge out of the specific descriptions.

In certain ways, the occupation and the military response to the Intifada have turned all of Gaza into one big prison. There are regular 8 pm curfews, and, at times, 24-hour, total curfews that can go on for days and even weeks. Computer-coded ID cards are required to get jobs and denied to those who are politically suspect. Display of the Palestinian flag or map, and gatherings of more than five men are all prohibited. A family's home can be demolished because a member is accused of crimes against the occupation, and a number of alleged organizers have been forcibly deported from their homeland in blatant disregard of the Geneva Convention on occupied territories.

Arrests are widespread, and torture during interrogation is commonplace. International Red Cross estimates showed that in the first 17 months of the Intifada, more than 16,000 men were arrested in Gaza, which has a total population of only 700,000. We get accounts of prisoners kept constantly awake for interrogation, and beaten while covered with a thick hood that leaves them in total darkness and disoriented. Sometimes the hood is soaked with water or with tear gas, nearly suffocating the prisoner. (Widespread torture continues to this day. On April 2, 1992, a leading Israeli human rights group, B'Tselem, released a report stating that torture of Palestinian prisoners has become routine: of the 20,000 Palestinians taken prisoner in 1991, about 5,000 were tortured or seriously abused.)

Gaza takes us to the notorious prison in the Negev Desert, Ansar III. There, prisoners are packed 25 to a tent of 16 feet by 32 feet, where temperatures can rise to over 100 degrees. Water is limited, and there are no showers; no one is allowed to leave the tent to go to the latrine at night, and many can't have family visits. Some of the Ansar III prisoners are among the thousands of detainees who are held without charges.

We learn of the very important work done by Israeli human rights activists like Tamar Peleg and Leah Tselel, who frantically try to locate prisoners who disappear, who mount what "defense" is permitted in military courts, who try to bring the light of public scrutiny onto the most outrageous abuses. *Gaza* also takes a look at the growing number of Palestinians killed by Palestinians. In an interview, "Hassim," a member of the Popular Army, argues the necessity of eliminating informants whose activities can lead to the imprisonment, torture, and death of many people. Hassim maintains that those killed, as informants, are also casualties caused by the occupation.

Emerson presents the United Nations Relief and Works Agency's estimates of casualties requiring medical treatment as a result of military and police action of Gaza's population, for 1989 alone: Beaten—10, 865; shot by live rounds—3,779; shot by plastic-coated metal bullets—2,738; shot by rubber bullets—410; hit by tear gas—3,155; fatalities—124. Thirty-eight percent of these casualties were under the age of 15, in what the Swedish Save the Children organization has called the military's "severe, indiscriminate, and recurrent" use of violence against the children of the occupied territories. Along with these harsh realities, the book is also permeated with the strength and dignity of the Palestinians interviewed and with their determination to be free.

[published in *Downtown*, June 10, 1992]

The Doherty Case

STANDING PROUD:
Writings from Prison
by Joe Doherty
New York: National Committee for Joe Doherty

> *In December 1971, I was awakened around dawn by the ominous sounds of approaching military armored cars. As I ran to reach my parents' bedroom, the front door was bashed and*

> *heavily armed British soldiers rushed into our home. The fear*
> *and pure terror...are ever etched in my family's mind...I watched*
> *the fright in the young faces of my sisters. After the rampage and*
> *destruction of our home, my father and I were forced at gun point*
> *to an awaiting armored car. Along with...many other neighbors*
> *picked up at that cold break of dawn, my father and I were taken*
> *to the local military barracks for screening.*

That's Belfast, Northern Ireland. The young Joe Doherty was soon released but warned by British intelligence that he would be arrested under the Special Powers Act as soon as he turned 17 (the Act has since been amended to permit internment of even younger nationalists). As promised, he was picked up a month later and taken to the infamous Girdwood military barracks.

> *Over the next several days in Girdwood barracks, I was taken*
> *into a world of tortuous horrors and psychological turbulence. My*
> *first few minutes there made me aware of the intense violence of*
> *the place. The smells, sounds, and colors are vividly in my mind.*
> *Over the next several days I was placed in complete isolation,*
> *forced to endure sensory deprivation. Even the forced strips and*
> *severe beatings were an escape from the mind torturing eternity*
> *of hooded darkness and the "white noise" that pierced the*
> *depths of your mind. I passed through those several violent days*
> *to an emotionally shocked and horrified unexistence.*

Like more than 3,000 other nationalists in the early '70s, Doherty was held in internment without even being charged, let alone given a trial. He was lucky to be released after a year. As soon as he got out, he joined the Irish Republican Army.

This volume of Joe Doherty's writings during the nine years he later did in U.S. prisons brings to life the human and historical issues behind the conflict in Ireland, the very realities buried by the media in their clamor to decry those who resist as "terrorists."

In what is perhaps the world's longest war, the initial Anglo invasion of Ireland goes back to 1169. The British and their Unionist allies (predominantly Protestant forces who support union with Britain) still rule over the northern six counties. The denial of Irish integrity and independence is more than an issue of abstract principle; it is also expressed daily in the harsh oppression of the Nationalist (predominantly Catholic) population in the North: "the ghetto where I was brought up was typical of all nationalist ghettos of English rule: high unemployment, up to 80 percent; poor housing, among the worst in Europe; inadequate educational facilities, as in common with the ghettos of Harlem, Johannesburg, Manila, and San Salvador."

The schools taught about the "glorious British empire, but never were we told of our own history, so beautiful, yet so cruel." Doherty left school at the age of

14, "somewhat illiterate." Yet, the mature IRA volunteer of *Standing Proud* writes eloquently and knowledgeably, not just about Irish history, but also about struggles for freedom around the world. His pieces on South Africa, El Salvador, Puerto Rico, and Haiti are deeply moving because of his strong empathy with the people. "We Irish Nationalists who live in our own quasi-apartheid society are stricken by the extremity of the persecution of our Black sisters and brothers in Azania (South Africa)." And he often goes beyond the simple solidarity sentiment to a serious study of these struggles.

Doherty's treatment of Irish history is fecund with contemporary lessons. For example, his beautiful tribute to one of the foremothers of the cause leads to this reflection: "Feminism has an important role to play in republicanism. Women have been the longest and most oppressed sector in society. Without full socio-economic freedom for women, Ireland will still be unfree."

Amazingly, he is able to view even his Unionist oppressors in a very human light: "it is important that we understand the insecurity of the Anglo-Irish Scots planter class, who have been made to fear the loss of their cultural identity," and he hopes that they can eventually be brought into a multiethnic and democratic Irish nationhood.

This staunch Irish volunteer was not necessarily born a soldier. He grew up in the '50s and '60s, when the IRA had laid down its weapons and was relatively inactive. A new surge of political activism developed in the late 1960s, a civil rights movement modeled on Dr. Martin Luther King, Jr. in the States. Like King, this nonviolent movement did not seek to overthrow the government, but only to achieve equal rights under it. But the marchers were greeted by mass arrests and beatings by police as well as violent attacks on the Catholic communities by Unionist forces.

Ironically, when British troops marched into Belfast in 1969, the 14-year-old Joe Doherty naively welcomed them, believing that they would stop the mob violence. He was quickly disillusioned when he saw the troops draw their guns on the victims in support of the ferocious Unionist mobs. And he learned the realities of an occupation army as he was daily placed spread-eagle against the wall (later, as another essay makes clear, there was strong evidence of army collusion with Unionist death squads). Small wonder that Doherty became a youthful supporter of Republicanism. Then, during that year of his first internment, British troops fired into an unarmed civil rights march in Derry, killing 14 persons, on January 30, 1972. That "Bloody Sunday" was a pivotal atrocity, convincing many Republicans that armed struggle was again necessary.

Doherty spent most of the 1970s in prison. His key encounter was in May 1980: his IRA unit, hoping to ambush a British military convoy, was instead surrounded by a much larger force of British elite troops. In the ensuing battle, British Army Captain Herbert Westmacott was killed. Doherty was subsequently convicted of murder. On June 10, 1981, he and seven IRA comrades made a spectacular escape, under a hail of machine gunfire, from the secure Crumlin Road prison. Doherty was free for two years until arrested by the FBI in New

York City. That bust began a nine-year legal battle as the U.S. government sought to return him to Northern Ireland.

There is a long-established principle of international law, also included in Anglo-American treaties, of the political offense exception to extradition. Doherty went to U.S. federal court and won a clear ruling that he represented the political offense exception in its most classic form. His actions were completely in service of a well-established political cause, his attack was on a purely military target, and he belonged to a clearly defined political-military organization. This ruling was the first of eight successive victories he won in the courts as the Reagan/Bush administrations held him prisoner for nine years while they tried one legal ploy after another. Finally, the Reagan-Bush Supreme Court gave the green light for an unprecedented use of executive power to turn him over to the British colonialists. On February 19, 1992, Joe Doherty was deported to a life sentence in the notorious Long Kesh prison of Northern Ireland.

Those frustrating nine years for him in the U.S. were tremendously enriching for all of us who became aware of him. It's a shame that, while many tried, we couldn't make our government abide by fundamental international law and free this courageous Irish political prisoner.

As Joe Doherty says in his poem, "Walls of Silence,"

> *Some say soon, my walls will fall*
> *in the dust I'll dance to the chorus of Mankind.*

[Joe Doherty was released following the 1998 Easter Peace Accords. The conflict is far from settled, though, and the road to justice and peace in Ireland continues to be a rocky one. One of the main sticky issues continues to be the disarmament of the IRA, which has since split into several factions following the peace accords.]

[published in *Downtown*, November 18, 1992]

Facts of Death

The truth about civilian casualties in the Middle East exposes a double standard.

At the mention of senseless civilian casualties in the Middle East, what comes to mind? If your first thought is solely, or even predominantly, the searing images of Israelis killed by suicide bombers—such as the 62 deaths on buses and in markets in March 1996—you are among the vast majority of U.S. citizens with a very constricted, one-sided view. Those massacres are real and terrible. Yet our human feelings are also being politically manipulated by what the media don't present.

We rightly respond to the tragedy for the Jewish families who lose loved ones. But how many of us have any idea that the number of Palestinian civilian deaths is six times greater? The loss for each of those families is just as painful. When civilian casualties around the Lebanese border are also considered, the Arab-Israeli ratio skyrockets even higher. The large numbers of people wounded, displaced, arrested, and tortured constitute additional categories of severe human rights abuses against Palestinians and Lebanese. To meaningfully support peace in the Middle East, we need to fully appreciate the humanity of all who live there.

The double standard concerning human life first struck me personally—like a lightning bolt—during the 1967 Arab-Israeli War. As a Jew born at the end of World War II, my consciousness formed in opposition to the supreme evil of the racism that produced the Holocaust. I grew up taking for granted that Israel embodied the best in humanitarian and democratic values.

That faith was shaken after a 1967 radio headline blared something like, "Seven Killed in Battle Today." The details of the engagement later revealed a far greater death tally. I was completely confused until I deciphered that the number seven referred only to Israeli losses; lives on the other side evidently weren't worthy of mention in a headline. That affront to my Jewish-engendered human sensibilities was the beginning of a more critical look at underlying issues of racism and the denial of Palestinian self-determination.

For today's conflicts, B'Tselem, a nongovernmental Israeli human rights group, compiles some of the more accurate figures. From the beginning of the Intifada (Palestinian uprising) in December 1967, the total number of Israeli civilians killed in Israel and the Occupied Territories was 234. Over the same time and space, Palestinian civilians killed by Israelis (security forces as well as civilians) totaled 1,468—including 200 after the Oslo "Peace Agreement." Of those, 69 were children under the age of 13.

The grim disproportion in civilian casualties is far worse in the Israel-Lebanon border area. Human Rights Watch (HRW) provides an in-depth assessment in its May 1996 report, *Civilian Pawns*. During Israel's July 1993 attack in Lebanon, two civilians in northern Israel were killed as a result of across-the-border shelling by the Islamic militant group Hizballah. In the same period, however, the invading Israeli Defense Forces (IDF) and its South Lebanese Army (SLA) killed 118 Lebanese and refugee Palestinian civilians there. The respective numbers of civilians wounded were 24 to about 500. During Israel's April 1996 assault, the approximately 150 civilian deaths were all on the Lebanese-Palestinian side, including 102 people killed when the IDF shelled the UN refugee compound in Qana.

The justification of that attack as a response to Hizballah attacks on northern Israeli towns doesn't hold up to scrutiny. HRW's detailed chronology reveals that during the 20-month period that began with the July 1993 agreement of both sides to not target civilians and ended with the rocket that first killed an Israeli citizen, IDF/SLA forces were responsible for the deaths of 13 civilians in five different incidents. And this figure doesn't include possible civilians among the 30 alleged Hizballah members who died in the Beq'a valley bombing raid.

The terrible toll on civilians can't be dismissed as "collateral damage." A major objective of both the 1993 and 1996 attacks was to drive the civilian population north to both deny the guerrillas a population base and pressure the Lebanese government to rein in Hizballah. As then Prime Minister Yitzhak Rabin explained to a Knesset Committee on July 27, 1993: "We want Lebanese villagers to flee, and we want to damage all those who were parties to Hizballah's activities."

An unmistakable pattern of village strikes drove an estimated 300,000 civilians north that month, while the civilians displaced in April 1996 numbered closer to 400,000. Those too old or poor to flee became the most vulnerable to village bombardments. Such consistent and conscious attacks on civilians violate several articles of international law—standards developed in large part in response to Nazi atrocities.

The U.S. government is implicated in these crimes as the major supplier of military aid and weapons to Israel, including some of the planes and helicopters—and perhaps even vicious phosphorous and flechette antipersonnel shells—used against civilians in southern Lebanon. Overall, U.S. military aid to Israel since 1948 has totaled $40 billion, about twice as much as the amount provided for any other country. For FY 1996, the $1.8 billion in grants to Israel accounted for 56 percent of all U.S. military aid.

The problem here is not, as some anti-Semitic propagandists depict it, that the U.S. government is a captive of "the Jewish lobby." Quite the contrary, it was the U.S. that quickly saw strategic value in building up Israel as a local guarantor of critical Western interests in the oil-rich Middle East. That was a pivotal point in the tragic process through which much of the just passion to overcome horrendous anti-Semitism was misrouted into a Zionist mission that entailed the inexcusable oppression and national negation of the Palestinians.

Any sincere concern about violence in the Middle East must move through the surface media images to reveal the roots of the problem. In the U.S., the crucial tasks are to demand that our government halt military and economic aid to Israel as long as human rights abuses continue and to fully support the Palestinians' right to land and self-determination.

Last November, in an exceedingly rare instance of holding security personnel accountable, an Israeli military court found that four undercover soldiers had violated guidelines and opened fire at a checkpoint without proper cause, killing 18-year-old Iyad Badran. The soldiers' punishment was a fine of one agora each, the equivalent of one-third of a U.S. cent.

There will be no chance for justice and a lasting peace in the Middle East unless we can effect a radical change in Israel's and the U.S.'s assessment of the value of Palestinian human life.

[published in *Toward Freedom*, September/October 1997]

Human Rights in Our World

HUMAN RIGHTS IN OUR WORLD:
Two 1995 Case Studies
1) Disappeared in Guatemala: The Case of Efrain Bamaca Velasquez.
2) Indonesia/East Timor: Deteriorating Human Rights in East Timor.
New York: Human Rights Watch (1995)

The Human Rights Watch (HRW) performs the invaluable service of exposing human rights abuses around the globe. It has issued a wide range of reports covering more than 100 countries, including the United States. This review looks at two important examples of HRW studies published in 1995.

Guatemala

The Guatemalan Army captured Efrain Bamaca Velasquez, a Mayan Indian and a commander in a revolutionary guerrilla organization, in March of 1992. Despite subsequent sightings of Bamaca alive, with obvious signs of torture and interrogation, the army denied that it was holding him. But, unlike untold previous cases of "disappeared" persons in Guatemala, Bamaca's plight received widespread attention in the U.S. and international media in the fall of 1994 because he happened to have a North American wife, Jennifer Harbury, and she courageously conducted a dramatic hunger strike in front of the National Palace in Guatemala City. HRW seized the opportunity of this one notorious case to shed light on the pervasive problem.

This account provides a clear definition of this particular weapon of terror:

> *'Disappearance' is a euphemism for an arbitrary or illegal detention that is denied by the authorities. The term was first used to describe a practice employed massively in Guatemala in the 1960s, when many political opponents were kidnapped by government forces and never seen again. The technique was used systematically by military regimes in Argentina and Chile during the 1970s, in El Salvador and Honduras during the 1980s, and is used in Peru, Colombia, and Guatemala today. A common thread in the practice is the involvement of specialized, highly secret bodies within the military, which, although directed through a clandestine chain of command, have the necessary credentials to prevent interference from public security forces. Victims are taken to secret detention centers where they are interrogated and tortured, beyond the reach of court inspections and controls. Often they are executed after interrogation and torture.*

Tens of thousands of Guatemalans—mainly civilians—have been "disappeared" in this way since the 1960s. To date, there has not been a single prosecution for such government-sponsored kidnap/torture/murder. The massive disappearances have abated since the advent of a (nominally) civilian government in 1986, but the process still continues in a more selective fashion. In 1994, 41 individuals were forcibly disappeared.

As a result of Harbury's efforts, evidence surfaced that showed that her husband had indeed been captured alive and then tortured, interrogated, and executed. In addition, confidential sources told CBS's *60 Minutes* that the U.S. government had known about this but had withheld the information from Harbury. She was able to obtain a document proving this charge after "Disappeared in Guatemala" was written. She also conducted a new hunger strike—in front of the White House in March 1995—which was the catalyst for a new revelation: Guatemalan Army Colonel Alpirez, who executed Bamaca and also murdered a U.S. citizen there, was on the CIA payroll at the time. The relationship between the U.S. and the systematic human rights abuses in Guatemala is far more intimate and integral than what HRW reveals. The succession of brutal military regimes in Guatemala was birthed by the 1954 CIA-organized coup against the democratically elected government of Jacob Arbenz Guzmán, because his policy of modest land reform and wage increases was seen as a threat to the very lucrative U.S. business interests there. The subsequent enforcement of extreme exploitation has required ruthless repression, including the disappearances. The U.S. has continued as the main sponsor of the Guatemalan military since the 1954 coup.

East Timor

The November 1994 Asia-Pacific Economic Co-operation summit meeting brought international media to Indonesia. Their presence afforded the East Timorese independence movement an opportunity to protest Indonesia's brutal rule. "Deteriorating Human Rights in East Timor," the latest of several HRW reports on that troubled land, exposes the intensified repression that came down after the media left: (1) The army executed six civilians in retaliation for an earlier guerrilla raid. (2) A minimum of 42 persons have been thrown in jail and are facing trial for protest activities. (3) Violent gangs tied to the government have emerged as a roving force that terrorizes supporters of East Timorese independence.

This critique, however, provides none of the history needed to understand the context and import of these events. While some elements of the background may have appeared in earlier HRW commentaries, a most glaring gap remains in HRW's entire approach: It doesn't deal with self-determination, a primary human right under international law. Indeed, this is so far from HRW's consciousness that this report endorses, on two different occasions, the Indonesian security forces' "right" and "obligation" to quell riots and other "criminal activity" for independence.

East Timor, located on an island about 300 miles north of Darwin, Australia, had been a longtime colony of Portugal until that country withdrew in 1974. The next year, the East Timorese held elections and declared independence—which was quickly followed by an Indonesian invasion and brutal, ongoing war of conquest.

In the greatest genocide relative to population since the Holocaust, an estimated 200,000 of the 690,000 East Timorese have been killed. Meanwhile, social conditions under the occupation leave the East Timorese with the highest infant mortality rate in the world and with 70 percent of their children malnourished (this summary is based on "East Timor: An Island Prison," by Pam Sexton, *Breakthrough*, 19:1).

The bloody handprints of the U.S. government are all over the mass murder scene. Hours before the 1975 invasion was launched, then President Gerald Ford and Secretary of State Henry Kissinger met with Indonesia's rulers; since then, the U.S. has provided Indonesia more than $1.5 billion in military aid; the U.S. has blocked international sanctions against the invasion. On an even more fundamental level, the Indonesian regime of President Suharto originated in 1965, with a CIA-supported coup that overthrew a popular government and massacred an estimated 500,000 suspected leftists. That coup began a close business and political partnership between the U.S. and Indonesia that continues to this day.

[Subsequent to this review, the Guatemalan government and leftist guerrillas signed a peace agreement in 1996. Over the preceding 35 years, more than 200,000 people, in a country of 13 million, had been killed or "disappeared." Almost all of these were civilians targeted by the government or its paramilitary allies. The peace accord brought some improvements in human rights but left the military/police terror structure intact and the pro-U.S. elite in charge politically and economically. East Timor, after considerably more struggle, bloodshed, and devastation, achieved independence on May 2, 2002.]

[published in *Downtown*, December 13, 1995]

In Times of Despair, Hatred and Vengeance Take Wing

PLAYING THE "COMMUNAL CARD"
Communal Violence and Human Rights
by Human Rights Watch
New York: Human Rights Watch. (1995)

The globe has been seething with a seemingly endless series of eruptions of violence between groups that define themselves by their differences of religion, ethnicity, language, or race—from Lebanon to Bosnia to Rwanda. The Human Rights Watch (HRW) summarizes such conflicts as "communal violence," which they see as "today's paramount human rights problem."

The widespread and costly hostilities are not only heartrending but also disheartening, because the only explanation we're offered asserts that these clashes are simply the product of "ancient animosities" and "deep-seated hatreds"—which can leave us in despair about "human nature." But such superficial platitudes hide the more complex roots of the various conflicts and thereby obscure the possibilities for more humane resolutions. HRW challenges the prevailing clichés with a more promising and productive thesis:

> *While communal tensions are obviously a necessary ingredient of an explosive mix, they are not sufficient to unleash widespread violence. Rather, time after time, the proximate cause of communal violence is governmental exploitation of communal differences.*

Playing the "Communal Card" looks at 10 major outbreaks of ethnic or religious violence to reveal the political power manipulations that propel them. For HRW—which usually limits itself to tabulating human rights violations—this book is a rare (and very welcome) foray into the historic and social conditions that breed such abuses. One striking thread runs through the majority of these situations: past colonial rulers consciously constructed and fomented religious and tribal antagonisms as a basic tactic of "divide and conquer."

Despite the limitation of covering 10 different areas within 153 pages, HRW does a remarkably good job with several of them. The chapters on Rwanda and Lebanon are gems, and those on the Israeli-occupied territories and Kenya are quite substantive. A good example of the value of the analysis is the discussion of the "Zulu/ANC" bloodshed in South Africa, a matter that, while seemingly put on the back burner after the 1994 elections, is still simmering with possibly volatile political implications.

On February 2, 1990, the president of the apartheid (white supremacist) minority regime in South Africa—finally bowing to the massive internal struggle and international pressure—lifted the decades-long ban on the African National Congress (ANC), which represented the African majority, and released its leader, Nelson Mandela, from prison.

This act began a transition period that culminated in the April 1994 election that finally ushered in majority rule with a landslide victory for Mandela and the ANC. While these events constituted one of the most hopeful "peaceful" seat changes in history, there was a deadly undertow: during those four years at least 14,000 people died in political violence. These casualties did not come from a direct struggle with white supremacy but rather from hostilities that pitted members of the ANC against followers of the Zulu-based Inkatha Freedom Party (IFP), led by Chief Mangosuthu Gatsha Buthelezi.

As always happens with strife in Africa, the Northern media relished portraying it as "tribal antagonisms"—or at least as an entire tribe against the ideologically nontribal but Xhosa-led ANC. But HRW cogently shows that there was a much more fundamental basis for the fractiousness: the history of and the ongoing manipulations by the apartheid regime. White supremacy set this fire and then fanned the flames.

The context was that the horrendous social conditions of Blacks under apartheid—the unemployment, humiliations, and misery—created a tinderbox of frustrated youth as potential recruits for violence:

> *The combination of economic immiseration, social disintegration and political repression resulting from [apartheid] led to brutal competition for resources between the poor and the very poor, the employed and the unemployed, those who lived in formal township housing and migrant workers from the hostels or shack dwellers from the squatter camps. As the overt machinery of apartheid was dismantled...the lid was taken off the boiling pot of black resentment created by these conditions.*

The more direct incendiary device was the use of Chief Buthelezi as a dupe to fracture black unity. He became the chief minister of a "KwaZulu homeland," which was established by apartheid as part of a series of "bantustans"—essentially reservations—to splinter the African majority into a multiplicity of subordinate minorities.

Liberation movements, people of color, and anti-racists around the world universally condemned this anathema. While the ANC was banned, the Buthelezi administration received millions of dollars and lots of weapons from the racist South African government. At the same time, he condemned the armed struggle, and even the mass actions of boycotts and strikes, of the liberation movement. The good chief even toured the U.S. to plead for an end to the international economic sanctions that were bringing apartheid to its knees. Later, in negotiations on the structure of a post-apartheid government, the IFP demanded an extreme form of federalism that would make its home region of Natal, and other provinces, largely independent. Such divisions coincide with a prime strategy of Northern neo-colonialism for preventing the emergence of strong African nations.

As the 1990–1994 violence surged, the South African authorities stood by when IFP gangs attacked ANC supporters, but the apartheid police and military intelligence were not inactive: as was later documented, they provided secret payments to the IFP, trained its hit squads, and even directly carried out acts of "tribal" violence.

While *Playing the "Communal Card"* doesn't take us past 1994, there are political implications of an ANC national and an IFP provincial government that are worth considering. For now, the predominant forces in the world, representing Northern business interests, are probably content to deal with an overall national government—and the promise of an integrated market—as long as it is amenable to providing cheap labor and raw materials. But should the ANC (or potential successors from the now very small, more militant Africanist parties) dare to respond to the urgent needs of the African majority with a radically populist social and economic program, the North has a spoiler waiting in the wings. Buthelezi and his IFP embody the threat of the devastatingly destabilizing role played by the Contras in Nicaragua or by UNITA in Angola.

HRW's chapters on Sri Lanka, the former Yugoslavia, Armenia, and Azerbaijan are not nearly as good. The recounting of the key events in such a brief space left this reviewer lost in the swirl of religious and ethnic violence. While politicians will maneuver for power in any situation, that in itself doesn't refute a communal basis for the conflict. More penetrating and specific analysis is needed.

We also have to look at the world context. One important configuration was presented in the book *Night-Vision* [reviewed in Chapter 8]: the ascension of a global economy where the key decisions are made by inaccessible and almost invisible international financiers and corporate executives. Political players below the world ruling-class level now have to scramble to carve out smaller areas of turf where they can exercise control, and they do so by mobilizing people through communal loyalties and hatreds. There is certainly plenty of powerlessness and frustration at the base that can be channeled in this direction. The local opportunists are often quite acceptable to the lords of international capital, who are happy to see the potential wellsprings for mass resistance splash—however bloodily—against each other.

The other major global factor is the string of painful setbacks to the national liberation movements since 1979—the result of the ruthless economic and military assaults orchestrated by the U.S., along with the emergence of tendencies toward bureaucracy and elitism within those movements. These losses, at least for now, have deflated hopes that the world's majority, in a common situation of oppression, was reshaping the world in a more humane fashion. In times of despair, hatred and vengeance take wing. Those of us disturbed by the horror of surging communal violence need to do more than wring our hands. We need to look for the ways, however small, to help regenerate hope.

[published in Aquarian Weekly, April 3, 1996]

Manufactured Genocide

Well aware of the susceptibility of foreigners explanations of "ancient, tribal hatreds" among Africans, (the genocidal regime) repeatedly underlined the supposedly "tribal" nature of the killings in an effort to mask the deliberate role played by the authorities.

—Human Rights Watch

Rwanda has experienced one of the world's worst eruptions of genocidal violence. Beginning in April 1994, more than 500,000 people—mainly from the Tutsi minority, but also Hutu who had been willing to work with them—were slaughtered in this country of 7.8 million. The four months of carnage only ended with the military victory of the predominantly Tutsi Rwandan Patriotic Front (RPF) in July of that year. As the RPF took power, some two million Hutu fled to neighboring countries, crowding into squalid refugee camps where more than 50,000 died of disease and hunger.

The horrific images of suffering are still seared into our consciousness: stacks of bodies, civilians who had been hacked to death, a human sea of refugees pouring down roadways, people in border camps wracked by cholera and dehydration. And there may be more: the desperate poverty of the RPF-led government, the mass of Hutu still chafing in refugee camps, and the rearming of the old genocidal leadership harbored there all create a tinderbox for a potentially new outbreak of brutal civil war.

This genocide could have been prevented, and the impending bloodshed can still be averted by concerted and compassionate action from the international community. But that won't happen as long as the nature of the crisis in Rwanda is misunderstood as simply a problem of deep-seated ethnic hatreds. That prevailing interpretation from the Western media and diplomats promotes the demoralizing and racist view that Africans are fundamentally incapable of governing themselves. Instead, what is needed is a more penetrating analysis of underlying causes that can provide a basis for constructive action.

There is nothing inherently "tribal" about this conflict, nor are the roots of the problem solely African. The Hutu and Tutsi, respectively 85 and 15 percent of the population, not only have a common language and culture but have also lived together and intermarried to the point where it's often impossible to distinguish between them. The hostile dynamic between the two groups was a conscious construct of first German and then Belgian colonialism earlier in this century, both using the Tutsi as elite strata for administering colonial rule. In fact, the division was such an artifact that Hutu who grew rich became "Tutsi," while impoverished Tutsi became "Hutu."

To solidify the distinctions, the Belgian colonial authority instituted ethnic identity cards in the 1930s and required every adult to carry one. That practice continued in the post-colonial era, and, during the 1994 massacres, those cards became death warrants for people identified as Tutsi.

By the time independence was achieved in 1962, antagonism between the Tutsi elite and the Hutu majority had become deep. Nothing exonerates the criminals who participated in genocide. But it's important to recognize how, on top of this colonial legacy, the economic vise of neo-colonialism creates an unforgiving context so conductive to catastrophes.

As is typical for African countries at the mercy of a world market controlled by transnational corporations and banks, Rwanda was hit hard in the 1970s by a sudden drop in the price of coffee, its chief export. In the 1980s, it was subjected to crippling "structural adjustment programs"—really a modern form of debt peonage on a world scale—imposed on indebted Third World countries by the International Monetary Fund and the World Bank. Those institutions spearheaded international economic forces that have left Rwanda dirt poor, with a yearly per-person gross domestic product of just $800.

The regime of General Juvenal Habyarimana and his chauvinist Hutu Republican Movement for Democracy and Development (MRND) came to power in a 1972 coup. Unable to deliver economic and social improvement, and unwilling to really even try, this corrupt and repressive administration resorted to consciously fomenting ethnic hatred as a means of maintaining a political base. In a clear precursor of the cataclysm to come, there were four massacres killing a total of 2,000 Tutsi between October 1990 and February 1993. The government radio broadcast false reports of murder plots in order to whip up an anti-Tutsi frenzy, and officials actively directed the killings.

The regime was greatly assisted by international arms aid. The number-one supplier was France, which also had at least 680 soldiers there by 1993, backing the government in its civil war with the RPF. The U.S. also supported the Hutu-extremist administration, although on a much smaller scale, with $2.3 million worth of military sales from 1981 to 1992. Foreign arms helped the MRND build the "unofficial" Hutu militias that became shock troops for the wholesale butchery of 1994. The prevailing poverty provided an added incentive; landless Hutu were promised the property of the Tutsi they killed.

The debacle was clearly predictable; in fact, Human Rights watch (HRW) sounded a clear alarm in a report published in January 1994, a few months before the bloodbath erupted. But that urgent call for a strong international peacekeeping force went unheeded. The report was also prescient in its indication that the extremist Hutu clique around President Habyarimana was strongly opposed to his new entry into negotiations to end the civil war. It now seems likely that this clique engineered the April 6, 1994, assassination of Habyarimana and then used the event to launch the merciless pogrom designed to retain its monopoly on power.

A public aware of France's role in the earlier arms buildup wouldn't have been fooled by the country's "humanitarian" gesture during the 1994 crisis. After doing nothing during the massacre of civilians, France rushed in 2,500 troops in June as the old regime crumbled. The resulting safe haven provided a refuge for fleeing war criminals, which at the same time panicked the Hutu population into a mass exodus. The same extremist forces now rule the refugee camps, retaining control over a large population base out of which they may yet build an exile army to resume the civil war.

The current RPF-led government in Rwanda hasn't been able to totally prevent revenge killings of Hutu, but its record on human rights is qualitatively better than the murderous regime it overthrew. At the same time, the RPF has made a concerted effort to build a coalition with moderate Hutu forces. But there's no hope that Rwanda will be able to rebuild and get back on its feet as long as the country is depopulated, and international reconstruction aid remains so scarce. Meanwhile, the old genocidal leadership, with help from France and other foreign powers, is rearming inside packed refugee camps that seethe with frustration.

Still, we need not simply despair while a new and deadly tornado brews. Instead, we can support HRW's call for major international aid to Rwanda. We also can work to get at the source of this and so many other human tragedies by supporting campaigns such as "50 Years Is Enough!" for a more equitable distribution and use of world economic resources.

[published in *Toward Freedom*, October 1996]

State of Seige

THE PALACE OF JUSTICE:
A Colombian Tragedy
by Ana Carrigan
New York: Four Walls/Eight Windows Press (1993)

It was perhaps the most spectacular and bloody assault on the judicial branch of any government in modern history. On November 6, 1985, 35 guerrillas seized the Palace of Justice in Bogotá, Colombia, taking hundreds of hostages, and the army immediately attacked the building. After the 27-hour battle and mop-up operations, more than 100 people were dead, including 11 justices of Colombia's Supreme Court and its Council of State.

An official version of events emerged very quickly, first leaked by the U.S. Embassy and soon trumpeted across the Western media: the M-19 guerrillas had been paid by Colombia's drug cartels to destroy judicial records that could be used to extradite drug lords to the U.S. The army claimed to have made every effort to save the hostages, but reported that many had been machine-gunned in cold blood by the guerrillas, who then committed suicide just before the army could get to them. As the months and years went by, no challenge to this official version ever saw the light of major media coverage.

Ana Carrigan, an award-wining journalist of mixed Irish and Colombian descent, was sent on a two-week assignment to do a story for the *New York Times*. What she wrote was never published by the *Times*, and her two weeks stretched into an eight-year project. The result is *The Palace of Justice*, a gripping book that is as terrifying and harrowing as any novel, but about a real-life and politically weighty tragedy. Her work more than equals the standards for investigative journalism set by Woodward and Bernstein—and under far more dangerous circumstances. Carrigan met secretly with survivors and with disaffected pathologists at the city morgue, obtained documents from the official investigation, studied the transcripts of police and army radio transmissions during the siege, and interviewed a range of people involved in the events to piece together what actually happened. There was no evidence of any collaboration between the guerrillas and the drug cartels (however, links have been proven to exist between high military officials and the training and arming of drug militias used as death squads against the revolutionary movements). And, while it suppressed the information, the government knew exactly why (from captured M-19 documents) the guerrillas went into the Palace of Justice.

M-19 (Movimiento 19 de Abril) took its name from April 19, 1970—the infamous day when the election was stolen from a populist alliance that won by millions of votes. Power was retained by the traditional elite when used the army to suppress peasants' and workers' movements and proscribed significant opposition. A group of activists decided they needed to build a guerrilla force. By 1982, M-19 had an 85 percent approval rating in public opinion polls. A 1984 Peace Accord was brokered between President Belisario Bentacur and M-19, with the latter laying down its arms in return for being allowed to participate in the legal political process. But the now-open ex-guerrillas were hit by a wave of death squad assassinations along with a disinformation campaign that blamed them for the breakdown of the peace process. Politically crippled and defamed by the media, their popularity plummeted as they were forced back underground. Their seizure of the Palace of Justice was a bold/desperate bid to expose the government's culpability for torpedoing the Peace Accord. Along with their weapons, the guerrillas carried a sheaf of legal documents on violations of the Accord and brought along their most respected negotiators. They selected the Palace of Justice precisely because the judiciary was the most independent and respected branch of government. Their plan was to have the Supreme Court preside over a hearing that would broadcast the truth to the nation.

While Carrigan is sympathetic to the causes of social justice for which M-19 initially picked up the gun, she doesn't treat them as heroes. She sees them as guilty of a cavalier attitude that resulted in serious errors throughout the process. The most staggering miscalculation was the naive belief that the army would respect the lives of the hostage Supreme Court justices. As a judge's wife later tells the author: "When the M-19 seized the Palace of Justice, they proved they knew precisely nothing about our national reality."

The army not only had a bloody record of massacres and of spawning death squads but also more specifically had an animus for the judiciary, which had recently ruled against the military in several cases about torture and abuse of power. What becomes absolutely clear from Carrigan's hour-by-hour reconstruction is that the army, with President Bentacur's acquiescence, adamantly thwarted any and all efforts to negotiate a peaceful end to the siege: the president never answers the urgent telephone calls from the chief justice, third-party efforts to set up communication are spurned, hostage judges shouting out to soldiers to ask for a cease-fire and negotiations receive gunfire in return, and a message about negotiations carried by a judge released to the military is never delivered to the civilian government. When public pressure finally leads to the token gesture of sending the head of the Colombian Red Cross, the military purposely delays him until after their final, lethal assault is launched. Radio transcripts show that the generals are frantic to complete this operation before public pressure forces the government to negotiate.

The army was not just obsessed with exterminating revolutionaries. At best, it didn't give a damn about the lives of the civilians; at worst, the military was out for judicial blood. From the beginning, the plan of attack was to fire high-powered rockets into the areas occupied by guerrillas and hostages alike. When army ordnance started a fire in one section and some judges tried to crawl out, army guns shot them down (in fact, later ballistic studies showed no bullets from M-19 guns in the many hostages shot to death).

In addition, tapes from military and police communications reveal that at least 17 persons were taken captive—none of whom were ever heard from again. Some of these prisoners were probably guerrillas, but about nine were from the palace cafeteria staff because the military was obsessed with possible inside help for M-19. As a clandestine report from disgusted members of military intelligence later revealed, the captives were brutally tortured during interrogation and then all murdered to erase any witnesses to torture.

On top of the physical carnage of charred bodies and tortured civilians, the military added another chilling dimension of horror with its post-massacre campaign to impose its version of events. Its efforts were so thorough that it was almost like erasing videotape and imposing another, virtual reality on top of it. The minister of defense solemnly assured the public that "the fundamental objective of the military operation" was to "at all times avoid any loss of life among the hostages." Within 48 hours, the U.S. government rushed to proclaim its support for President Bentacur's handling of the crisis.

To enforce this virtual reality, all tapes of a publicly aired interview with the chief justice (carried out over the telephone during the siege) disappeared, ballistics reports were suppressed, and bodies were dumped into a mass grave and burned with acid before legally required autopsies could be performed. To this day, no one knows the exact number of persons killed. A number of Colombian journalists who tried to investigate the alliance between sections of the army and the drug mafia have died, as have countless investigators for independent government agencies and human rights organizations. Many other independent journalists have been driven out by published "death lists." Most of these targets are also listed as "subversives" by the U.S Embassy, and thus are denied entry to this country and access to the media here.

While the Palace of Justice siege and massacre was a most spectacular event, the results reinforced the continuity of modern Colombian history: massacres of peasants continue apace, as do political assassinations and disappearances, outstripping the human toll from the Contra war in Nicaragua. Ironically, while some guerrilla movements fight on in the mountains, the remnants of M-19 finally did make peace with the government in 1989, and now hold some seats in Congress. These now-legitimate politicians have little desire to refocus public attention on M-19's greatest debacle, not to mention rekindling army hostility, by demanding a new inquiry into the events. Meanwhile, the government continues to be very much by and for the narrow elite. It is, as Connor Cruise O'Brien writes in the foreword to *The Palace of Justice*, "the façade of democratic institutions masking the reality of arbitrary and brutal military power."

[published in *Downtown*, March 30, 1994]

Democratatorship

COLOMBIA: THE GENOCIDAL DEMOCRACY
by Javier Giraldo
Monroe, ME: Common Courage Press (1996)

Quick, what is the first thing that comes to mind to complete the sentence, "The main cause of violence in Colombia is..."

If you thought "drugs" or "the drug cartels," you joined the vast majority of public opinion—in being completely wrong.

Colombia has the highest murder rate in the world, but only a tiny fraction of that is drug-related. For example, over a survey period between January 1991 and May 1992, only 0.18 percent (that's a rate of 1 in 550) of the murders there were drug related. Even more importantly, a similar survey showed that political assassinations outstripped drug murders by a ratio of 13 to 1. The source of those figures is a Colombian of unparalleled integrity and knowledge, Javier Giraldo. He is a Catholic priest who is the executive director of the intercongregational Commission of Justice and Peace. You can read his wrenching report and thoughtful explanations in *Colombia: The Genocidal Democracy*.

One point the author doesn't mention—but that is obvious to anyone familiar with recent history in Colombia—is that his own life is in danger for exposing the government's central role in the pervasive violence, in a country where even the rare prosecutors and judges who've engaged that issue have become targets for assassination. What has kept Giraldo alive so far is international attention. That glimmer of interest has to grow into the full daylight of disclosure and condemnation to put a stop to the overall "murder, incorporated."

The number of lives involved is no trifling matter. From 1988 through 1995, in this country of 38 million people, some 30,000 persons were killed in clearly political violence. There were another 37,000 unsolved murders that were most likely political. Of that total of 67,000, only 14 percent resulted from direct combat with antigovernment guerrillas. Giraldo attempts to humanize those stark figures with specific "scenes from the dirty war." For example, there was the massacre in the town of Trujillo in early 1990:

> Just before midnight on the 31st [of March], a combined army/paramilitary group dragged a large number of campesinos [peasants/farmworkers] out of their houses, took them to the hacienda [rural mansion] of a well-known drug trafficker and brutally tortured them, dismembering them with a chainsaw.

But the author cannot bring himself to write the details provided by eyewitness testimony "because their cruelty is enough to wound anyone's human sensibility. I can only say that the tortures carried out at the farmhouse were rooted in some of the worst barbarism in the annals of history."

Giraldo is not an elegant writer, at least not in this English version of his book. In any case, there is no decent way to bring such horrors to life. What his examples and analysis do make clear is that the typical victims are not guerrilla fighters but rather poor peasants, homeless street children, labor organizers, radical students, leftist political candidates, priests and nuns who work with the poor, and even journalists and judges who threaten to expose what's going on.

The introduction to the book, by Noam Chomsky, provides a brief sketch of the social structure that needs such brutal repression to survive: the top three percent of the land elite own 70 percent of the arable land, while 57 percent of the poorest farmers have to get by on under three percent; 40 percent of Colombia's population lives in the dire conditions of "absolute poverty," with some 4.5 million children—one-half of all those under the age of 14—going hungry.

Given that reality, the global media's sensationalism about the serious but relatively minor problem of drug violence does more than sell TV commercials. The dazzling artificial camera lights blind viewers to the far more fundamental and far-reaching problem: the rich's total war to rule over the poor. Thus, the U.S. State Department could get away with certifying Colombia, which has the worst human rights record in Latin America in recent years, as a "democracy." That qualified the regime to receive military aid, arms justified as needed to continue the war against drugs but more often used in atrocities against sectors of the population considered disloyal to the government.

Colombia is democratic in form, with a civilian government and periodic elections between two establishment political parties. But the military and police are given impunity to run the more divisive process of eliminating any serious opposition and of using terror to prevent the rise of powerful mass movements. In this, they are as ruthless and effective as any dictatorship. This dual reality is aptly captured in the term coined by Eduardo Galeano—"democratatorship." In recent years, to maintain the facades of democracy and respect for human rights, the bulk of the murders have been shifted from direct military operations to paramilitary groups—irregular forces initiated, directed, and often manned by the military and police but not officially part of those structures.

At the same time, the collapse of the Communist bloc has undermined the old rationale for such dirty wars as needed to stop "subversion." The new justifications are stamping out "terrorism" and combating "drug traffickers." But the reality on the ground contradicts the propaganda. Giraldo presents considerable documented evidence of cooperation between the military and some of the "drug Mafias." The narco-military link is not simply one of corruption but also involves class interests. Some drug cartels share the interests of other big businesses, such as oil, cattle, and commercial agriculture, in suppressing movements by the poor to acquire farmland or to win higher wages.

There is a double irony in the bitter reality. Colombia is a "democracy" maintained by savage terror directed against the majority; the rationalization for militarization is the "war against drugs," while the actual operations involve frequent and close collaboration with the real drug traffickers in organizing paramilitary attacks on the people. As Giraldo sums it up in his conclusion, "What exists is an unyielding Policy of State which is devouring our martyred country."

This book is also important because Colombia may be a grim harbinger of dangerous international trends: (1) a phony "drug war" to justify police state measures and (2) a public relations version of formal democracy that masks a brutal and manipulative rule by a narrow elite.

[published in Aquarian Weekly, December 18, 1996]

People's War or War on the People?

Revolutionary movements are routinely slandered in the bourgeois media. That reality has led radical movements to automatically rally behind any left movement fighting the power structure. Sadly, such a direct, simple response isn't adequate. The examples of Stalin in the Soviet Union and Pol Pot in Cambodia painfully demonstrate that some regimes that claim to be revolutionary end up committing atrocities and even genocide. Our loyalaty is not to the "left" label but rather to humankind. As such, we have a serious responsibility to be aware of and oppose movements that turn against the people. But it is usually very difficult to sort out when such allegations have a real basis and when they are purely imperialist disinformation. I read Peru: Time of Fear as part of an effort to sort out these issues in regard to the "Shining Path." At the same time, I tried to develop some general warning signs for when a left organization is liable to betray the people.

PERU: TIME OF FEAR
by Deborah Poole and Gerardo Rénique
London: Latin American Bureau

The most developed guerrilla war in the Western Hemisphere has been raging in Peru since the 1980 initiation of armed struggle by the Peruvian Communist Party—Sendero Luminoso ("Shining Path") (PCP-SL). In the ensuing 14 years, an estimated 27,000 Peruvians have died in political violence, which has also caused about $24 billion in property damage.

On April 5, 1992, Peru's President Alberto Fujimori carried out an "auto-coup"—dismissing Congress, disbanding the judiciary, and turning over nearly complete control to the military. (Fujimori is presently a fugitive in Japan, hiding from an international INTERPOL arrest warrant, for his numerous crimes in Peru.) Five months later, security forces captured the PCP-SL's supreme leader, Abimael Guzmán ("Chairman Gonzalo"), and other key members of the central committee. While the year following these arrests saw a 50 percent decline in the intensity of the war, it was still at a formidable 1,650 deaths that year, and the

PCP-SL still has an estimated 3,000 active combatants. In addition, the explosive mix with a $2 billion-a-year cocaine trade means that Peru is still a major venue in danger of U.S. military intervention.

For those of us here on the side of the oppressed people, it is hard to know what to make of the PCP-SL. They are demonized in the mainstream media as terrorists and mass murderers, but we know that the establishment is capable of going to great lengths of disinformation to discredit even the most humane of revolutionary forces. On the other hand, we cannot just dismiss the real danger that parties who say they fight for the people can become murderous tyrants themselves. A prime and tragic example is the Khmer Rouge, responsible for the killing of an estimated one million of Cambodia's 8 million citizens during its rule from 1975 to 1979. The problem of obtaining reliable information and analysis is not automatically resolved by turning to leftist critiques of guerrilla forces. Some reformist leftists feel threatened by examples that demand physical confrontation with the state, and will therefore do their best to discredit armed struggle.

Peru: Time of Fear went to press shortly after Guzmán's capture in September 1992 and is being distributed in this country by *Monthly Review*. Deborah Poole and Gerardo Rénique have a definite point of view. They argue that the PCP-SL is an authoritarian and violent force whose main targets have been peasants, shantytown residents, and competing left activists. "In 1990 alone, over sixty percent of Sendero's 1,249 recorded victims were peasants. Nearly 27 percent were slum dwellers. Fewer than five percent were police or military personnel." They see the main impact of the PCP-SL's war as the decimation of the once numerous and strong grassroots organizations that could have formed the base of resistance to the vicious social and economic policies of the government. In short, Poole and Rénique very much see the Peruvian masses as caught in the middle between the competing and ruthlessly violent actions of the PCP-SL and of the Peruvian state.

This reviewer has to admit to not having enough specific knowledge of Peru to form a definitive judgment. How can we tell, for example, whether the assassinated community activist María Elena Moyano was a feminist and leftist organizer, as the authors and other critics contend, or an active collaborator with the police, as Sendero's supporters charge? This book gains some credibility from the thoughtfulness of its social analysis and also from its sympathy for Peru's other guerrilla group, Tupac Amaru Revolutionary Movement (the MRTA is considered "Castroite", while the PCP-SL is avowedly "Maoist"). The sheer numbers of peasants and activists killed and the many examples presented in this book lend weight to the grave charges against the PCP-SL.

On the other hand, Poole and Rénique don't provide specific references on the character of the violence, which would help in evaluating the authenticity of the charges, and they don't give us any way to sort out how often massacres were committed by security forces posing as the PCP-SL. The authors also fail to provide adequate explanation for the PCP-SL's formidable accomplishment of large recruitment among the indigenous population (the long-suffering and long-forgotten, even by most of the left, majority of Peru) and of the strong participation of women. The most serious shortcoming of this book is that it balances the atrocities of the PCP-SL and of the state. But all independent human rights observers—while attributing serious abuses to the PCP-SL—report that the great bulk of the terror comes from government security forces. In addition, whatever one thinks of the PCP-SL, there is no question that the fundamental problem is the overwhelming misery and suffering imposed on the Peruvian majority by world capitalism and the repressive Peruvian regime.

The book's shortcomings do not, however, let the PCP-SL off the hook. While there has never been a perfect resolution of the tough contradiction between building a disciplined combat organization and developing a democratic process (both internally and in accountability to the oppressed), historical experience does tell us some of the warning signs for when an organization has shifted from fighting for the people to being dangerously drunk on its own power: (1) deification of a supreme leader; (2) seeing the party as arbiter of all right and wrong rather than as an instrument of the people; (3) prioritizing the struggle against "revisionism" (those who would turn the movement away from revolution) over the struggle against the state (while opposing revisionism is an essential part of the revolutionary process, obsession with it often serves as a cover-up for destructive competition for leadership with other left forces); (4) the position that there are only two sides—one is either with the party or an enemy; and (5) a direct goal of bringing down state repression on the people in order to raise revolutionary consciousness. The PCP-SL's own writings abound in all these disconcerting danger signals.

While there are real grounds to be wary of endorsing or supporting the PCP-SL as a leading revolutionary force, that cannot be an excuse for acquiescence to the terrible repression of political prisoners. Some 3,000 guerrilla suspects have been detained and secretly killed by Peruvian security forces in this dirty war. Rape is standard during interrogation of women, as is torture of all suspects. Thousands have been sentenced to long and onerous prison terms by secret military tribunals, including 220 life sentences in 1993 alone. Hundreds of political prisoners have been massacred by troops retaking control of prisons. Guzmán has been held in complete isolation while the lawyer who was defending him, Dr. Alfredo Crispo, was himself taken to a secret tribunal and given a life sentence for treason. These human rights abuses are abominations that must be strongly opposed. And, of course, the same methods can be, and are, used against the most legitimate of forces who fight effectively against the government.

But even more to the heart of the matter are the totally savage living conditions imposed on the Peruvian people. Here, the authors provide some of the relevant data, even if they fail to make it the compelling centerpiece of their book. After President Fujimori's 1990 "shock" treatment for the economy, the number of Peruvians meeting the UN's dire criteria of "absolute poverty" shot up from 7 million to almost 13 million persons, out of a total population of 22 million. Chronic malnutrition has jumped to 5,753,600 persons, including 40 percent of children under six. Eighty out of a thousand infants die before their first birthday. More than 90 percent of the working population is classified as unemployed or underemployed, and the average household income is $271 a year. In 1990, profits tripled to a scandalous 60 percent of the GNP, while wages and salaries comprised only 15 percent. There has been a collapse of the public health system and the reemergence in the 1990s of easily preventable epidemics that are rampaging because of poverty and neglect: cholera, tuberculosis, malaria, and many others.

According to the U.S. media, Fujimori's economic programs have been a grand success: inflation is down, debt payments have resumed to U.S. banks, and conditions are once again favorable for U.S. business investments in Peru.

Peru: Time of Fear does provide useful historical and political background and also ends with a very illuminating chapter on "Coca Capitalism and the New World Order." The authors point out how the Fujimori/International Monetary Fund (IMF) policies of withdrawing credit supports and encouraging imports forced small farmers out of growing corn and rice, leaving coca (from which cocaine is derived) as the only economically viable crop.

> *At one extreme of this economy are the U.S. working class Latino and Black youth who have been marginalized by Reaganomics and racism. At the other, are the Andean peasants whose economies have been destroyed by U.S.-backed IMF austerity measures and neo-liberal reforms. For both those disenfranchised populations, the drug economy offers their only source of security.*

While "the war on drugs" provides the rallying cry for militarization and police state measures—in Peru and in the U.S.—*Peru: Time of Fear* brings to light a player of particular interest—Fujimori's shadowy right-hand man, General Vladmiro Montesinos. With long-term and close ties to the CIA, Montesinos played a key role in assuring military support for Fujimori's 1992 "auto-coup" and in using that situation to strengthen the positions of military officers with known ties to the drug trade. North Americans need to be more than vigilant against any U.S. involvement in Peru under the rubric of "the war on drugs."

There are good reasons to be wary of the PCP-SL, its strategy, and its purpose. But our main fire must be directed at the abommable human rights abuses in Peru and the intolerable social system that is the main killer of its people.

[June 11, 1994]

But Today We Say ENOUGH!

The Zapatistas' January 1, 1994, uprising and subsequent "Encounters Against Neo-Liberalism" provided a key spark for igniting what the media later dubbed the "anti-globalization movement." More accurately, the struggle is for democracy and equality, as well as respect for the environment, in the world economy. It's still too early to know how well the Zapatistas will do in overcoming past setbacks to Third World struggles. Many questions of direction and strategy remain unresolved. But they place a welcome emphasis on democracy and deep roots among the people, and provide a vital example of continuing struggle.

VOICE OF FIRE:
*Communiqués and Interviews from
the Zapatista National Liberation Army*
edited by Ben Clarke and Clifton Ross
Berkeley: New Earth Publications (1994)

It was as though a long-dormant volcano had erupted, throwing an incandescent light into what had been a grim, dark sky for the struggles of the oppressed. On January 1, 1994, the first day that the North American Free Trade Agreement (NAFTA) went into effect, Zapatista rebels seized control of six municipal capitals in the dirt-poor state of Chiapas in southeastern Mexico.

The Mexican Army responded predictably enough with bloody repression. But some of the results were also surprising. The Zapatistas' skillful cultivation of international media attention, along with their call for intervention by the nongovernmental organizations (NGOs) of Mexico, forced the regime to agree to a cease-fire and to negotiate on the rebels' demands for democracy for the nation and for social justice for the poor indigenous people of Chiapas. The group, which was virtually unknown to the outside world, is the Zapatista National Liberation Army, known as the EZLN, for the initials in Spanish (Emiliano Zapata was the martyred leader of an indigenous army during the Mexican Revolution of 1910). We now have a chance to at least glimpse their heart and mind with a recently published collection of their communiqués and interviews. *Voice of Fire* has many, but not all, of the EZLN statements from January 1, 1994, to June 10, 1994. The translations from Spanish are done by various sources and, while not flawless, they are easily readable.

To people in the U.S., the uprising may have seemed like a shocking, spontaneous combustion, but it was actually 10 years in the making. A few non-indigenous revolutionaries from other parts of Mexico, including the now-famous masked spokesperson, "Subcomandante Marcos," came to live among the indigenous people in the jungles and mountains of Chiapas. The movement includes all six of the major ethnic groups among the Mayan Indians there. Thus, the roots and continuity of the struggles really go back a whole lot longer.

As the EZLN says in its January 2, 1994 "Declaration of War" from the Lacandona Jungle: "We are a product of 500 years of struggle. We have nothing, absolutely nothing, not even a decent roof over our heads, nor land, nor work, nor health, nor food, nor education. But today we say ENOUGH!"

Editors Ben Clarke and Clifton Ross wisely include one piece written by Marcos before the uprising that provides us with essential social and economic background. Capitalism bleeds Chiapas in a thousand different ways—sucking out the oil, gas, coffee, and timber and leaving "the imprint of capitalism as change: ecological destruction, agricultural plunder, hyper-inflation, alcoholism, prostitution and poverty."

Of the 3.5 million people of Chiapas, 72 percent do not finish the first grade, one and a half million don't have access to medical services, and 54 percent suffer from malnutrition. These overall statistics are much more dire for the two-thirds of the population that is rural and particularly for the one million who are indigenous. Chiapas also has the highest mortality rate in Mexico. The close to 15,000 deaths a year is overwhelmingly caused by readily curable diseases such as respiratory infections, parasites, malaria, and cholera. The "white guards," death squads that are financed by the big landowners and trained by the Mexican security forces, have brutalized campesinos who have tried to organize against these conditions.

NAFTA promises to make things much worse. While the debate in the U.S. revolved around the pros and cons for relatively well-paying jobs here, the primary crime of NAFTA is the way it will destroy the livelihoods of those living on the very edge of subsistence in Mexico.

To help integrate markets, the Mexican government revised Article 27 of its constitution to now allow land that had been reserved for small owners and communities to pass to large, private estates. Further, the new imports of cheap corn from U.S. agribusiness will totally flood the market and ruin Mayan campesinos—forcing more into starvation, driving many off the land, and undermining a culture in which the relationship to the land and to corn was a centerpiece. As Marcos says in an interview, "NAFTA...is a death sentence for the Indians, an international massacre."

This series of documents does not provide a detailed map of EZLN structure and strategy, but some fascinating facets do come to light. The Zapatistas explicitly distinguish themselves from earlier guerrilla groups where a small, armed vanguard aspired to lead a revolution. Instead, they emphasize the mass character of their movement, and insist that major decisions are made through democratic discussions and votes in the communities. They argue that change doesn't come from just armed action but rather through all forms of struggle, on many different fronts. While Subcomandante Marcos stands out as a spokesperson and as the presumed military leader, he stresses that he is fully subordinate to the collective political leadership of the Revolutionary Clandestine Indigenous Committee (CCRI), which is elected by the people and is 100 percent indigenous.

Editor Clarke asserts that Marcos is the author of most of the CCRI communiqués. But while Marcos's signed work has a refreshing, sardonic wit, many of the CCRI communiqués resonate more with the affecting lyricism that peeks out in the occasional interviews with Indian leaders. The CCRI statement "To 500 Years of Indigenous Resistance" is worth quoting at length:

> *In our heart there was so much pain, so much death and suffering that it no longer could be contained in this world that our ancestors gave us...and even the hearts of the plants and animals were filled with pain; and the hearts of the stones and all the world was filled with pain and suffering; and the sun and wind suffered and were in pain and the land was in pain and suffering. Everything was pain and suffering, everything was silent. And we saw, brothers and sisters, that it was DIGNITY that was all we had. We saw that we had to win a dignified death so that everyone would live one day, with good and with reason. Filled with fire...we rose to walk again, our step firm again. Our hands and our hearts were armed. "For everyone!" says our heart, not for only some, not for the few, "For everyone!" cried our spilled blood, flowing in the streets of the cities where lies and deprivation govern.*

This revolutionary movement offers a perhaps unique blend between local and national demands. The EZLN is completely rooted in the fight for social justice and human rights for the indigenous of Chiapas but still sees the primary issue as real democracy for the Mexican nation as a whole. Thus, they also differ from past guerrillas by disavowing any intention to seize power: "We don't want...to impose our ideas on Mexican civilian society by force of arms." Instead, their goal is to open up a free and democratic space of political struggle so that the proposals for society from the different classes will be resolved according to who convinces the majority of the nation. They are so strict in keeping the focus on democratic space that they don't put forward their own proposal or broad vision. Only once, in the pre-uprising essay by Marcos, is some indication given, when socialism is mentioned as "the only hope of this world on earth."

The central demand of the uprising is contained in the steps the EZLN sees as necessary to achieve national democracy: the resignation of the illegitimate government; the formation of a transitional government made up of respected and independent NGOs; their supervision to ensure new, clean elections throughout the whole country and at all levels. This program in effect calls for dismantling the current rule by a single party, the PRI, which has used bribes, repression, and fraud to guarantee continual electoral victories over the past 65 years. In addition to this fundamental goal, the EZLN put forth numerous, more specific demands—such as for schools, clinics, and cooperatives—to end illiteracy, curable diseases, and hunger.

The series of demands for indigenous women is of particular interest. The most outstanding issue is reproductive health, with the sky-high maternal mortality rate. Other demands include alleviating the onerous domestic workload, providing day-care centers, and helping women market their craftwork. The women also call for freedom from physical abuse, freedom to choose a spouse and how many children to raise, and access to decision-making power. Curiously, though, this entire section on women does not figure into the EZLN's later evaluation of the government's response to their demands. There were two women in the 19-member CCRI delegation to the negotiations, and this book reprints a valuable interview with them. Overall, we can infer that there have been important advances in women's participation while, of course, there is still a long way to go to achieve equality.

These voices and from the Lacandona Jungle are stirring. Their emphasis on political direction from the indigenous communities and their commitment to full democracy is welcome. Nonetheless, based on what is presented in this book, there are some major gaps and key unanswered questions. The call for national democratic space expresses an ideal, but there is very little offered on the formidable obstacles in practice. How can decisions truly be made by the majority when the means of public discussion are so thoroughly monopolized? The only specifics that appear in this regard are a demand for an indigenous radio broadcasting system and the favorable reference to plebiscites as a way the people can confront the power of the ruling party. But even plebiscites can be very undemocratically manipulated when wealth and power are essential to having a powerful national voice.

A related set of questions revolves around what strategy the movement will have when facing the all-out assault by state power. Can the EZLN's commitment to subordinate their military command to a community decision-making process hold up in conditions of full-scale war? A partial answer as to their view of political power can be seen in the EZLN's call to the range of NGOs to intervene in the struggle. It is almost as though they see themselves as an armed spark (and a guarantor against retreat) for a much broader, primarily peaceful and politically varied movement. This appeal to civil society proved to be a very effective tactic to stop the army repression in January 1994. But it remains to be seen if it can be forged into a winning strategy to actually break the hold of the ruling elite. Marcos recognizes in an interview that "there's the risk that the government will be able to politically isolate us at the national level," which is indeed the tack the regime has taken since the peace negotiations broke down.

This collection ends with the communiqués of June 10, 1994, which explain in detail why the Zapatistas rejected the government's proposals. Their critique, in essence, is that there was no substantive concession on issues of power: all that was offered was either commissions to study problems or small and localized concessions on social programs. Since then, the government held its elections as planned, on August 21, and the ruling PRI won in what international observers said was an election with many irregularities but "clean" relative to Mexico's past elections.

Many commentators feel that the PRI's victory, at the national level, was mainly the result of the opposition parties' inability to mount a credible alternative. But at the state level, the EZLN unambiguously charges that the PRI victory in Chiapas was imposed by outright fraud. In a communiqué issued on October 8, 1994 (subsequent to *Voice of Fire*), the CCRI alerts us that the

217

government has returned to a strategy of repression in Chiapas, including military provocations, evictions of people on occupied lands, and beatings and torture of campesino activists.

More recent news reports say that the Zapatistas tried to blockade a series of towns to prevent PRI's state government from taking office. And the *New York Times* of December 22, 1994 (in the "Business Section," since the focus was on what political unrest would mean for potential U.S. investors), reported the governor's claim that roads in and out of all 38 of the towns the rebels had infiltrated are now back under government control. As this review is written, Chiapas could be approaching another January 1st uprising. However, if the documents in this book are a guide, the EZLN will do everything in its power to draw full political attention to the injustices while trying to avoid a full-scale military engagement.

One particular value of *Voice of Fire* is how it highlights the special appeal to people in the U.S. for solidarity. After all, as the EZLN gently reminds us: "The North Americans have a lot to do with the conditions of misery in which the Indians live." And, "the Mexican federal government is using U.S. economic and military support to massacre Chiapas' indigenous people." The issue is not only for justice down there; they can also provide us some much-needed inspiration and direction. Another post-*Voice of Fire* communiqué could, in a way, speak for all of us: "Now is the time for hope to organize itself and to walk forward in the valleys and the cities."

[published in *Downtown*, January 18, 1995]

Chapter 10

Life in the Balance: The Environment

Life in the Balance

FIGHT FOR THE FOREST:
Chico Mendes in His Own Words
by Tony Gross
London: Latin American Bureau (1992)

When Chico Mendes was murdered in a remote town of western Brazil on December 22, 1988, it made headlines around the world. Mendes was not only a leader of the local rural workers' union, but also a frontline defender of the rapidly disappearing rain forests. Landowners assassinated him while pursuing their violent campaign to clear the land for cattle ranches.

The centerpiece of *Fight for the Forest*, which recently came out in a new edition with background material and updates by Tony Gross, is a long interview with Mendes, completed days before he was killed. "I don't get that cold feeling any more. I am no longer afraid of dying...the resistance would still go on and it might even be that much stronger." This remarkable and accomplished leader could not even read or write until he was 20. "My life began just like that of all rubber tappers, as a virtual slave bound to do the bidding of his master. I started to work at nine years old, and like my father before me, instead of learning my ABC's I learned how to extract latex from a rubber tree."

Rubber tappers are some of Brazil's poorest citizens, often refugees from other parts of the country, who make a living in the Amazonian rain forests by placing taps into rubber trees and harvesting the latex sap. In earlier generations, they were virtually serfs on rubber plantations, but synthetic replacements for rubber and international competition led to the decline of the Brazilian plantations in the 1960s and '70s. This situation meant more independence for the rubber tappers, but they continued to be held in a form of debt peonage by the merchants who controlled the marketing of the latex. The decline of the plantation also meant that the most powerful commercial interests shifted their focus to exploiting the land for cattle ranches.

Preservation of tropical rain forests is of global importance. Such areas, only 7 percent of the earth's surface, contain an estimated 60 percent of its plant and animal species. Even though only 1 percent of these plants has been studied for medicinal properties, they provide a quarter of all pharmaceutical products. Thirty percent of the world's remaining tropical rain forests are located in Brazil. When the ranchers clear and burn large tracts of this land, it has terrible consequences for biodiversity, global warming, and soil fertility; the preserves for many unique species are destroyed; trees that absorb carbon dioxide are removed; the land is laid bare to severe erosion. In contrast, rubber tapping is not only a livelihood for impoverished workers but also a sustainable way to make use of the forest without destroying the trees.

In 1975, despite threats, repression, and a dearth of finances, Mendes organized a union of the rural workers in his hometown of Xapuri in the county of Acre. He was also instrumental in the founding of the National Council of

Rubber Tappers 10 years later. The union fights for both the livelihood of the workers and the preservation of the forest. Key aspects of its program have included (1) popular education to bring both literacy and critical thinking to the rubber tappers, (2) health clinics to provide medical care in these remote rural areas, and (3) marketing cooperatives to free the tappers from dependence on the merchants. While these programs have had pockets of success, the union hasn't had the resources or backing to develop them on any scale. Also, repression and violence have been major problems from the beginning. After the open assassination of union leader Wilson Pinheiro in 1980—to which "law enforcement" turned a blind eye—the union has emphasized a more decentralized movement, less dependent on leaders and based on grassroots discussion and participation.

While education, health care, and marketing cooperatives are all crucially important, the heart of the movement's strategy is to force the government to set aside vast tracts of the rain forest as "extractive reserves"—areas under public ownership, where those who live on the land have the right to harvest it, but private commercial interests cannot come in and clear it. In addition to rubber tappers, there are local workers who harvest nuts, babacu (for palm oil and nuts), and jute (for fiber for cloth).

These workers are not the only ones who live in harmony with the land. While their population has been decimated, there is still an indigenous population of some 6,600 persons in Acre and southwestern Amazonas. Commercial interests have prevailed upon the government to drastically reduce the areas reserved for indigenous peoples. Relations between the Indians and the rubber tappers were not good in past generations because the workers were used by the plantation owners for man-hunting expeditions that massacred and enslaved the Indians. The modern union movement under Mendes, however, has recognized the importance of building an alliance, and since 1986 has worked closely with indigenous representatives around their common interest in preserving the forest. This book, however, would have served us better by including more on the indigenous perspective on these issues.

The rubber tappers' main tactic has been the *empate*, or "standoff." When word gets out that a community is threatened by deforestation, people gather and march en masse to occupy the area. Women and children play a prominent role, and their presence deters the police from firing into the crowd. The occupiers stand in the way of the chain saws and scythes and try to convince the workers to lay down their tools. The non-violent protestors are usually arrested and beaten by the police, but on a number of occasions the *empate* called international attention to the environmental destruction and forced the government to set aside the area as an extractive reserve.

The problem is that the ranchers, often with government complicity, have pursued a campaign of systematic violence against the movement. Chico Mendes was the best known but only one of more than a hundred Brazilian rural workers killed in labor and land disputes in 1988, and there is almost never any legal accountability (Mendes's international fame meant that, in his case, at least one of his assassins was convicted). Tony Gross offers an epilogue that sums up the partial reforms, and their limitations, that came in the wake of this infamous murder; he also describes some of the continuing violence against the movement. Gross, unfortunately, doesn't provide a grassroots view that can tell us whether the union achieved Mendes's goal of participation and initiative from the base, which can then move forward despite the killing of leaders. This perspective is best expressed in Mendes's own words: "Our movement grew out of the needs of the rubber tappers. We made a lot of mistakes but we learned from them. You know, people have to look after themselves, they have to fight and be creative. That's how we built this movement... we're involved because of our ideals and we'll never turn back. Our roots are too deep for us to think of giving up the struggle."

Those of us in faraway North America must also realize that these impoverished and uneducated workers of rural Brazil are fighting and dying on the front line of a battle that has life-and-death implications for all of us.

[published in *Downtown*, January 6, 1993]

Pollution at the Core

CONFRONTING ENVIRONMENTAL RACISM:
Voices from the Grassroots
edited by Robert D. Bullard
Boston: South End Press (1993)

When we think about the environment, our mind's eye immediately travels to scenes of pristine forests and cute but endangered species such as the spotted owl, and these are certainly important concerns. Yet the environment—the surroundings—for the vast majority of people in this country is either urban or suburban. These are plagued by dreadful pollution with a clear and present danger to human life. The worst cases usually get little media attention because they are foisted onto the communities with the least political clout—Native Americans, Blacks, Latinos, Asians, and Pacific Islanders.

Confronting Environmental Racism rips the veil off this disgrace, providing us with an eye-opening introduction to the problem and heartening initiatives to do something about it.

As editor Robert Bullard tells us, "The mainstream environmental movement has not sufficiently addressed the fact that social inequality and imbalance of social power are at the heart of environmental degradation, resource depletion, pollution, and even overpopulation."

It is hard to come up with compelling summary statistics because government agencies such as the Environmental Protection Agency (EPA) haven't done comprehensive studies on the hazards that most affect people of color. What

223

work that has been done reveals lethal environmental damage. To start with the air we breathe, 33 percent of whites, 50 percent of African Americans, and 60 percent of Latinos live in the 136 U.S. counties, in which two or more air pollutants exceed established standards.

Then there is hazardous waste, the storage of which creates one of the most difficult and costly conditions. The U.S. produces between 250 and 400 million metric tons of toxic waste each year. By 1985, the EPA had inventoried about 20,000 uncontrolled sites but still had little idea how many remained unidentified. The manifold toxic wastes not only entail risks through direct contact but also seep into the water table and leak fumes into the air.

The United Church of Christ Commission of Racial Justice's Study in 1987 showed that the most significant factor in the location of commercial hazardous waste sites is race. Three out of the nation's five largest such landfills were located in predominantly Black or Latino communities. In areas with either large or multiple facilities, the average minority percentage of the population was three times greater than for communities without such facilities. Overall, 60 percent of African Americans and Latinos live in communities with uncontrolled toxic waste sites.

Lead poisoning is a heartbreaking problem that is particularly harmful to children because it damages their developing brains and nervous systems. Even low-level lead exposure can lead to attention disorders, learning disabilities, and emotional disturbances that can affect children for life. It can also cause many long-term health problems such as kidney disease. A 1988 government study that focused on lead-based paint, without adequate attention to the also serious risks from industrial and incinerator lead pollution, found that 49 percent of African American inner-city children, and 16 percent of their white counterparts, are exposed to dangerous levels of lead (outside the large urban areas, it is 36 percent and 9 percent, respectively). Since then, medical studies have shown that even far lower exposures are harmful, which means that a far greater number of children are at risk.

Not all environmental racism is urban. The most hazardous profession in the U.S. is that of a farmhand. The two million hired workers, 77 percent of them minorities, get the most direct exposure to the more than one billion pounds of insecticides, herbicides, and fungicides applied yearly in U.S. agriculture. Many of these poisons are implicated in causing such health problems as several types of cancer, sterility, birth defects, and neuropathological disorders. The EPA has been exceedingly slow at evaluating, registering, and regulating these pesticides and serves more as an agribusiness collaborator than a health protector. The farm workers are on the front line of a chemical war that, in smaller increments, contaminates all of us.

Another type of rural setting is illustrated by the Chicano Ganados del Valle cooperative in northern New Mexico. This struggle has roots in the efforts to retain the land, particularly the traditionally communal lands, going back to the Mexican land grants of the mid-1800s. Much of this land was seized by a combination of fraud and force over the years, and has been depleted by commercial agriculture and grazing. More recently, the promotion of the tourism industry has engendered rising land costs that have made small-scale agriculture prohibitively expensive. This study describes a fascinating effort at a "proactive" form of environmental organizing, as the community has formed cooperatives to create ecologically sustainable development, a way to meet human needs without destroying the earth and its other life forms.

Part of this approach—such as demanding some grazing rights for communal herds in the National Forest—flies in the face of the purely preservationist impulse of the mainstream environmental movement, made up mainly of people who make good livings, at ultimately greater cost to the environment, in the city. But poor people need to make a living, too, and a carefully sustainable approach will provide greater long-term protection for the environment.

Ecologically sustainable development is also a key for resolving the environmental crisis in the Third World. While this book focuses on the U.S., there is a strong chapter on the global level, where environmental racism is played out with a lethal vengeance. This chapter sketches such problems as the impact of wars, and nuclear testing, and the rise of the international trade exporting toxic waste from the industrialized countries to impoverished nations.

We also learn why the trend to swap Third World debt for plans to preserve its forests is not always the benign solution it appears to be. Most importantly, this chapter highlights a core problem of economic development that is worth a book in its own right: The agro-export model through which international capital displaces local food agriculture to promote the export of cash crops. These cash crops are input (fertilizer and pesticides) intensive, are very land depleting, and displace peasants who are then forced to clear forestland to survive. This approach produces cheap exports for the transnational corporations at the cost of hunger and land degradation in the Third World. The unbridled consumerism and the monomania for economic growth of the industrialized nations is at the root of global environmental destruction.

As grisly as some of the realities are, *Confronting Environmental Racism* is a very encouraging and hopeful book because the other half of the story is the burgeoning of grassroots organizations to fight these problems in what has become the fastest growing sector of the environmental movement. For example, in 1989 the Citizen's Clearinghouse for Hazardous Waste worked with about 2,000 community groups; by 1991 it was over 7,000.

Unlike most mainstream environmental organizations, Third World community groups tend to be multi-issue, linking the environment to racism, distribution of wealth, and social priorities. Women usually lead these groups, frequently with a non-hierarchical and democratic style that is rarely practiced in national formations. While the mainstream environmental movement has been slow to recognize the importance of these issues, it has been pressed by the grassroots upsurge to be more aware and provide increasing support and sharing of resources.

Confronting Environmental Racism has its weaknesses. The tone, especially the opening by Bullard, is much too dry and academic (the reader bored by this should skip right to the four stunning essays, chapters 4, 5, 8, and 11). There's a strong analysis of the importance of grassroots efforts but, despite the book's subtitle, little sense of the energy and activism of working within them. The format of 12 different essays by different authors inevitably means some overlap as well as significant gaps. There's not nearly enough on Native Americans. While the book mentions that Navajo teenagers have a rate of organ cancer 17 times the national average, there is no chapter devoted to such major problems as nuclear waste on reservations and the industrial despoiling of the sacred four corners area in the Southwest. Despite these weaknesses, this book is a great introduction to a crucial arena of struggle rarely mentioned in the establishment media, and comes with an excellent bibliography for further reading.

To the degree that industry and government can, with the complicity of our unconscious racism, get away with imposing the most dire degradation on communities of color, the polluters are also creating large-scale and lasting environmental disasters that will eventually ripple out to all of us.

As Bullard argues: "No community rich or poor, black or white, should be allowed to become an ecological 'sacrifice zone'…we must be visionary as well as militant. Our very future depends on it." This book surveys an exciting frontier of activism, one that combines the overriding importance of the environment with the core social problem of racism in the context of grassroots and democratic upsurges that are often led by women. Welcome to what may well become one of the most urgent and promising movements of the 1990s.

[published in *Downtown*, September 15, 1993]

Chapter 11

Busting a Grape: Humor

To provide comic relief for myself and others, I've written dozens of satires. A few were spoofs on prison life. Most were in personal letters and particular to the person involved. Here is a sampling that readers might enjoy.

How I Busted a Grape

One of the first things that struck me about men's prisons is how much of the banter was about who was tougher, who could beat up the other. A typical, usually joking, exchange would be: "If you give me any problems, I'm going to bust your jaw." "Oh yeah? You couldn't even bust a grape." The story below shows just what a tough guy I am.

March 8, 1988

Dear _____

You may have heard about the dramatic events here. Before you judge me too harshly for the brutal action I was forced to take, please try to understand this environment. The worst thing that can happen to a prisoner is to get labeled as "soft"; then the predators will abuse him, steal his property, and even rob him of his dignity.

My problem started when that damn mouse ran into my cell. It wouldn't have been so bad except that there were guys standing out on the gallery who saw me when I jumped up on my bed and started shrieking. After that, the word started spreading like wildfire: "Dave is softer than baby shit." I knew things were getting bad when guys started asking me what size sneakers I wore; I just had to take decisive action to put it in check.

Deeply depressed, I was shuffling into mess hall one morning with my head hanging down when I saw my opportunity. There, lying on the floor was a grape. This was it. I would show everyone how tough I really was by busting a grape in front of the entire mess hall! (It's true that it was an old, moldy grape already splitting on the sides, but no one else had to know that.)

So I lifted my right leg high in the air, gave a blood-curdling karate yell, and came down with a full-body stomp on that grape. Unfortunately, my aim was a little bit off (I hadn't yet had my morning cup of coffee), and my heel just caught the very edge of the grape. Well, you know how slippery grape skins can be—my feet went skidding out from under me, and my body did a backward flip. Fortunately, I landed with the fleshy part of my backside squarely on top of the grape—totally smashing it. Even though the grape was under me, everyone could tell that I busted it...I, mean why else would everyone in the whole mess hall stand up, laughing and clapping? Unfortunately, I dislocated my back and broke a few limbs in the fall. While it may be true that after this fight I had to be carried to the hospital on a stretcher, I was clearly the victor: my opponent had to be, quite literally, scraped off the floor!

I know you probably want to boast to your friends about my great exploits, which is fine. But don't brag too much; there's no need to get into all the details—like which part of my anatomy I used. One other thing: please don't complain about my sloppy typing. You see, I'm lying in the hospital bed in a full-body cast and in 4-limb traction. I'm typing by holding a pencil in my mouth and moving my head back and forth to peck the keys. In fact, I'm getting pretty dizzy and have to bring this letter to a close. But don't ever let it be said that David Gilbert couldn't bust a grape.

Transfer Request

TO: Correction Counselor
FROM: D. Gilbert, 8316158, D-1-24
DATE: June 8, 1988
RE: Transfer Request

You informed me that as part of my periodic six-month review I am eligible to request a transfer to another facility. The issue for me has always been being behind bars at all—not which particular kamp I am in. And, as you know, it has not been my practice to ask the Department of Correctional Services for any favors. But, I have just heard about a facility that is so much more suited to my needs that I feel it is worth breaking with my past precedents to make this request. I believe that my outstanding disciplinary record over the years entitles me to favorable consideration for a transfer that would so markedly improve my conditions.

The facility I have in mind provides many times the cell per inmate than I currently have, and it affords all the outside recreation one could want. While the food is of comparable palatability, I understand that it provides a lot more in the way of fresh greens and whole grains, which are so important for long-term health. Evidently, there is also no problem in getting a shower every day. And this is one facility that absolutely does not tolerate any staff brutality against the inmates. Most importantly, the requested facility is much closer to my family and friends in New York City and has very liberal visiting hours. Amazingly, I'm even told that it permits you to share a large cell with your mate if she too is incarcerated!

For all those outstanding features and the qualitative improvement from my current situation, I am asking you to kindly approve me for a transfer to the Bronx Zoo.

Dearest Chesa

This one was a letter to my son when he started college and was prompted by a snafu that delayed my getting his new address there.

September 5, 1999

Dearest Chesa,

Hugs & Kisses to you. My apologies for not writing earlier but (if you can excuse this lame excuse) I didn't have your address. Of course it would have been much more considerate if I at least dropped you a quick note explaining why I couldn't yet write a letter, but you know what an insensitive brute I am. Besides, even though you are the cynosure of my universe, I wasn't quite 100% sure that a card addressed "Chesa, Somewhere in Amerika" would reach you.

Speaking of "Somewhere in Amerika," when I received no address within 10 days of your visit, I became convinced that you (a child of children of the '60s) had gone underground...and I don't know of any subway systems in New Haven. What I heard was that you (perhaps more confident than we had been) were calling it the "WON-U," which I took (given the grammatical level of today's Ivy Leaguers) to be your way of saying to the government "we'll defeat you." But then I found out that, literate fellow that you are, you took your inspiration from (instead of Marx and Lenin) Hamlet, and the acronym stands for the "Weather or Not Underground"—certainly less action-oriented than we but a lot more philosophical and nuanced (sp.? Or perhaps responding to the alienation of today's youth, it's "new-angst"?).

Needless to say, I've been terribly worried about you: out there in the big bad world on your own and cut off from your weekly inoculation of silliness from yours truly. Indeed, my *sui generis* humor is so tasty and substantive that it's affectionately known as "pop-corn." And we have an even softer, more cuddly version in Boston: "pup-corn."

Anyway, it's a relief to learn that you are safely ensconced at Yale. As I think about it, those "Elis"[1] were very shrewd in making it so hard for me to call you. Otherwise, obviously, I would do all your coursework for you (college math doesn't go beyond fractions, does it?) and you would get a Phi Beta Kappa without ever touching a key. But, genius that I am, I've valiantly overcome the communication delay by preparing all of your term papers in advance:

1. For creative writing—"An Action Story: The Battle with Blood-Soaked U.S. Capitalist Patriarchal White Supremacist Homophobic Imperialism and All Its Running-Dog Lackeys and Evil Gentry!"

2. For biology—"A Study in Parasitism: The Battle with Blood-Soaked U.S. Capitalist Patriarchal White Supremacist Homophobic Imperialism and All Its Running-Dog Lackeys and Evil Gentry!" Well, I won't ruin the suspense

for you by writing out the other titles, but I've also completed your history and economics papers, all in 1 fell swoop (or, from my political perspective, 1 swell whoop). And it goes without saying that the same paper will completely fulfill your "foreign language" requirement. With my work, you're guaranteed all "A's!" (A stands for "Anti-imperialism," right? I mean, what else could it be?)

Of course, there are no free lunches. In return, and to do something with your resulting free time, I have a major research mission for you. There are certain profound and fundamental enigmas of nature and science that have perplexed me for years. Now that you have ready access to a voluminous library and a gaggle of eminent professors, you should be able to find the answers:

1. Do cemetery workers prefer the graveyard shift? 2. Is there another word for "synonym"? 3. Why is "abbreviation" so long? 4. Why is "bra" singular and "panties" plural? 5. Can you be a closet claustrophobic? 6. What is the environmentally correct response when you find an endangered animal that eats only endangered plants? (Reference: the world's leading scientific journal, *Funny Times*).

Or perhaps in a pathetic paroxysm of parental pride (you know I'm prone to just P,P,P,P), I misunderstood what you meant by "Yale," and you're actually at the top brand-name locksmith school. Hey, don't knock it, that could open the door of opportunity. It's a good trade (i.e., an Ivy League B.A. for a locksmith's apprentice certificate). So keep on picking away.

Silly with love,

———————

1. "Elis" is short for a characteristic form of communication akin to E-mail but properly named "E-lies" because, like all bourgeois thought, it is full of Bull Doo (euphemistically cleaned up, with just 1 scoop of the pen, as "Bull Dog").

Linguistics and the Common Man

There are many injustices in the world today, but one in particular has always bothered me: a foreigner could study English at a university or language school for years and, despite his or her total mastery, still be totally incapable of communication with the common people. Imagine our visitor, straight from his or her Ph.D. in English, landing in New York City and asking a local denizen how, for example, the local sports team did that day. A typical response might be: "Those motherfuckers fucked that shit up so fucking bad that I don't give a third flying fuck about those assholes no more." Not only would our doctor of English not have the slightest clue as to what was being said, but he or she would thumb frantically through the dual-language dictionary or Berlitz book to no avail—years of arduous study and many thousands of dollars in tuition all down the drain! In fact, we have conducted a statistical survey of language use and have found, at least among the male of the species, that "fuck," or some variant thereof, constitutes 19.3 percent of all spoken words. What sort of "English course" is it that censors out one-fifth of the spoken language?

We cannot simply decry this gross injustice; we must do something about it. To remedy the matter, we've called upon the renowned professor of linguistics, Im-No Chumpsky, to prepare a course on "English as Spoken by the Common Man." To begin his fieldwork, Dr. Chumpsky was dropped unobtrusively, by helicopter, into the north yard at Clinton Correctional Facility. What follows is his first field report.

I arrived in the Clinton yard on Christmas day, with my tape recorder over my shoulder and my notebook in hand. There was one phrase on the lips of all the men who were out: "It's as cold as a motherfucker out here!" From this universal usage, I deduced that "motherfucker," a noun, was something known to be extraordinarily cold. Some inmates even discussed how "the warden's heart is colder than a motherfucker"; so, that particular person must have reached absolute zero (I'm forwarding this rare datum to the bio-medical dept. for further research). Just when I felt I had settled the matter, we all went into the blocks. Much to my surprise, the men on the top gallery began to shout, paradoxically, "Turn down the heat, it's as hot as a motherfucker up here!" "Motherfucker" had the polar opposite meaning in this context.

After days of perplexed observation I learned that someone could be as fat as a motherfucker or as thin as one, as strong or as weak, as rich or as poor. After much reflection it finally dawned on me: "motherfucker" plays a unique role in the language analogous to what "Accent" is with spices—it is an enhancer word that intensifies any quality to which it is appended. Of course "very" plays the same sort of role, but "very" can become very tiresome and (think about it) can't be said with much inflection. Moreover, "very" can only be an adverb, whereas the premier enhancer word, "motherfucker," can appear in the form of a noun, or adjective, or even as a verb (as in "motherfuck you"). This previously unparsed word is more colorful and versatile than any we can find in the Queen's English.

Our journey of inquiry led us to an even more amazing discovery: English (like Chinese) can be a tonal language. "Motherfucker," aside from its enhancer role, can have at least 4 different meanings (all that we have documented so far) depending on tone:

1. a lowlife or despicable person (as in "he was a dirty motherfucker"); 2. a regular guy (as in "I knew all the motherfuckers on 1 gallery"); 3. a solid and respectable person (as in "he was a down motherfucker"); and 4. with a dramatic change of tone, this same word can actually become an entire sentence (when said with an explosive opening MUTH-sound, followed by an artificial infusion of bass, and ending with a perhaps unintentional rising of pitch) meaning, "Let's fight!" We don't believe that our discovery of English as a tonal language has ever previously been recognized in a bona fide academic study—Nobel Prize committee, take note.

Dr. Chumpsky's field report is just the beginning of our life's work to construct a curriculum for real English. Part II will examine various conjugations of "to fuck" as well as look at the dialectical concept of "fucker" and "fuckee." Part III will examine some very elegant uses of synecdoche, as in "bring your ass over here." (The 3-letter word "ass" is so much briefer and more focused than the cumbersome "entire body and being"—and yet try to picture bringing your ass over without the rest following). Part IV will deal with the more esoteric use of oxymoronic scatology such as "that's some real clean shit."

While we are deeply committed to rectifying the terrible injustice of the now universal and bogus English courses, we implore the reader not to expect instantaneous results. Working in the field to develop a genuine linguistics can be a real motherfucker.

[December 1988]

Chapter 12

Children's Stories

David and Chesa, August 1984

The Bigfeet

What my son and I could do together in a prison visiting room was limited by the setting. So we developed storytelling as a major activity. Here is one I told him when he was four and asked for a "scary story." The main character ("Sean"), as in most of our stories, is him, and the childcare center represents the one he was attending at the time. The name of the story is "The Bigfeet."

Sean and all the children at the Sunshine Childcare Center made a very special summer trip, way across the Atlantic Ocean, to the Tree Top village—high, high up in the Pyrenee Mountains of Spain. They weren't going as tourists but rather to live and work among the people of the village.

Tree Top was a high and remote village. There was no airport up there or even roads that led into it. The children had to carry their belongs in backpacks as they climbed the steep and difficult mountain path. At times they thought they weren't going to make it. But they helped each other out and stuck with it all the way.

When they cleared the last mountain ridge, they knew immediately that it had been well worth the effort. They had never seen such a beautiful village before: high in the mountain clouds, with a crisp blue sky, a breathtaking view, and lush fruit trees all around. And the people of the village were very warm and friendly, with a glow that comes from leading a healthy life.

The sunshine children pitched right in with all the work—setting up tents, picking fruit, washing clothes, whatever. Despite the friendliness of the people, the Sunshine children began to detect a strange reserve or tension among the Tree Toppers.

"This is such a gorgeous place to live, it's perfect," gushed Sean.

"It could be," retorted John Tree Top.

It's so quiet and peaceful," exulted Audre.

"We long for peace," sighed Sarah Tree Top.

Something was amiss, some deeply held and frightening secret that the villagers were keeping from the children. The Sunshiners pressed the villagers, who finally answered:

"We didn't want to trouble you, our guests. but you have become like members of our community, and besides we won't be able to keep it secret much longer: the very survival of our village is menaced by the marauding Bigfeet!"

At the very mention of the word "Bigfeet," the whole village shuddered.

"Who are these Bigfeet and why are they so scary?" asked Audre.

"Why would they hurt the village?" queried Sean.

But the villagers were so obviously terrified that it seemed silly to even ask. Finally Sarah Tree Top said, "we will show you, you will see for yourselves."

Very quietly Sarah and John led the children as they slithered through the high grass to a place where they could hide behind some rocks. There, in a little valley below, they could see these giant and scary creatures tending to a herd of sheep.

"See what we mean?" hissed John. The Bigfeet were about eight feet tall, with pointed faces, very hairy, and with *giant* feet. They certainly looked like formidable enemies."

"We live here with you, and we will share your battles," said Sean bravely.

"And we have a way we can help you," added Audre. "We practiced archery at Sunshine. We're great with bows and arrows."

Quietly the Sunshiners broke out their bows and arrows and took very careful aim for the first surprise volley. But the Bigfeet must have have sensed the attack. They just reached up with their big, powerful hands and plucked the arrows out of the sky, throwing them back in the direction from which they came. Panic seized the kids and the villagers. They didn't slither back through the grass, rather they tore through it as fast as their legs would carry them.

Back in the village, they tried to evaluate what had happened. "Clearly these creatures are powerful," said Sean, "but we can use an even more potent weapon—fire!" So they carefully planned their move, and the next day they snuck up on the Bigfeet, setting a ring of fire around them, and watched as the wind blew the fire toward their enemies. But the Bigfeet felt the heat closing in and, all together, blew out a giant breath. This sent the flames shooting back at the attackers, singeing their hair and putting them on the run.

Back in the village, the people were even more frightened and discouraged. But Sean had one more idea: "We'll use the most powerful force in the whole universe—gravity!" Before sunrise the next morning, they snuck up to the hill overlooking the Bigfeet encampment, and amassed a giant pile of rocks. At the signal, they pushed the rocks down the slope, starting a giant rock slide. But the Bigfeet awoke with the sound and were strong enough to actually catch the rocks and throw them back at the attackers—who really panicked this time and ran so fast down the other side of the hill that they ended up tumbling and sliding most of the way on their backsides.

Now they were back in their village with singed hair and black and blue butts... and very demoralized. But they didn't have time to discuss it because they suddenly heard an ominous Thump! Thump! coming toward sthem. Every minute it got louder and louder: Thump! Thump! "Oh no, the Bigfeet are coming to get us!" Thump! Thump!

Quickly they tried to scramble out of the village, but the path out was already blocked by a phalanx of Bigfeet. They rushed toward the back way out of the village, but that way was blocked by the Bigfeet. In desperation, they tried to claw their way up the mountain, but the Bigfeet were there too.

Now they sat cowering in the center of teh village as the sound only became louder and louder—THUMP! THUMP! THUMP!—and they were completely surrounded by the humongous Bigfeet carrying giant clubs. Everyone was too petrified to say a word—except for one little boy who was so curious that he forgot his fear for just a moment: "Why?" squeaked Sean.

"Why!" roared back Yetta, the leader of the Bigfeet.

"Yeah, why?" added Audre. "Why do you want to hurt the people of this village?"

"Why?!" shouted Yetta, "Why?!" she sputtered with rage. "Aren't you the people who shot arrows at us, set fire around us, poured rocks down on our encampment?!"

"Yes we did," admitted Sean, "but we had to do that to protect ourselves against such a powerful enemy."

And at this point all the people in the village and all the Bigfeet burst forth with stories of how the others had attacked them. They all had many complaints, and each side claimed to be acting only in self-defense. As they talked and talked, the anger faded because they realized that they didn't have to be enemies. In fact, the Bigfeet offered some nice warm sheep's wool blankets (so wonderful for these cold mountain nights) that they would be happy to trade for some of the village's luscious bounty of fresh fruit.

When it came time for the children to return to New york, the Tree topers threw a big good-bye party, and invited their friends the Bigfeet. At the party, the villagers unveiled a plaque they had put up in the mountainside which told the whole story of what happened, with a special thanks to all the children of the Sunshine Daycare Center and a salute to Sean, a little boy who had the courage to ask "Why?"

The Vortex

During the long intervals between visits, the only way to be in touch with my son is the phone. But like many kids his age, he isn't into talking on the phone. I would ask him what he did at school that day, what games he was playing, etc., but he wouldn't have much to say. I guess for him it was boring to report on something that had already happened when he'd rather be doing something with me. So we created epic stories together that we could develop in episodes over successive phone calls. Phone access has varied over the years, but typically I could call him once a week, with a 20-minute prison time limit on the call. We would get a good start on a story during a visit and then keep it going with 20-minute episodes each week. I would try to end each week on a suspenseful point. One of our epics went on for 18 months. These stories are very much joint creations. Often my son will set the terms for what he wants included; at key crisis points I stop and ask him what the main character (which is he) does or says. Here's a condensed version of several episodes from an epic we developed when he was eight.

INTRO: "Sean" (my son), "Kwame" (his best friend), "Katie" (Kathy Boudin, my wife), and "Roland" (yours truly) were on a cross-country surveying trip to find ways to replace the missing ozone in the atmosphere. We got caught in a tornado in the Minnesota mountains and, after a harrowing escape, helped evacuate local people into a remote valley forest. The local people had always been terrified of this forest and never entered it. We soon found out why—in the center of the valley a giant vortex was sucking everything within range into it, like a mini-black hole on Earth.

Sean himself was almost sucked in and was only saved by clinging to a tree until we could get a rope around him. Then we noticed that our instruments were going wild—showing a severe ozone depletion in the area. Was that also a result of the strange vortex? We realized that the mystery of the vortex had to be explored. But only the government had the resources to do so, and they were strangely reluctant to look into it, ignoring all our reports. We had to mobilize widespread concern—through teach-ins, TV interviews, and demonstrations—to force the government to do something. The following episodes open with the resultant meeting with the government representative, Stevens.

Stevens said, "Yes, yes, we quite agree that the vortex must be investigated. But we have a little problem: all our trained explorers are tied up in a secret space project—so secret that you didn't even hear me mention it. We just can't spare anyone. We can provide the equipment but not the explorer. The only way the vortex can be examined is if Sean, the only person ever to be at its mouth and survive, volunteers to go down into the Black Hole."

Sean was about to shout back, "Are you crazy?! For an untrained person to go down there would be certain suicide!" But Roland gave him a kick under the table indicating that he should accept this government offer. Sean even made a macho little speech about how he loved adventure and was honored to take this risk for his country. That statement pleased Stevens, who said, "This is an outstanding example of our policy of accomplishing great things through government support for private initiative."

When the day for the exploration arrived, many people came to view it from the safe distance of a mile away. Katie was with Sean as the government outfitted him in a special explorer suit of high-tensile fabric that could withstand enormous pressure and heat. His face was protected by a thick plastic mask. Dressed in this high-tech outfit, Sean would be lowered into the vortex with super-strength titanium cables—and later (hopefully) pulled back out.

Once Sean was dressed, Katie said to the government man, "Please give me just ten minutes alone with my son before he leaves on such a dangerous mission." Stevens could hardly refuse. As soon as he was out of the room, Katie and Sean had to move fast—they quickly got Sean out of the suit and replaced him with a dummy. Sean had scrambled out of the room through a trapdoor. The dummy had a tape recorder in it, so when Stevens returned he heard Sean's voice from within the suit proclaim: "Let's get it on!"

Thousands watched with bated breath as the figure of Sean was lowered into the vortex. Just as "Sean" descended, a colossal explosion rocked the mouth of the vortex and the whole valley. The figure was blown to smithereens; all that could be retrieved was the broken end of the titanium cable.

Stevens went on national TV to proclaim his shock and heartbreak at the loss of such a heroic young explorer. The government declared a national day of mourning for Sean, but even that wasn't enough. Stevens said that the vortex had proven too dangerous for anyone to approach it ever again. It and the surrounding area were to be sealed off forever, guarded by troops, and renamed "The Sean Roberts Memorial Protected Area."

So, as it had planned, the government used the incident both to get rid of Sean and close off the vortex. But we had an advantage on our side: they thought that Sean was dead and that the three of us who remained were paralyzed with grief. As long as Sean stayed out of sight, we were now free to investigate. But how could four untrained people ever get to the secret of the vortex?

To be continued next phone call—

When the figure of Sean was lowered into the vortex, Kwame was sitting in the audience observing everything intently. He saw that it wasn't really an explosion but rather an implosion, with everything collapsing very rapidly inward. For all those hot gases to rush inward, there had to be an exhaust outlet somewhere farther down the line. Kwame estimated the volume, the direction, and the speed of the gases and calculated that there had to be an exhaust vent exactly 5.3 miles SSE of the vortex.

Dressed in black and carrying picks and shovels, we snuck into the area at nightfall. At first we found nothing. But as Sean stepped over what looked like a rock, he was blown high in the air by a rush of gas and landed unhurt. We had found the camouflaged exhaust outlet. There was no possibility of climbing down the exhaust against the outflow, so we dug alongside it and broke through the ceiling of a giant underground room. Katie secured a rope and leapt down, then helped the others. We were in the center of a mammoth underground laboratory, with a huge computer and a complex control panel.

But our moment of discovery wasn't such a delight—for in the same instant we felt round nozzles sticking into our backs. We turned to see the barrels of giant laser guns trained on us. These were no little handheld "Star Trek" guns but killer machines that could easily cut a person in half.

To be continued next phone call—

A strange, rumpled man emerged from behind the lasers asking "how dare we" intrude into his laboratory! We realized that our only chance for survival was to convince him that we had no idea what was going on. "You mean this isn't the engine room of the Grand Coulee Dam?" exclaimed Sean. "That tour guide really messed us up!" complained Katie.

The man, obviously relieved, introduced himself as Dr. Linnoleus and offered us a guest room for the night. To our (apparently) naive questions, he passed his project off as a computerized study of nocturnal flight patterns of bats, to which we responded with very bored yawns. He showed us to a guest room with cots.

Once inside the room, we saw that we were locked in; we also discovered that the room was bugged. Continuing to talk verbally as naive tourists, we used sign language to discuss our real plan of action. There had to be way to explore the area! We spotted a grating covering an air vent in the ceiling. But the crawl space was very small; only Sean and Kwame could possibly fit through it. They would have to go alone.

The vent system was complex, almost like a maze. Kwame and Sean tied a string to the grating and unrolled it as they went so that they could find their way back. After a long crawl through the dust and darkness, the main vent took them to a view of an incredible sight: a long, metallic tunnel passing through a lake of molten, bubbling metal. This was all surrounded by a strong magnetic field (they could tell by the effect on their watches), and there was a giant funnel for sucking in ozone.

Kwame and Sean crawled carefully back to our room, rolling up the ball of string as they returned. In the morning, Dr. Linnoleus let us out of the room and offered us breakfast. We asked a few polite questions about his bat study and he bid us farewell.

As soon as we left the area, we checked to make sure we weren't being followed, then made a beeline for the University of Minnesota. We couldn't wait to describe our discovery to two renowned scientists active in the ecology movement—Drs. Richard Greenberg and Elena Gonzalez.

"Amazing," said Dr. Gonzalez. "It has to be a giant particle accelerator fed through a lake of ionized metal, all magnetized and then boosted to a higher energy level by an ozone-fed explosion."

"We knew it was theoretically possible," exclaimed Dr. Greenberg, "but we never thought anyone would ever be mad enough to try it!"

"What do you mean? Try what?" asked Kwame.

"They're trying to create anti-matter. It must be a secret project to develop an anti-matter bomb!"

"What's anti-matter?" asked Sean.

Dr. Gonzalez explained: "At the birth of the universe, for every type of matter that was formed, its exact opposite was also formed—with the same structure but the opposite electrical charge and direction of spin. They're so perfectly opposite that if matter and anti-matter ever meet, they completely cancel each other out—boom, instant annihilation! Fortunately, matter gravitated to one universe and anti-matter to another. Otherwise we wouldn't have a universe at all."

"It's the ultimate Doomsday Machine," said Dr. Greenberg. "If they can create anti-matter, they can build a bomb that will make nuclear weapons look like firecrackers. Once they start an anti-matter reaction, no one knows for sure where it will stop!"

"These madmen in pursuit of their superweapons threaten the very survival of the world," Katie cried out. "We have to find a way to expose this project and stop it!"

"Let's go tell the newspapers and TV," suggested Sean.

"No one would believe such a fantastic story—and all based on the observations of two kids!" said Dr. Greenberg.

"And once we showed our hand, the government would get us out of the way one way or the other," I added. "No, we have to stay under cover until we can come up with definite proof to show the public."

At the very same time this discussion was going on, Dr. Linnoleus was boasting to his head of security, Ed Williams, in the underground complex.

"I sure fooled those dumb tourists," chuckled Linnoleus.

"Fooled them, my ass!" retorted Williams. "I suppose that's why my people spotted a string trail in the vent system—a trail that was there in the middle of the night but gone in the morning. Those 'dumb tourists' of yours have been casing the whole complex."

"Well, wh-why didn't you stop them?!" sputtered Linnoleus.

"Because I have a better plan," answered Williams. "Right now I'm having them tailed by a surveillance team. They're going to have to come snooping back here to get more evidence; we're going to need some cover for when we do our first anti-matter test. We're going to time it so that it goes off when they're here—that way we'll kill three birds with one bang: first, we'll get rid of the four of them forever; second, we'll cover our test by saying the explosion was caused by their meddling; and third, we'll discredit the ecology movement for all time!"

To be continued next phone call—

(Summary of Several Episodes: Drs. Gonzalez and Greenberg agreed to do more research on anti-matter, while we would sneak back to the site for more evidence. But before we had even gotten off the campus, Sean realized that he had left his gloves at the doctors' office. Grumbling, we all went traipsing back—only to find the office empty and the window wide open. Drs. Gonzalez and Greenberg had mysteriously disappeared! A student saw us and shouted: "Those are the four suspicious characters who were here before. Quick, call the cops." We hightailed it out of there. We became the objects of the most intense man-woman-and-children-hunt in history. We felt like an antelope that had stumbled into a lion's den. The police were after us for the kidnapping of the two scientists, while it soon became clear that the surveillance team from the anti-matter project was also on our trail. There were all-points bulletins out and descriptions of us on radio and TV. The only people who could clear our names were the two scientists, who were nowhere to be found. Over several episodes of the story we have a number of harrowing escapes. But, as the following episode opens, it has become clear that we cannot continue to elude them.)

Katie said, "It's time to turn the tables, from being the hunted to becoming the hunters."

"But how," queried Roland, "with just the four of us alone against the most powerful government on Earth?"

"We have something going for us," offered Sean. "Remember, everyone in the world believes I was killed in the explosion at the mouth of the vortex."

We sat down and formulated our plan. When it was done, Kwame said, "So the government wants to find us, eh?—well, we'll come to them, and right at the vortex."

We then proceeded to make phone calls—done quickly and from different phone booths—to TV stations and newspapers throughout the state. It was Sean, unmistakably his voice, saying: "This is Sean Roberts and I am very much alive. If you want to know how that could be, I will appear at the gate to the Sean Roberts Memorial Protected Area next Saturday at noon."

Soon the excitement about "the miracle of the vortex" spread throughout the country. Thousands of people started to make their way to the backcountry of Minnesota by bus, by bike, by foot, and even by hang glider. Of course, the government security forces were questioning everyone coming into the area. They claimed that there was a bomb threat, but their real purpose was to intercept Sean and spirit him away. What they didn't know was that Sean was already at the gate—in a hidden underground compartment that we had dug out three days before. Just at noon, when everyone had gathered, Sean popped out of his hiding place and shouted: "You want to see the miracle of the vortex? Just follow me!"

The 4,000 government troops, who had looked so imposing just a day before, were easily pushed aside by the 100,000 people. The government man, Stevens, was aghast, and ordered the troops to open fire. But the soldiers, whose families and friends were in the crowd, refused to shoot, and the crowd surged forward.

We knew that once the people actually saw the anti-matter complex they would believe us and that such exposure would end this dangerous project. But Dr. Linnoleus met the crowd at the entrance. "Be reasonable," he said. "Would I lie to you? This is just a peaceful industrial project, but if you enter you could all be harmed by the radiation." The crowd wavered and the moment of decision was about to be lost.

Just then a voice came on the intercom shouting, "Yes, he *would* lie to you." It was Dr. Elena Gonzalez, imploring, "People, people, please come in; it's important; you have to see what's happening here." Everyone rushed in and saw that she, along with Dr. Greenberg, had been tied up but had managed to get loose and get to the intercom system. Government agents had kidnapped them to try to force them to work on the anti-matter project, but they had steadfastly refused. The scientists led the people to the edge of the sinister complex, explaining to all exactly what it was and how it worked.

Sean felt a tremendous sense of relief after these frantic weeks of being hunted and knowing a terrible secret. Now that this dangerous and frightening project had been exposed, it would definitely be stopped.

At that very instant, they felt a deep and powerful rumbling well up from the ground below them.

"Oh, my God, I don't believe it," shouted Dr. Greenberg. "The government scientists have set off the anti-matter reaction!!!!"

To be continued next phone call—

P.S. Needless to say, we figured a way out of this one, too...

[published in *Hauling Up the Morning*, Trenton, NJ: Red Sea Press, 1990]

Chapter 13

Lessons to Help Liberate the Future

We study the past to draw lessons to help us liberate the future. Today's young activists are to be commended for showing much more interest than my 1960s generatio did in learning from earlier movements. Still, I want to alert you to two characteristic errors in such study:

(1) In looking at victorious revolutions in other countries, we mechanically applied lessons from far more advanced levels to our own embryonic stage.

(2) In looking at past U.S. struggles, we saw errors as mainly the result of wrong ideas in the heads of the leaders of the day. Thus, we implicitly flattered ourselves as outstanding individuals who would naturally be more principled and intelligent. This approach underestimates the material forces—such as the depth of white supremacy or the repressive powers of the state—that produce repeated errors.

This brief two-part history is neither detailed nor definitive. It is written by a participant and partisan, with the goal of contributing to today's struggles.

Students for a Democratic Society

The U.S. was rocked by widespread and tumultuous protests in the 1960s. SDS was the organization at the heart of the radical movement among predominantly white college students. It drew special vitality from its close relationship to the Student Nonviolent Coordinating Committee (SNCC), the mainly Black youthful and militant civil rights group doing the most courageous fieldwork in the South. SDS also became the spearhead for what became a massive movement against the war in Vietnam by organizing the first national demonstration against it on April 17, 1965. Back then, it was unheard of to challenge "our" government's "foreign policy," so just to call for such a protest was radical, and the turnout of 20,000 people was very impressive. The work for that march also led to a defining break from SDS's parent organization, the League for Industrial Democracy, when we defied their orders to exclude Communists.

SDS, founded in 1960, received its early definition from "The Port Huron Statement" of 1962. The core concept was participatory democracy: beyond electing leaders, people need to directly participate in discussing and determining the decisions that affect their lives, including in the economic sphere. The compelling issues were the Civil Rights Movement and peace (opposing the cold war and nuclear bombs). The defining early work of SDS, along with its alliance with SNCC, was the Economic Research and Action Project (ERAP). Students went to live in poor communities to "build an interracial movement of the poor." While organizing success was limited, the experience was profound.

SDS hummed with a youthful vibrancy. Most of us rejected both red-baiting and the Soviet model of "socialism." Both red (communist) and black (anarchist) flags flew at our conventions. And we tried to apply participatory democracy to our own organization, with mixed results. The challenge to hierarchy felt liberating, even if often chaotic and inefficient. But there was a real problem of "the tyranny of structurelessness," where decisions are made in an informal and thereby unaccountable way.

The escalations of the war in Vietnam and SNCC's dramatic advance, in the summer of 1966, from civil rights to Black power posed new challenges and led to some tension between the old guard, steeped in ERAP, and newly activated student militants. SDS wasn't prepared for how the anti-war movement would mushroom, but did provide a radical and militant presence within the much broader coalition. SDS still naively defined the system as "corporate liberalism" as we grappled to put together our anti-racism and anti-war impetus with an economic critique.

The impact when the Black Panther Party burst onto the national scene in the fall of 1966 was electric. Their armed self-defense of their community from police brutality and their community self-help programs (free breakfast for schoolchildren, free clinics, free schools) provided a living example of revolutionary nationalism and self-determination for oppressed people. Several other revolutionary nationalist groups, all drawing on the teachings of Malcolm

WHO DOESN'T BELONG IN THIS PICTURE? David Gilbert, left speaks to a crowd during the Chicago Days of Rage while an "inconspicuous" police official listens in.

X, emerged in this period. At the same time, the first photos were published of Vietnamese children burned by U.S. napalm bombs—which drove us crazy about stopping the war. SDS's slogan became "from protest to resistance," with a focus on draft resistance.

Meanwhile, the inspiration of the Civil Rights Movement, the key and assertive work of women in it, and the problems of sexism within the Left all led to a rebirth of women's liberation. An early example was SDS's first-ever all-women's workshop at our June 1967 national convention. The air crackled with the energy and creativity the women generated. But their report to the plenary got a raucous reception—including catcalls and paper airplanes—from many SDS men. Given that there had been little history of struggle, it isn't surprising that men were still very sexist, but such blatant hostility was shocking for an organization that prided itself on always siding with the oppressed. That debacle was an example of the problems that pushed many women to leave the "Left" and contributed to an unfortunate tension between anti-imperialism and feminism, which weakened both. Many principled women—strengthened by the often, unsung examples and leadership of women of color—continued to struggle on both fronts, but it took an Amazonian effort to do so.

A high tide of struggle crested in 1968, with the Vietnamese's powerful Tet offensive and more than 100 ghetto uprisings in the U.S. after Dr. Martin Luther King, Jr., was assassinated. These events inspired SDS-led student strikes that shut down scores of colleges. We began to name and analyze the system as "imperialism." Che Guevara's slogan of "2, 3, many Vietnams" pointed to how such a colossus could be overextended and eventually defeated. The Black rebellion was accompanied by militant upsurges of Native Americans, Chicanos, Puerto Ricans, and Asians in the U.S.

The government's response was a vicious campaign of disruption and violence, called COINTELPRO for "counterintelligence program" (see *Agents of Repression* by Ward Churchill and Jim Vander Wall). More than 30 Panthers were killed between 1968 and 1971, and more than 1,000 were jailed. Many other groups and activists were attacked as well. While that level of repression generally wasn't used against whites, we did experience harassment, arrests, and the threat of a wartime draft. More importantly, we identified with the Panthers and had vowed to stand by them. As rapidly as the movement had grown, we were still a small minority in white America. We had started out thinking all that was needed was to "shake the moral conscience of America." We now found ourselves confronting the most powerful government in world history.

Under this tremendous pressure, SDS split apart along the basic fault line of the U.S. bedrock of white supremacy: between the desire for a potential majority base among white Americans and the urgent need for militant solidarity with Black and other Third World struggles. One side (invoking a Eurocentric Marxism) said that revolution was about the working class and used that as a left cover for retreat from fighting alongside Vietnam and the Panthers, claiming "all nationalism is reactionary." The other side (inspired by Marxist-led Third

World struggles) rightly saw solidarity with national liberation as a priority for any revolutionary movement worthy of that name. However, we wrongly abandoned efforts to organize significant numbers of white people, which also limited our base for anti-racist activism.

While the split moved along the horns of a real dilemma, there was a chance— although it certainly would have been difficult to achieve—for a larger and more working-class movement base without pandering to racist trade union traditions. That strategy would have entailed reaching the growing youth rebellion with anti-imperialist politics, as well as allying with the emerging women's movement.

We were too overwhelmed by the stark life-and-death challenges, combined with our own inexperience and weaknesses, to implement such a strategy in practice. SDS splintered apart in 1969-1970. One result was a series of formations that more or less reproduced the traditional white left opportunism toward the white working class. Another result was the Weather Underground Organization, an unprecedented, if seriously flawed group that carried out six years of armed actions in solidarity with national liberation struggles.

The Weather Underground Organization

In a society where every single movie and TV program showed that the FBI "always got their man," the Weather Underground eluded capture and sustained armed action for six years. In white supremacist Amerika, where historically just about every promising radical movement among whites (populism, women's suffrage, trade unionism) slid into compromising with racism, the WUO was known, at least at its best, for solidarity with national liberation. In a world where "legitimate" governments bombed villages and assassinated activists but decried any armed resistance as "terrorist," the WUO carried out more than 20 bombings against government and corporate violence without killing anyone or so much as scratching a civilian.

The springboard for these advances was the historical context. The '60s and '70s were unprecedented in world history for the number of revolutions in a short time, as national liberation movements in Asia, Africa, and Latin America overthrew colonialism and neo-colonialism; it was also a high tide of Black and other Third World struggles within the U.S. These events spurred growing radicalism among white people. The WUO was not formed as a narrow conspiracy but instead was a focal point within a much broader surge of anti-war militancy, as thousands of military buildings and Bank of America branches were burned to the ground, and as hundreds of thousands of people joined demonstrations that broke government windows, disrupted meetings of bigwigs, and resisted arrest.

Weather's exciting breakthroughs coexisted with costly mistakes. The earliest and most visible came during the first six months (late '69 to early '70), while we were still aboveground: our sickening and inexcusable glorification of violence, which grievously contradicted the humanist basis for our politics and militancy. We thereby handed effective ammunition to all who wanted to discredit our priority on Third World struggles and our move toward armed struggle (AS). To this day, almost all "history" about the WUO makes the mania of those six months the whole story, without looking at our correcting of that error and the ensuing six years of solid and humane anti-imperialist action.

In my opinion, the basis for our early aberration was in the life-and-death crisis that split apart SDS. We were white middle-class kids who—witnessing saturation bombings of Vietnam and the murder of the Black Panthers we admired—felt compelled to make the leap into AS. Instead of admitting our fear and inexperience and developing a suitable transitional strategy, we psyched ourselves up by glorifying violence and with macho challenges about individual courage. This frenzy was accompanied by basic, related errors: (1) sectarianism—a scathing contempt for all who wouldn't directly assist AS (the sectarianism was mutual, as most of the white Left vehemently sought to discredit AS); (2) militarism—making the military deeds and daring of the group all-important rather than the political principles and the need to build a movement on all levels.

Early Weather's grave sins of commission were glaringly visible. The opposite movement sins of omission, which usually aren't even noticed, can be even more lethal. The terrible passivity of most of the white Left to the early attacks on the Panthers gave the government a signal that it would not face widespread political costs for proceeding with its full-fledged COINTELPRO campaign, which killed scores and jailed thousands of Black, Native, and Latino activists.

Weather's militarism culminated in March 6, 1970, when a frantic bomb-making effort, including anti-personnel weapons, resulted in an accidental explosion in a safehouse (known as the townhouse explosion) that killed three of our own beautiful young comrades. This tragedy set off intense internal struggle that resulted in a qualitative change to a more integrated use of AS to help mobilize and radicalize a potential mass base among white youth. Just two months later, young people poured into the streets more than a million strong in angry response to the state's killing of four anti-war protesters at Kent State University, and student strikes occurred on nearly 1,000 campuses across the U.S. At the same time, the dire need for anti-racist leadership was painfully revealed by the failure to respond in a similar way when the police killed two Black students at Jackson State.

The WUO's recovery from militarism didn't magically put everything into perfect balance. While seeing a potential base in youth culture was right, we quickly repeated traditional missteps based in white supremacy. For example: (1) our dearth of material aid for Black, Latino, and Native armed groups (even underground, whites had much greater access to resources, and faced much less danger of random police harassment); (2) to appeal to white youth, we endorsed "soft drugs" (pot and LSD), with little appreciation of drugs as a form of chemical warfare against the ghettos and barrios; (3) we failed to respond to the Panther 21's very constructive criticism of our initial backsliding on drugs and militancy; (4) there were subsequent moments of awful inaction, such as during the Native American occupation and government siege of Wounded Knee in 1973.

Not surprisingly, our other major internal weaknesses were based in sexism, heterosexism, and classism. Women's participation and percentage of leadership were very strong, but in practice, a woman had to be part of a heterosexual couple to be a top leader. We had little political program around women's liberation, and we failed to make a serious effort for the needed alliance between anti-imperialism and feminism. Internal struggle on sexism was very inadequate, which dovetailed with a *de facto* homophobic culture. While many lesbian and gay comrades felt the strength to come out while underground, there wasn't real space for an affirming L/G culture; out L/Gs didn't make it to leadership positions; and we had no political program around L/G issues. Similarly, our middle-class background meant that we did a poor job at outreach to more working-class sectors of youth.

There were related problems in our internal life. We embraced the theory of democratic centralism, but in practice, the organization was very hierarchical. Leadership tended to become manipulative and commandist, while cadre tended to curry favor with leadership. Criticism/self-criticism was used to compete and maneuver for power rather than to build people. While a strong organization was key to survival (and lone fugitives had a much harder time), the above-mentioned reality made social ostracism a potent bludgeon against political dissent. As far as I know, there is still no clear-cut successful model for combining the two critical needs of a fully democratic internal process and of tight discipline for fighting a ruthless state.

To me, a crucial lesson is that activists must consciously grapple with the powerful pull of ego that can lead us to put our own position and leadership above advancing the interests and power of the oppressed. Organizationally, we need to strive to live our political ideals—anti-racism, feminism, democracy, humanism—in our personal relationships.

Despite these serious weaknesses, six years of impressive successes resulted from what was right about anti-imperialism. Contrary to the spy movie mystifications that are all about sophisticated techniques and technology, our survival underground was based on popular support from radical youth and the anti-war movement. That was the key to solving needs such as ID, money, and safehouses. There were moments when the FBI hunt was breathing down our necks, but popular support meant that information was kept from the state and instead flowed to the guerrillas.

Our stage of struggle was "armed propaganda," with no illusion of yet contending for military power. Instead, the purposes of actions were to (1) draw off some of the repressive heat concentrated on Black, Native, and Latino movements, (2) create a leading political example of white solidarity with national liberation, (3) educate about key political issues, (4) identify the institutions most responsible for oppression, and (5) encourage others to intensify activism despite state repression. We also provided examples of non-armed struggle (e.g. spray painting), pursued dialogue with the aboveground movement by writing to and reading responses in radical newspapers, and even created our own underground print shop. We wrote and published the book *Prairie Fire*, a well-developed statement of the politics of revolutionary anti-imperialism.

The WUO's more than 20 bombings included the U.S. Capitol Building after the U.S. expanded the war in Indochina by invading Laos in February 1971; the New York State prison headquarters after the September 1971 massacre at Attica; and Kennecott Copper Company on the anniversary of the bloody 1973 coup against the democratically elected president in Chile. Every action was accompanied by a well-reasoned communiqué articulating the political issues. While there are no 100 percent guarantees, we placed the highest priority on avoiding civilian casualties and fortunately succeeded.

The FBI never broke the WUO, but in 1976–1977 we imploded from our own weaknesses. The downfall came from drifting back into the traditional failures of the white Left with the politics of the "multinational working class," and a plan to surface from the underground to be central to "leading" the "whole U.S. revolution." These positions negated the independent and leading role of people of color within the U.S. and at the same time undercut autonomous women's formations. When those forces sharply criticized us, we—with our vitality sapped by the lack of internal democracy—couldn't deal with it, and instead split apart amid harsh recriminations.

The WUO was born in the era of the breathtaking rise of national liberation, in opposition to the U.S. foundation of white supremacy, and on the heels of exciting movement victories met by fierce government repression. Our demise was also rooted in heavy historical realities: (1) COINTELPRO (along with internal weaknesses) had decimated the Black, Native, and Latino leadership that had inspired progressive motion among whites; (2) our strongest base, the anti-war movement, shrank drastically after the U.S.'s 1973 withdrawal from Vietnam; and (3) we didn't realize that we hadn't done nearly enough to develop anti-war consciousness into a deeper anti-racism and anti-imperialism.

In learning from history, we need to break from the mainstream culture that defines people as either purely "good guys" or purely "bad guys," which can lead to the self-delusion that getting certain basics down guarantees that everything else we do is right. The WUO made giant errors along with trailblazing advances. Hopefully both are rich in lessons for a new generation of activists.

[These two essays, were originally written for and published in *ONWARD*, an anarchist newspaper, in the spring and summer 2001 issues. They have since been published in pamphlet form by Abraham Guillen Press/Arm The Spirit, titled *SDS/WUO*. They were revised for this book.]

How I Met Marilyn Buck

Marilyn Buck is an anti-imperialist political prisoner with an 80-year federal prison sentence for activities in solidarity with the Black Liberation Army. This reminiscence was first written in December 1985 and then slightly revised in December 1998 for an event honoring Marilyn.

The year 1967 was a hothouse for rapid and intense changes in SDS (Students for a Democratic Society, the main radical student organization that allied with the Black struggle and spearheaded the anti-war movement). The guiding slogan of the day was "move from protest to resistance," and we were in the midst of a soon-to-be-successful struggle to get the organization to define the system as U.S. imperialism. It was also the year that SDS held its first national workshop on women's liberation. The way women's liberation was put on the agenda for the national convention was almost accidental (there had been almost no explicit struggle within the "New Left" about male supremacy at this point). At a spring planning meeting, a long list of workshops was proposed for the summer convention; women's liberation was added to the list without discussion or much thought about its significance.

But as the women-only workshop was meeting at the convention in Ann Arbor, Michigan, it became clear to everyone around that something very significant was happening. When their report was later presented to the organization as a whole, the plenary session was chaired by a representative from the workshop—Marilyn Buck.

The reaction in the plenary to the mere announcement of a report on women's liberation was the most disconcerting experience of my years in SDS. Men hooted and whistled from the floor, threw paper planes at the chair, and shouted things like, "I'll liberate you with my cock." Some men and most women were supportive of the report, but the initial response was defined by this raucous attack.

The memory of that scene is still vividly with me some 18 years later (in 1985). I was sitting in the plenary session (trying to get called on to speak), shocked and chagrined by the reaction. SDS was supposed to be an organization defined by siding with the oppressed against the oppressor; even with little previous struggle, one would have hoped for at least an initial openness to and support for women's issues. Clearly there was a lot of struggle yet to go.

Another strong impression was of the dignified and determined way in which Marilyn chaired that session. She never lowered herself by responding in kind to the catcalls and snide remarks hurled at her, nor did she ever retreat an inch in the face of this unruly attack. She calmly and firmly insisted that the report be completed and seriously discussed, and this goal was achieved despite the disruptions.

The report from the women's workshop at the 1967 convention was an important watershed for our movement. It was the first major salvo to open up the issue of women's liberation within the New Left; it also exposed the appalling depths of male supremacy within our ranks; it was a beginning point for a tremendous amount of struggle, struggle on which we still have a long way to go. For me personally, it was also a very striking introduction to the extraordinary and deeply committed comrade who chaired that session.

Later, while underground in the 1970s. I occasionally spotted bits of news about Marilyn. Given that first encounter, it came as no surprise (but this is certainly never a given) that she became our movement's finest example of a white person fighting in solidarity with Black liberation, someone whose commitment and consistency we all needed to emulate. People at this gathering have some idea of what I'm talking about. But now, with more recent common work as political prisoners, I have the pleasure to add that—along with her visible political practice that is so thoughtful and principled—Marilyn Buck is a wonderfully warm, caring, and creative human being.

The Townhouse Explosion Taught Hard Lessons

Ted Gold...usually I first see his warm smile, then sense his intensity— whether on the basketball court or in a meeting—feel his earnestness in discussing strategy. Then I also remember his exuberance in enjoying music or performing guerrilla theater, at times even recall his depression after a breakup with a lover. On occasion his presence has vividly come back to me in a dream. The memories are still strong 20 years later, not only because I loved him but also because he influenced me greatly, partly shaped who I am. How painful it was to lose Teddy, Diana Oughton, and Terry Robbins—so young, and because of a wrong strategy at odds with our deeper revolutionary commitment.

I remember Ted at Columbia in 1968 as he set aside the ego problems of being part of an overturned and disdained "old leadership" to work enthusiastically to build the strike because he sensed what a shining moment it was to shut down that elite institution in solidarity with Harlem and Vietnam. A few months later, he was part of Teachers for a Democratic Society and breaking into schools, which had been chained shut as part of a racist teachers' strike against community control, to hold freedom classes with the community.

It was Ted who recruited me into the New York Weather collective and in so doing defied the contempt that could go with sponsoring someone who was then considered "out of favor." I remember the first (and all day and night) criticism/self-criticism in that collective, hours of which focused on Ted's male chauvinism. We had never been challenged so deeply on sexism before, and it was clearly very difficult for Ted, but he really hung in there, wanting so badly to be fully revolutionary. I left the next morning thinking that it was insane to hold a 24-hour criticism session, yet feeling wonderfully hopeful that we could change.

After I moved to Denver in October 1969, I only saw Ted three more times. Again, he was completely warm and friendly toward me even when it wasn't politic in the organization to do so. When the townhouse explosion took Teddy's, Diana's, and Terry's lives, I was literally overwhelmed with grief; it was the one time in my life when I felt on the edge of a mental breakdown.

For some sectors of the movement, it was impossible to reconcile Teddy's humanity and rationality with his embrace of violent struggle. The solution to their dilemma was an interpretation that he was driven by middle class "guilt." This position was very quickly and articulately expressed in an April 1970 *Nation* article by J. Kirkpatrick Sale—who never knew or even met Teddy. Guilt is a psychological category frequently used to discredit our politics.

Speaking for myself, I never felt guilty that I had enough to eat, adequate medical care, and education, but I did feel very bad—and I still do—that so many people are denied these necessities. What the pundits on guilt seem to miss is that we can identify deeply with oppressed people, that it can come from love rather than guilt, that our sense of our own humanity could be totally bound up with that of a peasant in the Philippines, or a young comrade in Soweto, or a mother of a disappeared person in Guatamala, or Eleanor Bumpers in the Bronx. The identification, far from stooping to uplift Third World people, meant that we had a lot to learn and benefit from their struggle.

That identification and excitement was best crystalized and enhanced by Teddy's 1969 trip to Cuba. My fondest and most vivid memories of Teddy are from the period right after he returned—happy, brimming with energy, convinced that revolution was on the ascendance in the world and even eventually possible here. I don't think I ever saw him, or any other student, feeling less alienated. He had thrown himself deeply into his delegation's meetings with the Vietnamese and Cubans, trying to absorb their analysis and apply those lessons to our own situation.

One of the wonderful expressions of his energy and optimism was the delightfully creative lyrics he wrote to match the music of our favorite rock 'n' roll songs. He sang them, we all did, with great gusto at meetings and marches.

Sharing Ted's thoughts and feelings after his Cuba trip, I know that what compelled him to embrace armed struggle was his identification with Black and other Third World people; his respect for national liberation struggles, his belief that their advances could also open the potential for revolutionary change here. In particular he did not feel that we could sit idly while the U.S. military rained the most horrendous saturation bombing in history on Vietnam and while COINTELPRO assassinated or jailed all the Black leaders who had inspired us. We felt the need to fight this murderous system, including with arms, not only as a mandate of solidarity but also as necessary terms for building a revolutionary movement among whites.

This reaffirmation of Ted's love, identification, and commitment is not meant to excuse the terribly wrong politics that led to the townhouse explosion, that proved so costly. Under the pressure of those times and still expressing our very competitive culture, we made many serious and interrelated errors:

romanticization of violence, sectarianism, dismissing the potential to have both an underground and a militant mass movement, substituting status ratings on who is most "revolutionary" for honest political debate, perpetuating macho values, and failing to work with and foster potential allies for Black liberation. These errors, this wrong politics, were not only extremely costly in our loss of three bright, lovely, idealistic young lives, but were also a setback in the broader struggle against imperialism.

When activists take on armed struggle, the setbacks and costs are searingly visible. But this does not mean that true wisdom automatically lies in not assuming those risks. Those sectors of the movement who were far too passive toward the government's campaign of annihilation against the Black Liberation Movement also made a very serious error and had wrong politics with very high costs in human lives. Our movement as a whole, after making some marvelous breakthroughs and advances, fell short of the needed synthesis of passionate anti-racism and a willingness to fight the repressive power by building a growing mass base for anti-imperialism.

Twenty years later it is clear that we are still very far from having the answers. Even the struggles that most inspired us have had an infinitely harder time than we could have ever imagined in trying to build humane and economically viable societies in newly liberated nations. Right now, the media have focused world attention on the dramatic and sweeping changes in Eastern Europe—with their incredible mix of progressive and reactionary aspects that don't neatly fit into our established terms of analysis.

For all the sobering blows to our revolutionary optimism and changes in other areas of the world, reality has taken nothing away from the critique of imperialism—which is still, and even more so, an incredible daily assault on the human life and dignity of the world's majority. Not only have the conditions of life worsened terribly for people in the Third World and domestic colonies, but today we can add perilous ecological destruction, criminal negligence around AIDS and homelessness, and renewed attacks on the rights of women to our urgent critique.

Ted Gold wasn't a saint. He shared the problems of arrogance, competitiveness, and *machismo* that plagued our movement. But neither can his life be trivialized as that of a guilt-ridden sad sack or fool. Ted was an extraordinary person: warm and expressive with friends; intense in playing sports; exuberant about music, dance, and love; humorous and creative. Most of all, Ted felt a deep commitment to all oppressed people, found their continued suffering intolerable, and admired their leadership and struggle for liberation, feeling that there were many lessons and much potential to also help us transform our own society. He had that love and commitment and was willing, no matter how imperfectly, to take risks to pursue it.

In the spirit of Ted Gold, I hope that we who today remember the townhouse explosion never lose our sense of identification with the oppressed and never give up the effort to contribute to forging the possibility of a revolutionary alternative.

[published in the Guardian, March 14, 1990]

Political Prisoners in the U.S.

The last thing the U.S. government wants to admit—as it preaches to other countries about human rights—is that it holds political prisoners and prisoners of war. But in reality there are more than 100 such prisoners here in the United States, including in the New York State prisons. Such prisoners range from the freedom fighters of the Black Liberation struggle to pacifists trying to dismantle nuclear weapons.

What Is a Political Prisoner?

A political prisoner is anyone whose incarceration is a result of his or her actions taken, or positions espoused, on behalf of a political cause—specifically a political cause on behalf of the oppressed and downtrodden in society and against the powers that be. For example, many remember that literally thousands of Black Panther Party members were thrown in jail on trumped-up "criminal" charges.

There are several types of political prisoners:

Prisoners of War: These are captured freedom fighters from the Black, the Puerto Rican, and the Native American struggles. They consciously fought against the oppression of their people; they fulfill the obligation (recognized by international law) to oppose racist and colonial regimes. Indeed, they are soldiers in just struggles for national liberation. These include POWs from the Black Liberation Army (BLA) and the Puerto Rican Fuerzas Armadas de Liberación Nacional (FALN), among others.

Resistance Fighters: These include white revolutionaries who have allied with Third World movements, and see this social system—with its racism, its sexism, its wars, and it economic exploitation—as fundamentally unjust. The Ohio 7, accused of bombings against U.S. corporate support of apartheid and against U.S. military intervention in Central America, is one of several examples.

Civil Disobedience Activists: There are those who refuse to abide by unjust laws and who have carried out acts of civil disobedience. These include draft resisters as well as pacifists who took direct action against nuclear weapons. For example, four "Plowshares" activists received sentences ranging from 8 to 18 years for trying to render a nuclear missile unusable.

Prisoners of Conscience: There are prisoners of conscience such as church workers jailed for providing sanctuary to refugees from U.S.-sponsored dictatorships in Central America. Also, in the past three years, some 45 people were imprisoned simply for refusing to talk to grand juries conducting political investigations. Such grand juries were usually focused on clandestine political groups such as the BLA or FALN, and also sought a range of information to be used against movements for social change. The grand jury resisters have received sentences of up to three years simply for the "crime" of silence based on political principles. Another example is the women and men who have been charged with "crimes" for their efforts to register Black voters in the South. There are numerous instances when people have been framed on criminal charges because the authorities wanted to stop their political work.

All of the above people were imprisoned by the U.S. or state governments because of conscious political actions and stands against oppression. They struggle against social conditions that are themselves truly criminal. To give but a brief indication: The infant mortality rate, a basic reflection of access to medical care and nutrition, is twice as high for Black babies as for white babies, and one-third of Puerto Rican women have been sterilized, a result of U.S. policies to "control" Third World populations. The unemployment rate is well over 50 percent on many Indian reservations while the Native Americans' means of livelihood have been decimated. Women workers receive only 57 percent of the pay that men earn, and then have the added burden of housework. Effective control of the economy is in the hands of 2 percent of the population, while it is the Third World and working-class youth who are used as cannon fodder for war. These "dirty" wars are used to enforce the economic exploitation of Asia, Africa, and Latin America, where 15 million children die each year from malnutrition and easily preventable diseases.

The outside community should have a deep concern for political prisoners, for their incarceration is due to their active concern for the community. Historically, one crucial function of prisons has been to silence and eliminate effective opposition to the government. Prisons have been a weapon in particular to "neutralize" militants from Third World struggles and to intimidate entire communities. If people on the outside allow such activists to be locked up and forgotten, it will strengthen the government's strategy to tighten the screws against protest and social change on the outside.

The Politics of Prison

There is another, much broader category of political prisoner. These people are not in prison as a result of direct, conscious political activity, but their incarceration is political in the sense that it resulted from political conditions in society such as racism and economic inequality. There are innocent people convicted due to racist frame-ups or due to the financial inability to mount a proper defense. There are also prisoners who were driven to crime by the needs of economic survival. Overall, it is very political who is in prison and who isn't: A Black man is six times more likely to land in prison than a white man, while the rich hardly ever go to jail at all. Meanwhile those who commit colossal crimes—like stealing whole countries or profiting from war and hunger—live in luxury and ease.

Since these extremely political criteria determine who is put in prison and who is honored with wealth and power, the outside community has an important interest in examining the terms and functions of the criminal justice system. We must be careful, though, not to use the political character of prisons to excuse many acts that do in fact hurt the oppressed and poor communities: sale of drugs, violence, and theft within those communities; the use and abuse of women and children, etc. Just as it is important for the outside community to support those of us in prison, we must learn to respect and fight for the people of our communities. In this way, all prisoners can strive to become conscious political prisoners and thus eventually turn around the conditions that led to imprisonment in the first place.

[February 1986]

The Anti-War Movements, Now and Then

The following interview by Bob Feldman appeared in the June/July 1991 issue of the New York City's Lower East Side alternative newspaper The Shadow.

Q: How did the Columbia Independent Committee on Vietnam get started?

David Gilbert (DG): We started in March 1965, about a month after President Johnson began the regular bombings of North Vietnam—LBJ had bombed North Vietnam earlier, after the rigged Tonkin Gulf incident in August 1964, but we were fooled into seeing this as a oneshot out-burst—I was sure that some of the more established campus groups and leaders would form something. But when nothing happened after about a month, I called together a small group of people who had long been troubled by U.S. policy toward Vietnam.

Q: Did anti-war sentiment predominate on campus?

DG: Not by a long-shot. Back then it was almost unheard of to question the government on foreign policy. Initially, the vast majority of students accepted what the government and media told them. But it was also a wonderful time of new openness and ferment: students' social awareness and moral sensibilities were blooming due to the Civil Rights Movement.

The first thing the Independent Vietnam Committee (ICV) did was set up literature tables on Low Plaza. We'd be out there for hours and hours each day debating the war—debating, rather than discussing, because most students opposed us. But there was definitely a burgeoning anti-war sector, and events themselves were changing people rapidly. By 1968, more than two-thirds of the students at Columbia University opposed the war.

Q: What was the relationship of the ICV to Students for a Democratic Society (SDS)?

DG: SDS was a national organization. Their work included support for the Civil

Rights Movement, organizing in poor communities, and actions against apartheid. With the benefit of a little more-developed analysis they had, a few months earlier—December 1964—put out a call for an April 17, 1965, march on Washington against the war. When the systematic bombing started in February, interest in this march mushroomed, and it ended up with, for then, a tremendous size of 20,000. Columbia, incidentally, sent 650 people, despite it being spring vacation—the largest single delegation in the march.

Those of us who started the ICV really liked SDS because it combined the issue of the war with a program against racism and also had some sort of vague socialist perspective. So we started a small SDS chapter at Columbia. Still, there was such energy and awakening around the war that we felt we had to put our main effort into the ICV to provide a vehicle for the broader range of anti-war views and energy.

By 1967, so many students were seeing the connections between the war and the underlying nature of society that SDS became the main organization, at the same time raising the level of militancy—e.g., by disrupting CIA recruiters.

Q: Why do you think there was such extensive New York City Police Department Red Squad surveillance of the ICV at Columbia in the '60s? Do you think there is much spying on Columbia's campus today?

DG: Well, it was both the Red Squad and the FBI. What struck me—I think it was even clearer in my FBI files than in the Handschu files—is how early the surveillance began. They started their files on me in 1963, when all I had done was go to some civil rights meetings and a couple of picket lines. The file on the ICV starts right from the beginning, with my very first leaflet on the war, long before they could have had even the remotest conception that we would consider illegal activities.

One lesson is that their surveillance had nothing to do with law enforcement but was simply because they saw any significant dissent as a threat. Second, the surveillance wasn't just to keep an eye on us: they initiated disruptive activity against us almost from the beginning—usually trying to foment splits and distrust among us.

One of many examples I remember: an ICV member came to me with a list she said she found while working at some government agency that had the names of five ICV members who were actually police informants. If I had gone for this faked information and accused these people or tried to kick them out, at the very least we would have lost five fine activists; more likely we would have had a major and bitter split in the ICV. Luckily, I knew too much about some of the individuals' background and integrity to go for the bait.

Many examples became clear in retrospect once COINTELPRO—the government's illegal program to destroy the Black movement and the New Left—was exposed. But there are still situations we're not sure about—to what degree was it our own weakness and misunderstanding or to what degree had disinformation been consciously planted?

To maintain perspective, the infiltration of the ICV was minor compared to what was done to the Black movement. There, infiltration began a lot earlier, was much more pervasive, and moved beyond character assassination to outright violence.

As for the surveillance at Columbia today, I don't really know how to assess it from here. The government is so worried about the re-emergence of a student movement, I'd be surprised if they weren't at least keeping tabs on developments there.

Q: How do you compare the anti-war movement then to the one now [the first Gulf War in 1991 against Iraq]?

DG: That's a giant question—there are many connections and also major differences. To start with, the U.S. defeat in Vietnam has lain like an insufferable nightmare on the consciousness of the ruling class—like a demon to be exorcised—and has guided almost every detail of what they did in the Iraq war. On the other hand, the legacy of Vietnam—the wellspring of sentiment against interventions in the Third World—meant that this time around we had massive and broad-based anti-war activity before the fighting even began. And the hundreds of thousands of people who marched against the war on January 19 and 26 [1991] certainly dwarfed the 20,000 we found so impressive in April 1965.

The similarities in the wars are that (1) the U.S. government is determined to crush any significant threat to its hegemony, and (2), each war was fought to set an example to other Third World nations and movements.

But there are vast differences, too. For one thing, Vietnam was fighting a national liberation struggle with deep historical roots. With Iraq, while Hussein did connect with important sentiments of Arab nationalism and support for Palestinians, the war developed more suddenly, and involved his own maneuvers for power and aggrandizement. The Vietnam War was very protracted, and we were pretty sure Vietnam would win. With Iraq, it's just impossible to make up for the vast differential in military technology if you're not fighting a people's war—a war with deep roots in the people and for a cause they passionately believe in.

Q: But perhaps another reason for the one-sided slaughter is that Hussein—for all the demonization of him in the U.S. media—was actually not willing to be as ruthless as Bush, whose massive bombings killed tens or hundreds of thousands of civilians both directly and through the destruction of sanitation and medical infrastructures. Hussein did release the hostages he initially held as a shield against attack. And he didn't unleash his chemical weapons or order suicide missions in Europe.

DG: You're right. And the whole media demonization of Hussein is something we should discuss further on. But first, without in the least justifying the

U.S./Allies' invasion, I was trying to make an analytical point that you just can't fight a protracted war with any chance of success against a vastly superior military machine unless it's a people's war—a guerrilla war with deep popular support for a cause fully embraced by the people.

Another major difference in the context was the impact of the Civil Rights Movement and the Black Liberation Movement in the '60s. It opened people to seeing the need for social change and to questioning the very foundation of this society. It also created an atmosphere where moral questions were much more in the forefront. By contrast, in the '90s, it seemed that the only issue—and some sectors of the anti-war movement played into this—was how many U.S. body bags came home. It is really shocking to see how little feeling or concern there is for the something like 300,000 Iraqis who were killed in this war.

Even with the impact of civil rights, the '60s anti-war movement proved inadequate at incorporating anti-racism and in responding to leadership from Third World movements within the U.S. These necessary building blocks are certainly urgent tasks for the anti-war movement of the '90s.

Another important difference is the role of women. Women played active and leading roles in the '60s, but they had to do so against all odds. All too often women weren't listened to, and were shut out of leading positions. Today [in 1991], as I understand it, women are playing prominent and often predominant roles at all levels of leadership and activities.

Q: What about the role of the media?

DG: As much as the media functioned as an uncritical cheerleader for the government in the Iraq War, it was even worse in the early stages of the Vietnam War. This statement may seem strange to students because of the now-pervasive myth that the media were staunchly anti-war in the '60s. But that myth was consciously created to convince the U.S. public that the war in Vietnam was lost because the media and anti-war movement handcuffed the military. They need that myth so that people here don't see the reality that the U.S. military was defeated by a people fighting for independence. They also use the myth to intimidate the media, which had developed a tad of independence late in the war, back into total lockstep with the government.

This time around the media were much more conscious about burying and downplaying news of anti-war activity. I think in the mid-'60's anti-war activity was somewhat of a novelty. But they learned from that experience that once people saw what was happening, the movement could really grow. So this time around they were much more conscious about suppressing or at least containing that news.

I know what it was like in the early '60s. I remember the footage of Walter Cronkite cheering the troops on in Vietnam. I remember the many times when the media dutifully suppressed news of illegal, clandestine U.S. military operations in Indochina. But here, I'll just spell out one particularly striking example.

When President Johnson commenced those February 1965 bombings of North Vietnam, he went on national TV and justified it by citing the 1954 Geneva Accords. He said quite clearly that he was doing it to uphold the Accords because they provided for or guaranteed an independent South Vietnam.

That didn't fit with my sense of the history, so I went to the international law library and looked up the Accords. They were quite explicit—the division into North and South was in no way a permanent boundary but was only for a temporary regrouping zone. This was to let the French colonial troops get out without a rout. The Accords called for an election to reunify Vietnam in 1956. The U.S. and its client regime blocked the election because their intelligence estimates told them, as later recounted in President Eisenhower's autobiography, that Ho Chi Minh would win overwhelmingly.

I was amazed. LBJ's whole justification for this bloody escalation pivoted on a claim that the Accords called for an independent South Vietnam. The Accords in fact said just the opposite. It wasn't a matter of interpretation; it was very clear, black and white. I was sure that the next day there would be blaring headlines that the president had lied about the Geneva Accords. Instead, it wasn't mentioned in any establishment media. We made copies of the Geneva Accords and started passing them out by hand on Columbia's campus.

By 1967-1968, the media began presenting some more critical material for two reasons. First, the drain of the war on U.S. power and prestige produced a split in the ruling class with significant sectors now wanting the U.S. to get out before it was further weakened and discredited. Second, there was a big enough underground alternative press to potentially embarrass established media for too blatantly suppressing certain information. At its height, the alternative press had four million readers—and it too became an object of an FBI-led COINTELPRO campaign to destroy it. For example, the established media never showed pictures of children who had been napalmed until *Ramparts* broke that open and created a sensation.

In the context of a losing war, the anti-war movement played a secondary but still important role. We helped legitimize the alternative of getting out. We helped shorten the range of brutal escalations that wouldn't have changed the outcome but would have cost even more Vietnamese and U.S. lives. But the main brake on the air war was the heavy losses of U.S. planes to Vietnamese anti-aircraft fire. The main barrier to the "nuclear option" was fear of Soviet and/or Chinese response.

Q: What about the charges that the anti-war movement vilified the troops returning from Vietnam?

DG: Honestly, when I first heard reports of people vilifying troops returning from Vietnam, I thought it was a pure propaganda creation. I just never heard anything like that happening in our sectors of the anti-war movement. We realized that GI's—disproportionately Black, Latino, and poor—were being used as cannon fodder for the rich man's war. GI organizing became an important part of the anti-war movement. Of course, we urged GI's not to kill, and we did condemn war crimes. But it was those who ran the war who were the enemy, and they were the ones victimizing the GI's.

Nonetheless, I've now met a number of Vietnam vets who were pelted with fruit or cursed or spat upon when they returned, and that is wrong. My guess is that this came from sectors of the population that became disgusted with the war but, unlike the active anti-war movement, didn't have a clear analysis of who was responsible for the war.

Q: Were you surprised that the U.S. establishment was willing to slaughter so many Iraqis to accomplish its political objectives?

DG: No. After studying its international and domestic actions over the years, I wasn't at all surprised. I was surprised and chagrined, however, to see the U.S. public so readily manipulated into colossal callousness about Iraqi lives.

Q: What about the argument that Hussein was another Hitler?

DG: I guess you should phrase that as "Hitler of the year," since the U.S. propaganda machine has churned out quite a few "Hitlers"—Khomeini, Qadaffi, Arafat, Noriega—lately. One crucial element of defining Hitler objectively in history is that he was the leader of a major imperial power out to dominate the world. In that light, we need to worry a lot more about George Bush [Sr.] than Saddam Hussein—and the same is true if we look at racial impact and scope of deaths caused by their military and economic policies.

Hussein, even after trying to claim the very honorable mantle of Arab nationalism, is no sweetheart when it comes to human rights and international law, but he certainly doesn't stand out as worse than scores of dictators that the U.S. has installed in various countries around the world. The way I look at it, Hussein is a small-time local bandit. Bush [Sr.] is a big-time global bandit.

Q: What do you think was the Bush administration's main motive for the war?

DG: One thing for sure: it sure as hell wasn't about upholding international law and the principle of non-intervention. I mean, the U.S. government under Reagan and Bush, alone, invaded both Grenada and Panama; walked out of the World Court when it ruled that U.S. aggression against Nicaragua to be illegal; intervened militarily in Lebanon, Libya, the Philippines, and El Salvador; has been the main supporter of Israel's illegal occupations of the West Bank, Gaza Strip, and Golan Heights and its invasion of Lebanon; for a long time circumvented UN sanctions on South Africa; and has supported Indonesia's brutal invasion of East Timor—to name just some of the examples. The idea that Bush was acting to uphold international law is a joke—a sick and bloody joke. Calling in the U.S. to deal with Hussein's transgressions is like calling in the Mafia to clear out a local shoplifter.

In analyzing the real causes, I've been a little disappointed with the three positions I've seen most frequently in the left press: (1) it was a war for oil, (2) it was a war to maintain the high level of military spending crucial for the domestic economy, and (3) it was a way for the U.S., a declining economic power, to maintain its importance relative to Europe and Japan.

Each of these positions deals with elements of reality, but I don't think that any of them gets to the heart of the matter. Sometimes analysts who have correctly absorbed the importance of economic factors (or, better put, class interests) too often simplify every situation to something that can be calculated on a cash register. The way I see it, broad economic interests are usually behind the formulation of a political strategy that has a scope and coherence that goes beyond the cash flow of a particular situation.

Oil is certainly central to why the Middle East has been seen as vital to Western interests, but Western oil interests were well provided for and would have been rescued by the terms of several diplomatic initiatives—especially the Soviet/Iraq proposal—that Bush brushed aside. Military spending is important for the economy, but the military has always been able to come up with creative fictions for this purpose, and for many reasons such spending is problematical as a solution to the current set of economic problems. The focus on the economic competition with Europe and Japan misses just how much these three poles have had a common interest in keeping the entire Third World open for joint exploitation.

Bush was determined to fight a war. He frantically discredited and brushed aside credible diplomatic initiatives, terrified that peace might actually "break out." Bush was hell-bent to fight a war because fighting a successful major war was the capstone to what has been the ruling class's central strategy for the past 15 years: to move the U.S. public and world opinion past the "post-Vietnam syndrome."

To understand the ruling class's obsession, you have to know something about the world economy and recognize just how fundamentally the wealth and power concentrated in the West is predicated on the thorough and abject exploitation of the Third World. Moving past the Vietnam syndrome was so crucial to them because you just can't maintain a vast economic empire— especially imposing the living conditions that prevail in the Third World—if you are not capable of using decisive force and terror against any "upstarts."

They prepared the way step-by-step, first with the invasion of teeny Grenada in 1983 and then little Panama in 1989. Hussein's move into Kuwait gave them their opportunity to finally have well-orchestrated popular support for a major war that they could count on winning.

Q: How do you see the state of the anti-war movement today [in 1991], and the tasks ahead of it?

DG: Well, it is certainly discouraging to be living in such a wave of war euphoria. While that wave is wide, it is not very deep. The ruling class had a broader agenda and long-term goals behind this particular war. We need to have a long-term perspective. The logic of the system will lead to other interventions, and we want to be able to start from a stronger place to try to stop the next one.

During the past 10 years, there have been a number of important, although small, movements on international issues: around Central America, around apartheid, around Palestinian rights, and the recent surge of mass anti-war activity. I wonder what the possibilities are for pulling this all together into a strong and ongoing anti-interventionist front. To be successful, such a front would have to be firmly rooted in anti - racism and in challenging social priorities at home.

Q: Any closing thoughts?

DG: Despite the current orgy of jingoism, we need to maintain a sense of history, a sense of perspective. As human beings, we can never accept the depreciation of human life because the people happen to be Iraqi or Salvadoran or Angolan. If we maintain our sense of identification with humanity, especially the majority of human beings, who live in the Third World, we won't—even in the face of the most sophisticated media barrages—lose either our moral bearings or our sense of purpose.

Strategies for Movement Building

Resistance in Brooklyn (RnB): Given some of your history, what are some of the achievements or errors of the anti-imperialist movement and its armed clandestine organizations that you participated in?

David Gilbert (DG): Our first outstanding accomplishment was piercing the myth of government invincibility. In 1970, the conventional wisdom was that the Weather Underground Organization (WUO) wouldn't last a year because "the FBI always got their man"! But the WUO functioned for seven years—until we split and disbanded due to internal political weaknesses—and carried out more than 20 bombings of government and corporate buildings without so much as injuring a single civilian. Including other formations such as the United Freedom Front, there was a 15-year history of white anti-imperialists carrying out armed action.

Our other main achievement was the political example of fighting in solidarity with Third World struggles. Our practice in this area was inconsistent and inadequate, but we did succeed at times in making this work a visible priority. It was also significant that so many women participated and were leaders in the clandestine organizations, although this did not mean that we were able to overcome our sexism in terms of our program or personal relationships.

A main problem was various forms of racism. It's amazing how deep this stuff runs, that even while consciously opposing it, we continued to make racist

267

errors. In some periods, we just built our own organization, enjoying the greater resources and the protection of being white without offering significant support to Black or Latino or Native armed struggle groups under attack. At our worst, we even pretended to an overall leadership of a "multinational U.S. revolution." The opposite swing of the pendulum was to put ourselves under "direct Third World leadership." But that became a way of intervening in their struggles by throwing our resources to the group of our choice, before the strategic issues involved had been resolved by the national liberation movement as a whole. It's not that there is a set blueprint for the correct way to relate, but we need a better consciousness to avoid both the arrogance of total unaccountability and the interventionism of picking the Third World leadership. These apparently opposite forms of racism have a common element: our wanting to be validated as "the most revolutionary white folks going"—either through our own claim of leadership or, once that was discredited, through getting the stamp of approval from a "heavy" Third World group.

Another serious error has been militarism, which makes the military deeds and daring of a small group all-important, rather than the political principles and the concerted effort to build a movement at all levels. This error is usually bolstered by sectarianism and contempt for those leftists who don't engage in armed struggle or who have a somewhat different political line. These errors are dangerous because you cut yourself off from potential allies, and at the same time you tend to try to prove yourself by upping the military ante beyond what you can sustain. As costly as all the above errors were, they tended to recur in one formation after another.

Looking at the repetition of these well-identified errors, I have to say—it might not sound very political, but I think that it is—that ego is one hell of a problem. You can be attracted to a cause for the most idealistic of reasons and can endure personal sacrifices to build an organization, only to get caught up in all kinds of maneuvers for power and status. Once you're into this dynamic, it is easy to rationalize that your only concern is for the cause. Very decent people, once in leadership, became highly manipulative; former iconoclasts, once they became cadre, abandoned their critical faculties in order to curry favor with leadership. These patterns recurred so often that I think recriminations over which individuals were better or worse miss the point—there's been a deep problem around process for building a revolutionary movement.

By process, I mean how we conduct political discussion, how we make and implement policy decisions, how we treat each other as individuals. The Leninist theory of democratic centralism sounded beautiful, but in my experience the result was always overly hierarchical organizations. So I can only conclude that the theory itself is seriously flawed. I don't know of any well-defined solution to these problems. The women's movement has done some valuable, if uneven, work in this area, and perhaps the Christian-based communities in Latin America have as well. It is very difficult to achieve, simultaneously, a disciplined combat organization and a fully democratic and humane process—yet both are emphatically necessary. There is an important sense in which we have to try to implement "the personal is political." The ideals we express in our politics must also be put into practice in our human relationships.

Why hasn't there been more written on our errors? The obstacle of not giving up security details to the state can be readily overcome by focusing on the political themes and lessons. So I believe the main problem has been our reluctance to face up to and analyze our errors, along with the lack of consensus about them. There is no way to sugarcoat it: this dearth of self-criticism and analysis is a serious failure to carry out our responsibilities to the movement.

RnB: What are your thoughts on the current political climate and on possible strategies for movement building?

DG: This is a very dangerous period. The mass frustration in society—with the breakdown of the economic security that was previously guaranteed to the majority of whites—has been channeled against those with the least power: immigrants, women and children on welfare, prisoners. Such shameless and racist scapegoating, when fully developed, is a defining characteristic of fascism. While that has been mainly directed by those in power, there is also an armed white supremacist movement that is not simply a creation of the state. Some of those formations sincerely and vehemently oppose the government (which juggles to fulfill the ruling class's range of international interests) with a program that, in essence, calls for a return to the pioneer days' ethos that any white male had the right to lay violent claim to Native American land, New Afrikan labor, and female subservience. Such movements can become a radical right "alternative" to and savior for a failing capitalism, like the Nazi party was during the 1930s depression in Germany.

The Left has been tarred with the right-wing's brush of "big government," due to the policies of liberals on the one hand and Stalinists on the other. But actually, with our commitment to self-determination and our struggle against the warfare and police state, revolutionaries have been the most consistent opponents of the massive repression functions of government. We now urgently need an activist movement that counters racist scapegoating by dramatically shining the floodlights on the real sources of the problems: (1) the lion's share of public welfare that goes to the rich via staggering interest payments on government debt, bank bailouts, pork-barrel military contracts, etc. (2) the unaccountable big bureaucracies of the transnational corporations, run by a handful of corporate executives who determine the life choices of the vast majority of people worldwide. (3) the Structural Adjustment Programs (SAPs) imposed by the World Bank and the International Monetary Fund on more than 70 Third World countries. These are, in reality, draconian austerity measures designed to extract debt payment and cheap raw materials for the banks and industries of the North. The SAPs are the cutting edge for destroying human life and well-being in the world today; (4) the growth of big government in its most virulent form—prisons, police, military might, and the concomitant attacks on civil liberties.

The alternative has to be all about humane use of social resources, controlled by grassroots organizations within the oppressed communities. Early ACT-UP and others efforts around AIDS in the gay community provided a positive example; the environmental racism movement in many Third World communities is another very good example.

There is a lot of social activism going on, just not that much sense of a coherent or forceful overall movement. It seems that a big part of the challenge before us—I really don't know how to do it—is to find ways to connect the range of different oppressions, against our common enemy, imperialism, and to find ways to synthesize grassroots activism with a global consciousness and solidarity.

[from *Enemies of the State*]

Chapter 14

Epilogue: September 11 and Beyond

September 11: The Terrorism
That Terrorism Has Wrought

Like most people in the U.S., I was horrified by the incineration and collapse of the two towers at the World Trade Center (WTC). Thinking about the thousands of people, mainly civilians, inside, I was completely stunned and anguished (even the attack on the Pentagon, certainly a legitimate target of war, felt grim in terms of the loss of so many lives, and of course the sacrifice of civilians on the planes). In the days and weeks that followed, the media, as well they should, made the human faces of the tragedy completely vivid.

At the same time, the affecting pictures of those killed, and the poignant interviews with their families, the constant rebroadcast of the moments of destruction all underscore what the media completely fail to present in the host of wide-scale attacks on civilians perpetrated by the U.S. government. With the pain to 9/11 so palpable, I became almost obsessed with what it must have been like for civilians bombed by the U.S. in Hiroshima and Nagasaki, Vietnam, Grenada, Panama, Iraq, and Yugoslavia—and what it would soon be like for civilians in Afghanistan, already just about the poorest and most devastated country in the world. (While the media have very deliberately downplayed the issue of civilian casualties from the bombings in Afghanistan, they already exceed those at the WTC.)

Terror Incorporated

The U.S. bombing campaigns in Iraq and Yugoslavia not only killed hundreds of thousands of people but also deliberately destroyed civilian survival infrastructure such as electric grids and water supplies. And these are countries that don't have billions of dollars on hand to pour into relief efforts. The subsequent U.S. economic embargo of Iraq has resulted in, according to United Nation agencies, more than one million deaths, more than half of them children.

In addition to bombing campaigns, the U.S. is responsible for a multitude of massacres on the ground. September 11 was the 28th anniversary of the CIA-sponsored coup in Chile that overthrew the democratically elected president; the military then tortured, "disappeared," and killed thousands in order to impose a dictatorship. The U.S. instigated terrorist bands and trained paramilitary death squads that have rampaged throughout Latin America for decades. In little Guatemala alone (with a population of 12 million) over 150,000 people have been killed in political violence since the U.S.-engineered coup against their democratically elected president in 1954.

Listing all the major examples would go well beyond the length of this essay (see William Blum, *Killing Hope: U.S. Military and CIA Interventions Since World War II*). But what's worse is that these bloody actions are taken to enforce the greatest terrorism of all: a political and economic system that kills millions of human beings worldwide every year. To give just one example, 10 million children under the age of five die every year due to malnutrition and easily preventable or curable diseases. Talk about anguish: how would you feel as a parent helplessly watching your baby waste away?

Since the early '60s, I actively opposed these U.S. terrorist attacks. But without the videos, the personal interviews, the detailed accounts, I never fully experienced the human dimensions. Now, seeing the pain of September 11 presented so powerfully had me trying to picture and relive the totally intolerable suffering rained down on innocent people in these all too many previous and ongoing atrocities.

A Gift to the Right

What made the immediate grim event all the worse was the political reality that these attacks were an incredible gift to the right-wing in power. George W. Bush entered office with the illegitimacy of losing the popular vote by half a million. The report on the detailed recount of votes in pivotal Florida was about to come out. (When it did, the post-9/11 spin was that the recount the Supreme Court stopped would have left Bush in the lead. What got less attention was the finding that a complete recount of all votes would have cast Bush as the loser.) The economy had started to tank. The Bush administration was making the U.S. in effect a "rogue state" in the world: pulling out of the treaty on global warming, refusing to sign the treaty against biological warfare, preparing to scuttle the Anti-Ballistic Missile Treaty. And the U.S. and Israel had just exposed themselves, badly, by walking out of the World Conference Against Racism.

September 11 and its aftermaths became a tidal wave washing away public consideration of the above crucial issues. Not only did the crisis lead people to rally around the president, but it also provided the context and political capital to rush through a host of previously unattainable repressive measures that had long been on the Right's wish list. We've also seen an ugly rash of anti-Arab and anti-Muslim hate crimes and a new-found public support for racial profiling.

I won't attempt to summarize here all the serious setbacks to civil liberties. The one measure that struck closest to home for me was not covered in the mainstream media. Within hours of the first attack, the federal Bureau of Prisons (BOP) moved about 20 of the political prisoners (PPs)—prisoners from the struggles for Black liberation, and Puerto Rican independence, Native American and Asian activists, anti-imperialists, and peace advocates—held by the BOP into complete isolation. Most of these PPs weren't even allowed to communicate with their lawyers—an extremely dangerous precedent. Once established, it clears the way for sensory deprivation and torture to try to break people down.

The BOP's ability to move so quickly in prisons around the country means that this plan had to have been on the drawing boards already—just waiting for the right excuse. What makes the "terrorist" label placed on these PPs all the more galling is that the Department of Justice knows full well that (1) while the CIA had past connections to the September 11 suspects, these PPs certainly never have and (2) while the perpetrators emulated (albeit on a smaller scale) the U.S.'s cavalier attitude about "collateral damage," these PPs have always placed a high priority on avoiding civilian casualties. Indeed, it was precisely the U.S.'s wanton slaughter of civilians—carpet bombings, napalm, and Agent Orange in Vietnam; COINTELPRO assassinations of scores of Black Panther and American Indian Movement activists at home—that impelled us to fight the system.

In pushing through the host of repressive measures without serious debate, the government has carried out a giant scam: a perverse redefinition of the dreaded term "terrorism." Instead of the valid, objective definition of indiscriminate or wholesale violence against civilians (by which measure U.S.-led imperialism is the worst terrorist in the world), the political and legal discourse has twisted the word to mean use of force against or to influence the government. If their "newspeak" goes uncontested, the long-term implications for dissent are dire.

Global Strategy

More broadly these events have been a tremendous boon to what I believe has been imperialism's number one strategic goal since 1973: "kicking the Vietnam syndrome." You just can't maintain a ruthless international extortion racket (to describe the imperial economy bluntly) without a visible ability to fight bloody wars of enforcement. The imperialists have taken the U.S. public through a series of calibrated steps: from teeny Grenada in 1983, to small Panama in 1989, to mid-sized Iraq in 1991, and to Yugoslavia in 1999. But public support for these ventures was only on the basis of short wars with minimal U.S. casualties. Now the real sense of "America under attack" has generated widespread (if still shallow) support for accepting a more protracted war, even with significant U.S. casualties.

Other repressive forces around the world have been quick to capitalize on these events. A key example is Israel's prime minister, Ariel Sharon. Talk about terrorists...as defense minister in September 1982, he was in charge of Israel's occupation of southern Lebanon when local, Israeli-sponsored militias were given free rein for three days of butchery in the Palestinian refugee camps of Sabra and Shatila; 1,800 Palestinians were murdered. Now as prime minister, he very deliberately encouraged and provoked Islamic militants opposed to the peace process to attack. He then immediately cried "terrorism!" (the Palestinians are always labeled as the terrorists even though it is Israel who occupies their lands, and Israelis have killed almost four times as many Palestinians as vice versa) in order to discredit and isolate Chairman Yasir Arafat, who's taken great risks to try for a peace agreement. Sharon's strategy, as he continues to tighten the occupation and escalate the violence, seems to be to completely finish off the peace process, either by liquidating the Palestinian Authority or by forcing the Palestinians into a heartbreaking civil war that would bleed their nation to death.

Funding and Fostering Terrorists

The U.S. government played a key role in cultivating and empowering the forces charged with the September 11 terror attacks. It's not just a question of whom the U.S. supported after the December 1979 Soviet invasion of Afghanistan; CIA aid to guerrilla groups preceded that by more than a year, while U.S. interference through its client regime (until toppled in 1979), the Shah of Iran, went back at least to 1975. The goal was to destabilize a government friendly to the Soviets and sharing a 1,000-mile border. As the U.S. national security adviser of the time, Zbigniew Brzezinski, boasted years later, "The secret operation was an excellent idea. Its effect was to draw the Russians into the Afghan trap." Brzezinski also justified the harmful side effects from this medicine: "What was more important in the world view of history? The Taliban or the fall of the Soviet Empire?"

Even though baited, the Soviet's invasion was inexcusable. The CIA, of course, seized the opportunity with its largest covert action operation ever, aside from Vietnam. It did not, however, simply support existing national resistance forces. Progressive Islamic forces, tolerant of other sects and religions and supportive of education for girls, got no aid and withered. The CIA instead deliberately and directly cultivated the "fundamentalists" who interpreted Islam in the most sectarian and anti-woman fashion. I'm wary of the term "fundamentalist" lest it play into U.S. biases about Islam, although in the same context as the reactionary Christian and Jewish fundamentalisms, it would apply. I prefer Ahmed Rashid's terminology of "Islamic extremists" for forces who have interpreted or, as he argues, distorted Islam as hostile to women and generally intolerant.

One reason for this U.S. preference was apparently the belief that the best way to mobilize people against a pro-Soviet regime that had offered land reform and education for girls was on the basis of religious opposition to such policies. Another reason was that most U.S. aid was channeled through Pakistan's Interservice Intelligence (ISI), which had close ties with these extremist factions. A prime example is Gulbuddin Hikmetyar, who started with virtually no political base but became a major power thanks to U.S. arms and funds. U.S. aid breathed life into numerous reactionary and power-hungry warlords. It's no wonder, then, that a devastating civil war raged in Afghanistan long after the 1989 Soviet withdrawal. In short, the U.S. didn't have the slightest concern for Afghans' rights and lives; they were simply cannon fodder in the cold war. When this chaos gave rise to the Taliban, it was were backed by the U.S. and Pakistan as a counterweight to neighboring Iran, based on Taliban antipathy for Shia Islam. Also the U.S. made an early bet in 1994 on the Taliban as the force that could bring the unified control and stability needed by the U.S. company Unocal to build its projected multi-billion-dollar oil and gas pipelines through Afghanistan. This hope unraveled by 1998 but now has become quite realizable with the U.S. military victory there. Bush's new special envoy to Afghanistan, who will spearhead U.S. efforts to put together a post-Taliban government, is Zalmay Khalilzad. This Afghan-born U.S. citizen was, in the late '90s, a highly paid consultant to Unocal on how to achieve its Afghan pipeline.

The *jihad* against the Soviets in the 1980s attracted Muslim militants from around the world, including Osama bin Laden. In 1986, he helped build the

Khost tunnel complex, which the CIA was funding. As he later stated, "I set up my first camp where these volunteers were trained by Pakistani and American officers. The weapons were supplied by the Americans, the money by the Saudis." From 1982 to 1992, 35,000 Muslim radicals from 43 different countries participated in the war in Afghanistan, many training at CIA-supported camps. Tens of thousands more were involved in education and support work. Now, the U.S. demonizes one individual, but it is very unlikely that one man or one organization controls the range of groups that spun off from that baptism of fire—and therefore very unlikely that "neutralizing" bin Laden will at all contain the current cycle of violence.

The results of 20 years of U.S.-abetted wars in Afghanistan—even before the Taliban came to power—were two million deaths, six million refugees, and millions facing starvation in that nation of 26 million people. Infant mortality is the highest in the world, as 163 babies die out of every 1,000 live births, and a staggering 1,700 out of every 100,000 mothers giving birth die in the process (most of the background and data in the above section comes from Ahmed Rashid, *Taliban: Militant Islam, Oil and Fundamentalism in Central Asia*). What a bitter irony that the U.S., which did so much to foster the most anti-woman forces and to fuel the ferocious civil war, now the justifies bombing that devastated the country in part as a defense of women's rights (see Naomi Jaffe, "Bush, Recent Convert to Feminism", in *Sojourner: The Women's Forum*, November 2001).

While the direct aid to the now demonized groups is sordid, the U.S. has had a much more major role in breeding such terrorism. Imperialism's top priority has been to destroy progressive national liberation movements, which sought to unite the oppressed and end the economic rape of the Third World. Since 1989, the U.S. has achieved major strides against national liberation with a counterrevolutionary offensive that uses both relentless brutality (such as sponsoring various terrorist "contra" guerrillas) and sophisticated guile (a key tactic is to divide people by fanning tribal, ethnic, and religious antagonisms). But the conditions of extreme poverty and despair for billions of people have only gotten worse. Thus, the very successes against national liberation have left a giant vacuum now being filled by real terrorists indeed.

The Emperor Has No Clothes

The dominant power has discredited as unspeakable some truths essential to an intelligent response to the crisis: (1) the horrible poverty and cruel disenfranchisement of the majority of humankind constitute the most fundamental violence and are also the wellspring for violent responses; (2) the reasons given for the September 11 attacks don't at all justify the slaughter of civilians, but they do in fact have some substance: U.S. military presence and bolstering of corrupt regimes in Muslim countries (not to mention throughout the Third World); the brutal occupation of Palestine; the large-scale, ongoing killing of civilians in Iraq; (3) the Pentagon and the WTC are key headquarters for massive global oppression.

The system's massive terror does not at all mean that anything goes in response. As the Panthers used to say, "You don't fight fire with fire; you fight it with water." Ghastly examples from Mussolini to Pol Pot have proven, at great human cost, that articulating real grievances against the system does not automatically equal having a humane direction and program. True revolutionaries spring up out of love for the people, and that's also expressed by having the highest standards for minimizing civilian casualties. In the wake of September 11, the example of the Vietnamese has become even more inspiring. They suffered the worst bombardment in history but always pushed for a distinction between the U.S. government and the people, who could come to oppose it.

As painful and frustrating as U.S. dominance is, the simplistic thinking that "my enemy's enemy is my friend" does not advance the struggle. All too many battles in the world are between competing oppressive forces. U.S. embassies may be legitimate targets, but blowing up hundreds of Kenyan and Tanzanian workers and shoppers is unconscionable. And even within the belly of the beast, groups that would cavalierly kill so many civilians and that would hand such potent ammunition to the right-wing are not forces for liberation. At the same time, we can't let our human commitments be blinded by floodlights that shine solely on this one tragedy. By any objective standard based on concern for human life, U.S.-led imperialism is by several orders of magnitude—the biggest and bloodiest terrorist in the world. We cannot let the immediate horror, which the U.S. did so much to engender, then be used to strengthen its stranglehold on humankind. Our first and foremost human responsibility is to oppose U.S.-led imperialism.

The Challenges Ahead

It was encouraging that the anti-war movement here didn't just collapse under the deafening roar of jingoism. But with the public's attention on the U.S. juggernaut in Afghanistan, it's been hard to maintain the momentum of the anti-war, anti-globalization, and anti-racist movements. In many ways, it feels like a bleak time in the U.S. because of the dramatic lurch to the right and the public support for many "anti-terrorist" measures that can be used in the future against dissenters. Nevertheless, even if the U.S. completes this phase without a hitch, we are likely to be in for a protracted, if irregular, war as U.S. action escalates the cycle of violence. While the situation is scary, it would only be scarier to give up, because that would clear the way for continuing this highly dangerous skid into war and repression.

Even the most formidable fortresses of domination develop cracks over time. Contradictions in the war on terrorism as well as stresses in the economy and social fabric are likely to develop. Our task is to keep a voice alive for humane alternatives rather than let every setback add fuel to the imperial fire. We are not as isolated as in 1964, when it was completely unheard-of to publicly challenge such interventions. However, in other ways our task will be more difficult than the decade-long struggle to end the war in Vietnam. This time, people in the U.S.

do feel directly attacked, and those now labeled as the "enemy" are not a progressive national liberation movement.

To me, the most apt, if somewhat gloomy, analogy is to the "War on Drugs." In both cases these points apply: (1) The CIA actively fostered some of the worst initial perpetrators. (2) The "war" response only makes the problem worse (making drugs illegal makes them much more expensive, which is the main factor promoting crime and violence; waging a "crusade" against Afghanistan and "Muslim fundamentalists" and backing Israel's suppression of Palestine are likely to result in many more terrorists). (3) Both wars pit unsavory foes against each other whose respective actions justify and animate the opposing side. (4) While each war is a colossal failure in terms of its stated aim, each is a smashing success in building public support for greater police/military powers and in diverting people's attention from the fundamental social issues. (5) Finally, sky-high barriers have been erected to challenging these insane wars. You can't raise the question of decriminalizing drugs or of addressing the roots of terrorism without getting hooted off the public stage. One difference, unfortunately, is that the war on terrorism is likely to become bigger, and more violent and lead to an even worse loss of civil liberties. A difference from facing the McCarthyism of the 1950s is that, hopefully, recent currents of organizing and activism provide a basis to begin challenging such reaction from its onset.

Building an Anti-War Movement

The starting point is a love for and identification with other people. We don't have to become callous about the lives lost at the WTC, even though the government has used them so cynically. Instead we have the job of getting those who've awakened to this pain to feel the injustice and suffering of the many other atrocities that have been perpetrated by the U.S. As hard as that may seem, many Americans were asking, "Why do 'they' hate us so much?" While the government and media have done their best to shut down public discussion of this pivotal issue, we can offer genuine and substantive responses, which resonate with the widely held value of fairness. We have to break through the colossal double standard and insist fully on stopping all violence—whether bombings or hunger—against civilians, and to be very clear on all the major examples. There's a related specific need to puncture the dangerous misdefinition of "terrorism."

In the discussion I've seen about building an anti-war movement, I wholeheartedly agree with those who insist that it must be anti-racist at its core. White supremacy is the bedrock for all that is reactionary in the U.S.; in addition, the current gallop toward a police state will be used first and foremost against people of color. To be real about this, white activists have to go beyond the necessary process issues for making people of color feel welcomed at meetings and events. We also need to ally with and learn from their organizations and to develop a strong anti-racist program and set of demands.

It also seems crucial to develop strong synergy with the promising "anti-globalization" movement—not only because that's where many young people have become active, but even more importantly because the only long-term alternative to "the War on Terrorism" is to fully address the fundamental issues of global social and economic justice.

We face an extremely difficult period, without much prospect for the exhilaration of quick successes. But we don't have the luxury of despair and defeatism—that only hands an easy victory to the oppressors. To draw a lesson from the past, we now celebrate the many slave rebellions, going back centuries before abolition became realizable, because they weakened that intolerable institution and kept resistance and future possibilities alive. History, as we've seen, goes through many unpredictable twists and turns. Principled resistance not only puts us in touch with our own humanity but also keeps hope and vision alive—like spring sunshine and rain—for when new possibilities sprout through the once-frozen ground.

[This piece written in the aftermath of September 11, circulated widely on the internet, and appeared in several movement papers. It was revised for publication here.]

Postscript

No Surrender is going to press in the aftermath of the U.S.'s calculated brutal display of military might against Iraq. While much of the above epilogue remains relevant to the dialogue on building an anti-war movement, here are a few additional thoughts.

Imperialism has had some stunning successes over the past two decades: on one hand in decimating progressive national liberation struggles, on the other in fostering reactionary allies such as Noriega (in Panama), Osama bin Laden, and Saddam Hussein—who then, with just the snap of the fingers, can be made over into evil incarnate enemies used to justify U.S. interventions in the Third World.

As with every war, there are always a few former peace advocates who publicly convert to today's jingoism. To help cut through the government's protean rationales, look at the historical record: (1) Before 1917, gunboat diplomacy was required to "prevent anarchy." (2) From 1917 through 1989, the same kind of interventions (involving wholesale massacres and installation of bloody dictators) were mandated to "stop Communism." (3) After the collapse of the Soviet bloc, the terms shifted, without missing a beat, to the need for military action against drugs, terrorism, and human rights violations (all of which the U.S. has promoted). The three apparently disparate eras ideologically have the same underlying constants: securing U.S. business interests and the related strengthening of U.S. military and political power.

This most recent invasion is a particularly dangerous precedent. Not only has the U.S. proclaimed the right of "preemptive" war, but it did so in the midst of a United Nations process dealing with the alleged problem and in clear contravention of the UN Security Council. Indeed, it seems that Bush was in such a rush because inspections were in danger of working.

Readers of this book most likely already know about the hype and outright fraud in U.S. and British charges (not to mention the crass hypocrisy regarding Hussein's U.S.-condoned chemical warfare in the 1980s) about weapons of mass destruction. (At this writing the allies' failure to turn up such weapons or any concrete links to Al Quaeda has led to some tepid public "criticism" of Bush and Blair. I still expect some such "find" to be created, but in any case it's chilling to see popular domestic support for a conqueror whose excuses are so threadbare.)

"No blood for oil" is a great four-word slogan, but necessarily an oversimplification in terms of analysis. In my view, a major impetus for this war was the growing shakiness of the repressive, U.S.-client regime in Saudi Arabia. Its potential fall would have placed all three (with Iran and Iraq) of the major oil producers of the region—and the heart of OPEC (Organization of Petroleum Exporting Countries)—under hostile governments. War on the "evildoer" Hussein not only brought Iraq's huge oil reserves under direct imperial control, but even more importantly provided the basis for a permanent, strong U.S. military presence in the Gulf and on the borders of both Saudi Arabia and Iran.

But this war had an even broader strategic purpose. A position paper written in 2000 for the Project for a New American Century by many of the key policymakers-in-waiting for the new Bush regime called for an awesome display of the U.S.'s unrivaled power in the post-Soviet world (for fuller discussion and analysis, see *Behind the Invasion of Iraq*, by the Research Unit for Political Economy, Monthly Review Press). Then September 11 made this imperial vision politically feasible. Less than two years later, U.S. imperialism has catapulted from the strategic priority of "kicking the Vietnam syndrome" to an agenda of total world domination.

The quick victory in Iraq comes as no surprise. (1) The disparity of forces was so great that, as Noam Chomsky noted beforehand, "war" is hardly the right word. (2) Hussein was indeed a tyrant (empowered in part—from the '60s through the '80s—by the U.S.) who therefore could not lead or inspire broad-based popular resistance. Nonetheless, the U.S. military juggernaut is indeed staggering, and the rapid conquest inevitably took a lot of wind out of the billowing protest sails.

Today's tasks are daunting: the corporate media glosses over well-documented lies, blatant violations of international law, and the cruel realities of civilian casualties. The majority of the U.S. public still supports Bush, and there is a host of new repressive measures in place that can be used against dissent. It's scary. But to keep things in perspective, this anti-war movement started light-years ahead of the opposition to the war in Vietnam, when the taboo on criticizing foreign policy wasn't breached until the (for then very impressive) 20,000-strong March on Washington of April 17, 1965, four years into the active U.S. military presence there.

The worldwide outpouring of 11 million anti-war protestors in February 2003 was breathtaking. And the emerging synergy with anti-globalization is a very promising step toward fully taking on the military, economic, and political aspects of one integral imperialism. As argued in the above epilogue, putting anti-racism at the heart of our efforts is crucial and urgent.

The current moral and political discourse has been hijacked. The politicians and media won't even allow discussion of the U.S. wrongs that may have provoked the nonetheless unjustified massacre of 3,000 civilians at the World Trade Center. Yet consider this statement by then Secretary of state Madeleine Albright on *60 Minutes*, CBS, May 12, 1996. When asked about the deaths of 500,000 Iraqi children (under five years old) by the devastation to civilian infrastructures (water supply, medical, food) from the combination of the 1991 bombings and the subsequent economic blockade, she replied, "We think the price is worth it." That is one of literally thousands of egregious examples.

In facing this colossus, remember: the pharaohs of mighty Egypt were gods on Earth; the Han dynasty of ancient China, eternal; the Roman Empire, invincible. Every empire, no matter how powerful, eventually falls due to the contradictions sown by the very extent of its oppression. While we can't say exactly when, the same is true of today's sole superpower. What worries me is how costly the demise will be and what will replace it. Our job is to keep alive a vibrant voice and a clear direction for fully human alternatives. The keys, in my view, are anti-racism; opposition, in both our politics and our lives, to all forms of oppression; and a deep sense of history of the protracted nature of the struggle ahead.

Right now there are several potential problems for those in power. (1) As we are seeing in Afghanistan as well as Iraq, conquest is one thing, pacification another. (2) The massive worldwide resentment of imperial penetration is growing. (3) U.S. justifications are belied by support for Israel, whose conquests, occupation, weapons of mass destruction, and violations of international law far outdo Hussein's. The resulting intense and heartrending conflict won't go away. The only solution is full and viable nationhood that provides for the rights and needs of all Palestinians displaced or occupied since 1947. (4) The U.S. economy looks shaky. (5) Skewed social priorities at home are becoming increasingly blatant. (6) More people may become concerned about the grave attack on civil liberties.

Even without a single drawn-out and costly war, there is the grim prospect of a series of unsavory conflicts that fuel an endless cycle of violence. The anti-war movement embodies the best alternative: the struggle for global economic and social justice.

We don't have a chance for a decent future for all children unless we can change public terms and perceptions to get across that every human life is precious. Staying in close touch with our love for people and for life on the planet can both impel and sustain us. As Che Guevara urged decades ago, "We must stand firm but without losing our tenderness, ever."

The struggle continues,
David Gilbert
August 14, 2003

Political Prisoner Support Organizations

Anarchist Black Cross Federation
c/o Montreal ABCF
2035 St. Laurent, Montreal, Quebec, H2X 2T3, Canada
email: montrealabcf@ziplip.com
website: www.montrealabcf.org

Anarchist Black Cross Network
website: www.anarchistblackcross.org

Anarchist Prisoners Legal Aid Network (APLAN)
818 SW 3rd Avenue PMB #354, Portland, Oregon, 97204, USA

Break the Chains
P.O. Box 12122, Eugene, Oregon, 97440, USA
email: breakthechains02@yahoo.com
website: www.breakthechains.net

Critical Resistance
NATIONAL OFFICE
1904 Franklin Street, Suite 504, Oakland, California, 94612, USA
phone: (510) 444-0484
fax: (510) 444-2177
email: crnational@criticalresistance.org

NORTHEAST REGIONAL OFFICE
968 Atlantic Avenue, 1st floor, Brooklyn, New York, 11238, USA
phone: (718) 398-2825
fax: (718) 398-2856
email: crne@criticalresistance.org

SOUTHERN REGIONAL OFFICE
4041 Tulane Avenue, Suite #103, New Orleans, Louisiana, 70119, USA
phone: (504) 488-2994
fax: (504)488-8578
email: crsouth@criticalresistance.org

website: www.criticalresistance.org

Friends of Marilyn Buck
c/o Legal Services for Prisoners with Children
1540 Market #490, San Francisco, California, 94102, USA
email: fombuck@yahoo.com

**International Concerned Family
and Friends of Mumia Abu Jamal**
4601 Market Street, Philadelphia, Pennsylvania, 19143, USA
phone: (215) 476-8812
email: icffmaj@aol.com
website: www.mumia.org

Jericho Amnesty Movement (East Coast)
P.O. Box 340084, Jamaica, New York, 11434, USA
phone: (718) 949-3937
email: info@thejerichomovement.com
website: www.thejerichomovement.com

Jericho Amnesty Movement (Bay Area)
P.O. Box 3585, Oakland, California, 94609, USA
email: jerichosfbay@lycos.com
website: prisonactivist.org/jericho_sfbay

Leonard Peltier Defense Committee
P.O. Box 583, Lawrence , Kansas, 66044, USA
email: lpdc@freepeltier.org
website: www.freepeltier.org

Out of Control Lesbian Committee to Support Women Political Prisoners
3543 - 18th Street, Box 30, San Francisco, California, 94110, USA

Political Prisoner Calendar Committee
c/o QPIRG Concordia
1420 Sherbrooke Street West, Suite 404, Montreal, Quebec, H3G 1K5, Canada
email: freeppcalendar@inquilino.zzn.com

Prison Activist Resource Center (PARC)
P.O. Box 339, Berkeley, California, 94701, USA
phone: 510-893-4648
website: www.prisonactivist.org

Resistance in Brooklyn
309 Park Place, Brooklyn, New York, 11238, USA
email: mmmsrnb@igc.org

Sundiata Acoli Freedom Campaign
P.O. Box 1959, Newark, New Jersey, 07101, USA
email: saparole@aol.com
website: sundiata.afrikan.net

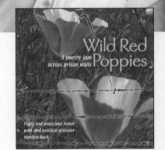

AIDS CONSPIRACY THEORIES - David Gilbert $3 US/ $4 Cdn

BEHIND THE TWENTY-FIRST CENTURY INTIFADA $4 US/ $5 Cdn

COMMUNE IN CHIAPAS? MEXICO AND THE ZAPATISTA REBELLION $4 US/ $5 Cdn

CREATING A MOVEMENT WITH TEACH: COMMUNIQUES OF
THE GEORGE JACKSON BRIGADE $3.50 US/ $4.50 Cdn

ENEMIES OF THE STATE
Interviews with Marilyn Buck, David Gilbert, Laura Whitehorn $5 US/ $6 Cdn

500 YEARS OF INDIGENOUS RESISTANCE - Oh-Toh-Kin newspaper $4 US/ $5 Cdn

GUSTAFSEN LAKE CRISIS - Statements from Ts'Peten Defenders $3 US/ $4 Cdn

LOOKING AT THE WHITE WORKING CLASS HISTORICALLY - David Gilbert $3 US/ $4 Cdn

MESSAGE TO THE BLACK MOVEMENT:
Political statement from the Black underground - Black Liberation Army $4 US/ $5 Cdn

MINI-MANUAL OF THE URBAN GUERRILLA - Carlos Marighella $4 US/ $5 Cdn

ON THE BLACK LIBERATION ARMY (BLA) - Jalil Muntaqim $3.50 US/ $4.50 Cdn

ORGANIZATION MEANS COMMITMENT OR COMMITMENT IS THE KEY $3 US/ $4 Cdn

ORGANIZATIONAL PLATFORM OF THE LIBERTARIAN COMMUNISTS $3 US/ $4 Cdn

THE POWER OF THE PEOPLE IS THE FORCE OF LIFE,
POLITICAL STATEMENT OF THE GEORGE JACKSON BRIGADE $3.50 US/ $4.50 Cdn

A RADICAL VOICE FROM PALESTINE
Recent documents from the Popular Front for the Liberation of Palestine $5 US/ $6 Cdn

REVOLUTIONARY ARMED STRUGGLE - Anonymous $3.50 US/ $4.50 Cdn

STATUTES OF THE FORCES OF NATIONAL LIBERATION (FLN) $3 US, $4 Cdn

SDS / WUO, STUDENTS FOR A DEMOCRATIC SOCIETY
AND THE WEATHER UNDERGROUND ORGANIZATION - David Gilbert $3 US/ $ 4 Cdn

TRIAL STATEMENTS OF RAY LUC LEVASSEUR - Ray Luc Levasseur $4 US/ $5 Cdn

WE ARE OUR OWN LIBERATORS - Jalil Abdul Muntaqim $12 US/ $15 Cdn

ABRAHAM GUILLEN PRESS
C.P. 48164
Montréal, Québec
H2V 4S8, Canada